D1499613

Keats
and the Victorians

*A Study of His
Influence and Rise to Fame
1821 - 1895*

BY

GEORGE H. FORD

ARCHON BOOKS
HAMDEN   LONDON
1962

COPYRIGHT, 1944, BY YALE UNIVERSITY PRESS
REPRINTED 1962 WITH PERMISSION
PRINTED IN THE UNITED STATES OF AMERICA

[*Yale Studies in English, Vol. 101*]

PR
4837
.F6
1962

HUGH STEPHENS LIBRARY
STEPHENS COLLEGE
COLUMBIA, MISSOURI

TO MY FATHER

113733

PREFACE

IN his well-known study *Byron in England,* in which Byron's fame and after-fame are traced, Professor Chew remarks on the great need for a parallel study of Keats. *Keats in England* would be a very tempting title for the present essay, but, aside from rather obvious considerations, I have decided that it would not be very apt. The methods which I have used to trace Keats's rise to fame differ considerably from those used by Professor Chew. Unlike that of Byron, the curve of Keats's reputation assumes an almost unbroken rise after 1830, and so instead of developing it in simple chronological order, I have placed more emphasis upon an account of the influence of his work on the major Victorian authors, sketching in aspects of his rise to fame in connection with each of them. When dealing with Arnold, for example, I have touched on Keats's biographers; when dealing with Rossetti, I have discussed certain shifts in Victorian taste. Because I was concerned with Keats's influence as well as with his reputation, this seemed to me the most workable method.

Anyone addicted (as I am thoroughly addicted) to reading the entertaining and informative footnotes of Douglas Bush's *Mythology and the Romantic Tradition* might be impressed, in his remarks on the Victorian poets, with the multiplicity of references to Keats. Like Sir Herbert Grierson and several other literary historians, Bush draws attention to the great impact of Keats on later writers and implies that his poetry is one of the most important links between the romantic and Victorian periods. Yet, except for this general awareness on the part of some critics, the real importance of Keats's role in the Victorian scene has not been examined in careful detail. With respect to his reputation, the only contributions are a few brief pages by Sidney Colvin and three or four short magazine articles which I have listed in my bibliography. The latter (with the exception of one by Professor Chew) are elementary.

The story of Keats's influence has fared somewhat better. English and American scholars seem to have passed over it, but in France it has received some attention. Lafourcade's essay on Swinburne and Keats is excellent, and a brief thesis by Mlle. Léonie Villard (*The Influence of Keats on Tennyson and Rossetti,* Paris, 1914) is very helpful. To the former especially I am under obligation in the sections concerned. Miss Louise Rosenblatt's study, *L'idée de l'art pour l'art en Angleterre,* also has some interesting comments on the importance of Keats in later nineteenth-century literature.

As a witty critic warns us, the real danger in research is, that unless we are very careful, we always find what we are seeking.[1] This is doubly true in problems of literary influence. To discriminate between genuine imitation and mere coincidence is always something of a juggling feat, but common sense is still the best criterion. When, for example, Tennyson writes in *St. Agnes' Eve:*

> My breath to heaven like vapour goes,
> May my soul follow soon,

we may reasonably assume that he had in mind the picture of the beadsman in Keats's *Eve of St. Agnes.* On the other hand, the following example, one of many ponderously collected by a German student for his thesis, seems to represent some bad concordance-hunting combined with an inadequate sense of the language:[2]

> Stay'd in the wandering warble of a brook;
> (*The Last Tournament,* 254)
> And wandering sounds, slow-breath'd melodies.
> (*Hyperion,* I, 208)

The other part of the present study has also its Scylla and Charybdis. It is sometimes hazardous to attempt accurate generalizations about the reputation of a writer at any given period. In the Victorian age it is not that information is lacking but that its quantity is almost overwhelming. As Lytton Strachey remarked concerning the expanse of materials open to any investigator of the Victorian scene, "the industry of a Ranke would be submerged by it, and the perspicacity of a Gibbon would quail before it."[3] I am aware that the evidence which has gone to make up this study might be expanded *ad infinitum,* but such additional information would not, I think, seriously affect its major conclusions.

In its original form, this study received the John Addison Porter Prize in the spring of 1942 when it was presented to the Graduate School of Yale University in candidacy for the degree of Doctor of Philosophy. About the same period, I enlisted in the Canadian artillery and my wife very gallantly took over the whole task of revision. The phrase "without her assistance" has become a platitude, but in this instance, it would unquestionably have been impossible for me to have considered publication without her acting as editor-in-chief. An occasional week-end since then has been my only contribution: the rest of the task was hers entirely.

The subject was first suggested to me a number of years ago by Mr. J. R. MacGillivray, whose continued assistance with Keats prob-

---

1. H. N. Fairchild, *The Noble Savage,* New York, 1928, p. 5.
2. Paul Leveloh, *Tennyson und Spenser,* Marburg, 1909, p. 52.
3. See O. F. Christie, *The Transition from Aristocracy,* London, 1927, p. 12.

lems has been very helpful. I should like to thank especially W. C. DeVane, my director, whose careful criticism and patient kindness have both been without stint, and also E. K. Brown, whose many suggestions are of long standing. Mr. Carl Rollins has generously allowed me to make use of a Kelmscott Press item from his collection. In the sphere of elusive split infinitives, I am grateful for the assistance of Miss Sara deFord. For supervision of the manuscript in the printing stages, I am much indebted to B. C. Nangle.

GEORGE H. FORD

BIBLIOGRAPHICAL NOTE

FOR Keats's poems, I have used the definitive text edited by H. W. Garrod; for Rossetti the 1911 text, and for Tennyson that edited by W. J. Rolfe. For Arnold, the *Collected Works of Matthew Arnold* were used when referring to his letters and less familiar essays. Other references to Arnold are from the readily accessible Macmillan editions of *Essays in Criticism,* Quiller-Couch's edition of his poetry, the 1883 text of *On the Study of Celtic Literature,* and Dover Wilson's edition of *Culture and Anarchy.* Texts of other writers are as listed in the bibliography.

ACKNOWLEDGMENTS

FOR permission to quote certain passages from the works concerned, I am indebted to the following publishers: to the Harvard University Press for Douglas Bush's *Mythology and the Romantic Tradition* (Cambridge, 1937), and for Dante Gabriel Rossetti's *The House of Life,* edited by Paull Franklin Baum (Cambridge, 1928); to W. W. Norton & Company, for Lionel Trilling's *Matthew Arnold* (New York, 1939); to The Odyssey Press, Inc., for Dante Gabriel Rossetti's *Poems, Ballads and Sonnets,* edited by Paull Franklin Baum (New York, 1937); to Lothrop, Lee & Shepard Company, for Albert Guérard's *Art for Art's Sake* (New York, 1936); to The University of North Carolina Press for Dante Gabriel Rossetti's *The Blessed Damozel,* edited by Paull Franklin Baum (Chapel Hill, 1937); to the Duke University Press for *An Analytical List of Manuscripts in the Duke University Library,* edited by Paull Franklin Baum (Durham, 1931); to Faber & Faber Ltd., for T. S. Eliot's *The Use of Poetry and the Use of Criticism* (London, 1934), and Georges Lafourcade's *Swinburne's Hyperion and Other Poems* (London, 1927); to Methuen & Company, and the Executors of E. V. Lucas for E. V. Lucas' *The Colvins and their Friends* (London, 1928). Messrs. Macmillan & Company have kindly granted permission to reproduce an illustration of *The Eve of St. Agnes* from Holman Hunt's *Pre-Raphaelitism and the Pre-Raphaelite Brotherhood* (London, 1906).

CONTENTS

PART THREE

ROSSETTI

PART FOUR

MORRIS, SWINBURNE, AND SOME OTHERS

ILLUSTRATIONS

KEATS AND THE VICTORIANS

I

Preliminaries: 1821–1840

What porridge had John Keats?

i

AMONG the poets of the nineteenth century, there are few who have reputations so well and firmly established today as that of John Keats. While Byron's meteoric popularity lingered on the continent well on into the century, it flickered out very rapidly in his own country, and in spite of grumblings among his many surviving votaries, it has never been successfully revived.[1] Shelley is certainly suspect, and if T. S. Eliot's bitter attack on him is symptomatic of any widespread feeling, the Sun-treader may share the comparative neglect accorded to his unreliable friend. And while our steady admiration of Wordsworth has been considerably enhanced by recent studies, it is nevertheless still qualified by a certain distrust of the emphasis which he placed on systems of epistemology and naturalism. In the midst of these shifting reputations, the bright star of Keats has assumed its place, as he himself modestly believed it would, steadfast and secure.

The evolution of Keats's reputation and influence constitutes an illuminating chapter in English literary history. His fame developed slowly, somewhat in the manner described in the ponderous opening sentence of *Modern Painters:*

If it be true . . . that nothing has been for centuries consecrated by public admiration, without possessing . . . some kind of sterling excellence, it is not because the average intellect and feeling of the majority of the public are competent . . . to distinguish what is really excellent, but because . . . the opinions formed on right grounds by those few who are in reality competent judges . . . communicate themselves gradually from mind to mind, descending lower as they extend wider, until they leaven the whole lump. . . .

---

1. The conflict between the insular and the continental still goes on. Maurice Baring speaks of meeting a Russian in 1913 who complained to him: "All you literary people in England are so munched and drained by the offsprings and tradition of the Sensuous school of delicious language—Keats—Tennyson—Yeats tradition, that you are quite incapable of doing justice to a poet such as Byron, who whatever you say is grossly underrated, and who whatever you say is a great poet." See E. V. Lucas, *The Colvins and Their Friends*, London, 1928, p. 324.

At the time of Keats's death in 1821, the few "competent judges" were indeed in the minority. By 1895, one hundred years after his birth, their verdict had been fully sustained in all the courts, but it was only after a long and arduous struggle. I shall touch here on the earlier stages of the struggle somewhat briefly, reserving more attention for the Victorian period during which Keats's poetry came into its own.

One of the small band of "competent judges" who defended Keats's poetry and character was the painter Joseph Severn (1793–1879). Severn, who had shared the dying poet's last hours in Rome, was especially resentful about the reception which his friend's writings had received. Forty-two years later, he looked back bitterly to those days after Keats's death when, he says, jesting Englishmen were fond of adding to the epitaph "Here lies one whose name was writ in water" the tag, "and *his works in milk and water*."[2]

Crabb Robinson, although likewise something of an early admirer of Keats,[3] felt rather differently about the matter. He was convinced that Keats's enemies were not numerous, and he remarked in 1830 that too much "fuss was made about his death."

Keats had probably as few enemies as any young poet. Through bad taste his genius was not appreciated, and from party spirit . . . his works were treated with unjust and stupid contempt in the *Quarterly Review. Voilà tout.*[4]

But this explanation is surely not *tout*. We may take Robinson's word for it that the scoffers were few, yet he does not go on to explain the real point at issue, that is, why the readers of this "genius" were perhaps even fewer. The neglect of Keats was more significant than the attacks made upon him. Two facts are inescapable. For nineteen years after his death not a single reprint of his poems appeared in England. Furthermore, it was not until 1848 that his first biography was published. The work of no other major English poet had received such neglect as Keats's.

Our account requires certain qualifications. In 1829 the Galignani edition was published in Paris, and between 1821 and 1840 his poems appeared occasionally in anthologies and gift books.[5] Yet generally speaking, the prospects for his future position in English poetry were not very promising in the years following his death. Even the warm

2. Joseph Severn, "On the Vicissitudes of Keats' Fame," *Atlantic Monthly*, xi (1863), 402.

3. Although Robinson preferred Wordsworth, he had some good words for Keats. See Henry Crabb Robinson, *On Books and Their Writers* (ed. E. J. Morley), London, 1938, i, 258–9. For his later view, see ii, 784.

4. *Ibid.*, i, 389.

5. E.g., Croly's *Beauties of the British Poets* (1828); *The Poetical Album* (1828); *Specimens of Lyrical Poets of Great Britain* (1828); *The Gem* (ed. Thomas Hood, 1829); *A Collection of English Sonnets* (ed. Housman, 1835).

enthusiasm of his publisher, John Taylor, was cooled by public neglect. "I should like to print a complete Edition of Keats's Poems" he
wrote in 1835, ". . . but the world cares nothing for him—I fear that
even 250 copies would not sell. . . ."[6] As Lounsbury notes, even
throughout the fourth decade of the century, Keats was comparatively unknown. When his name appears in critical literature "it is
frequently, perhaps in most cases, spelled wrongly."[7]

The causes of the neglect of Keats were numerous. For one thing,
there was the legend that he had been "deliberately murdered" as
Landor said, by the reviewers.[8] *Who killed John Keats?* We do not
take much stock in the *Quarterly* story today but it was fostered by
most of Keats's friends except Severn,[9] and seems to have been widely
believed. In some cases it worked to the poet's advantage. It attracted
the warm-hearted sympathy of Shelley, and his great elegy was
inspired by it. *Adonais* was a striking tribute to Keats, but we must
remember that Shelley's work was hardly more widely read than
that of the poet whose death he commemorated.[10] Furthermore, when
Adonais became known, it probably did more harm than good to
Keats's reputation. It took many years before Shelley's questionable
picture of the poet could be effaced, the poet

> . . . who grew,
> Like a pale flower by some sad maiden cherished,
> And fed with true love tears, instead of dew. . . .[11]

The legend, as I said, may have gained Keats some readers, but for the
most part it made him appear ridiculous, as in Byron's famous lines:

> John Keats, who was killed off by one critique,
> Just as he really promised something great,
> If not intelligible, without Greek,
> Contrived to talk about the gods of late,
> Much as they might have been supposed to speak.
> Poor fellow! his was an untoward fate;

---

6. Edmund Blunden, *Shelley and Keats as They Struck Their Contemporaries*,
London, 1925, p. 82.

7. Thos. R. Lounsbury, *The Life and Times of Tennyson*, New Haven, 1915, p. 161.

8. See *The Complete Works of Walter Savage Landor*, London, 1927–36, XVI, 221.

9. Crabb Robinson, *op. cit.*, II, 520. Much interesting material on the growth of
Keats's fame among Severn's friends in Italy is to be found in William Sharp's *Life and
Letters of Joseph Severn*, London, 1892, esp. pp. 159 ff. In the matter of the reviews, I
refer later to Leigh Hunt who also minimized their importance as a factor in Keats's
death.

10. The publication of Shelley's poetry was long delayed by the opposition of Sir
Timothy Shelley. In general, see the final chapter of Roger Ingpen's *Shelley in England*,
New York, 1917; also F. C. Mason, *A Study in Shelley Criticism*, Mercersburg, Pa.,
1937, chap. II.

11. Shelley had *Isabella* in mind when writing this passage, but his use of it is not
very happy.

'Tis strange the mind, that very fiery particle,
Should let itself be snuffed out by an article.

(*Don Juan,* Canto xi)

The story had some effect on Carlyle's estimate of Keats as well. Keats's poetry was despised by Carlyle as showing a "weak-eyed maudlin sensibility,"[12] and for Keats's character he had nothing but contempt. "Keats is a miserable creature" he said, "hungering after sweets which he can't get; going about saying, 'I am so hungry; I should so like something pleasant.'"[13] In Carlyle's essay on Johnson (1832), an obvious contrast is drawn. "Johnson, for his part, was no man to be killed by a review."[14] Until the story of Keats's "murder" was finally disproved by his biographers in the latter half of the century, his reputation suffered considerably on the score of his supposed weakness. Even sympathetic readers referred to him not as "Keats" but as "*poor* Keats."[15] I shall return to this aspect of his reputation in a later chapter.

Another reason for the neglect of Keats was, of course, the slashing treatment to which his work had been subjected in the hands of some of his reviewers. As Taylor stated in a letter of 1820:

We have some trouble to get through 500 copies of his work, though it is highly spoken of in the periodical works, but what is most against him, it has been thought necessary in the leading review, the *Quarterly,* to damn his [Poems]. . . . Damn them [I say] who could act in so cruel a way to a young man of undoubted Genius. . . .[16]

Taylor testifies here that the majority of the early reviews had been favourable to Keats. Jeffrey, for example, was genuinely indulgent.[17] So too *The Champion, The London Magazine,* Hunt's *Examiner* and others. But as Lounsbury shows, the journals which carried the greatest weight with the reading public of Keats's age were *The Quarterly* and *Blackwood's.* Outnumbered numerically, their adverse criticism was nevertheless important enough to hamper considerably the

---

12. Thomas Carlyle, *Critical and Miscellaneous Essays,* London (Chapman and Hall), n.d., I, 277.

13. T. W. Reid, *Life of Richard Monckton Milnes,* New York, 1891, I, 435.

14. Thomas Carlyle, *op. cit.,* III, 116. On Carlyle's dislike of Byron, Shelley, and Keats, see F. W. Roe, *Thomas Carlyle as a Critic of Literature,* New York, 1910.

15. Harriet Martineau, *Autobiography,* Boston, 1877, I, 508.

16. Edmund Blunden, *op. cit.,* p. 77. Taylor also stated that the five hundred volumes of the 1820 edition had gone into remainders. Concerning the relations of Taylor and Keats, Blunden's more detailed study *Keats's Publisher* (London, 1936) is useful.

17. *Edinburgh Review,* xxxiv (1820), 203–13. Cf. Sidney Colvin who considers Jeffrey's review to be insincere (*John Keats,* New York, 1917, pp. 478–80). About the earlier reviews, see Roberta D. Cornelius, "Two Early Reviews of Keats's First Volume," *PMLA,* XL (1925), 193–210; also G. L. Marsh and N. I. White, "Keats and the Periodicals of His Time," *Modern Philology,* xxxii (1934), 37–53.

growth of Keats's fame.[18] Keats's mind was not snuffed out by an article, but his work was, at least for a time. As late as 1833, Lockhart was still delighted with the success of the cudgelling which he had dealt *Endymion* in 1818.

Let us take this occasion to sing our palinode on the subject of *Endymion*. We certainly did not discover in that poem the same degree of merit that its more clear-sighted and prophetic admirers did. We did not foresee the unbounded popularity which has carried it through we do not know how many editions; which has placed it on every table; and, what is still more unequivocal, familiarized it in every mouth.[19]

The Scorpion could well afford to be sarcastic. But in reality he could hardly lay claim to all the credit for Keats's neglect. The main reason for it had nothing to do with the reviews or with the legend about Keats's having been killed by them. It was simply that his poetry was ahead of its time. His work suffered for a period by virtue of its very originality,[20] and Keats had to wait for a reading public which would catch up to him. Meanwhile, until 1830 at least, Byron held the field. Scott and Moore also had their followers, but to most readers between Waterloo and the first Reform Bill, poetry meant *Childe Harold* and *Don Juan*. All other verse seemed pale beside Byron's. As one of Landor's characters exclaimed in 1823, "Be sparing of your animadversions on Byron. He will always have more partisans and admirers than any other. . . ."[21]

In the light of this evidence, Keats's rise to fame in the latter half of the nineteenth century is, to say the least, remarkable. It was occasioned primarily by four factors: a shift in public taste (which becomes marked after 1850), his immense influence on the leading poets of the day, the resurrection of his personality by such biographers as Milnes and Colvin, and the appreciation of his poetry by various essayists including Arnold, Masson, Lowell, Bridges, and many others. The operation of these several factors is especially noticeable after 1850, but from 1821 until the first reprint of Keats's poems in 1840, the ground is prepared for such developments.

18. See Reynolds' comment quoted by Sidney Colvin, *Keats* (E.M.L.S.), London, 1915, p. 141.
19. *Quarterly Review*, XLIX (1833), 82. The question of Lockhart's authorship is discussed in the next chapter. His first article on Keats appeared in *Blackwood's Magazine*, III (1818), 519–24.
20. See Amy Lowell, *John Keats*, New York, 1925, II, 347. There is also an interesting discussion of why the generation of 1820 failed to recognize Keats, in Somerset Maugham's *Fifty Modern English Writers*, New York, 1934, p. 549.
21. *The Works of Walter Savage Landor*, V, 168.

ii

WHEN *La Belle Dame sans Merci* was first published in Hunt's *Indi-cator* (number XXXVII), it was signed rather oddly with the name "Caviare." "Caviare to the general" it might well be, but there were those who cherished its qualities. After Keats's death, most of his friends endeavoured to convert others to share their taste for his work, in some cases with important results.

Among these was Charles Lamb, who although not an intimate friend of Keats, was a great admirer of his poetry. Among his favour-ites, he ranked Keats next to Wordsworth.[22] Lamb used to urge Keats upon his friends, even on one occasion trying to convert Wordsworth to Keats's poetry, but not, we may imagine, with much success.[23]

Of more concrete assistance was Leigh Hunt. To have one's name associated with that of Hunt was certainly not an unqualified bless-ing,[24] but the leader of the Cockney School nevertheless carried con-siderable influence in some quarters. In his widely-discussed work of 1828, *Lord Byron and Some of his Contemporaries*, Hunt included a very sane chapter on Keats. In it he defended Keats's work by means of a series of quotations which indicate better taste in Hunt than that with which he is often credited. One of these quotations is the *Ode to a Nightingale*, which Hunt quotes at length, adding that he does so because "Mr. Keats's poems are in few hands, compared to what they will be." The remark suggests the poet's status at the time. A few years later, Hunt felt considerable private resentment against Keats, but his various notices on the poetry itself made him a useful herald.[25]

Another of Keats's friends, Charles Brown, was indirectly of con-siderable importance in the same development, for it was Brown who

22. See E. V. Lucas, *The Life of Charles Lamb*, London, 1905, pp. 543–4, and Crabb Robinson, *op. cit.*, I, 258.

23. The incident is mentioned in *The Prose Works of Thomas Hood*, New York, 1878, p. 395. See also Leigh Hunt's chapter on Keats in *Lord Byron and Some of his Contemporaries* where Lamb's enthusiasm is described. The latter account is the source of the remark which Wordsworth passed on *Endymion*, "a pretty piece of paganism." For further evidence of Wordsworth's lack of interest in Keats, see C. D. Thorpe, "Wordsworth and Keats," *PLMA*, XLII (1927), 1010–26.

24. For example, when Hunt praised Keats in 1828, he stimulated Lockhart to attack Keats again in the *Quarterly*: "Our readers have probably forgotten all about 'Endymion, a poem,' and the other works of this young man [Keats], and the all but universal roar of laughter with which they were received some ten or twelve years ago . . ." (*Quarterly Review*, XXXVII [1828], 416).

25. W. B. Scott speaks of meeting Hunt in 1837 and observing his resentment against Keats (*Autobiographical Notes*, New York, 1892, I, 128). This personal resentment is apparent in Hunt's *Autobiography* (London, 1850, II, 201–14), but his remarks on Keats's poetry here are much the same as those which he made in 1828 and at other times. On Keats's character, Hunt may often be prejudiced, but, like Severn, he had the good sense to realize that the reviewers were not responsible for his death.

seems to have introduced Keats's poetry to Walter Savage Landor.[26] Landor became a much more reputable champion of Keats than Leigh Hunt could ever have claimed to be. Throughout the *Imaginary Conversations* and poems there are various references to the qualities of Keats. Landor seems to have especially liked *Hyperion* and what he called the "Grecian" in Keats's work, which he contrasted with Byron and also with Wordsworth:

> Keats, the most Grecian of all, rejected the meter of Grecians;
> Poesy breath'd over *him*, breath'd constantly, tenderly, freshly;
> Wordsworth she left now and then. . . .
>
> *(Works,* xv, 168)

As early as 1828 he published a poem in honour of Keats,[27] some lines of which rise above the usual level of this class of poetry (which becomes all too common in the Victorian age), and in the *Imaginary Conversations* of that year he says:

In Keats, I acknowledge, there are many wild thoughts, and there are expressions which even outstrip them in extravagance: but in none of our poets, with the sole exception of Shakespeare, do we find so many phrases so happy in their boldness.[28]

Perhaps the most important service which Landor rendered to the growth of Keats's reputation occurred in connection with Milnes's undertaking to write Keats's biography, but this may be reserved for later consideration.

Other friends also rendered assistance in the early part of the century. Charles Dilke, for example, used his influence as editor of *The Athenaeum* to secure publicity for Keats.[29] Another was John Hamilton Reynolds, who introduced Keats's work to his friend and brother-in-law, Thomas Hood, with some important results.

When in 1827 the editors of *Blackwood's* published Hood's poem *Ode to the Moon,* they perhaps unwittingly paid a compliment to a poet whose work they had savagely attacked a few years previously.

26. I have been unable to find any references to Keats in Landor's writings previous to the time of his meeting with Brown in 1824, and at a later date Landor acknowledges that he obtained most of his knowledge about Keats from a friend about to publish a *Life of Keats* (1836). I assume that this refers to Brown, not Milnes. (See *Works of Walter Savage Landor,* xvi, 221 n.)

27. *Works,* xv, 140.

28. *The Works of Walter Savage Landor,* ix, 121. See also v, 307. Concerning Landor's general position as a critic, see Stanley T. Williams, "Walter Savage Landor as a Critic of Literature," *PMLA,* xxxviii (1923), 906–28.

29. S. C. Chew notes that *The Athenaeum,* which had seemed unfriendly to Keats in 1829, began to change in 1830 and that in 1832 it published an elegy on his death written by Barry Cornwall ("Keats After a Hundred Years," *The New Republic,* xxvi [1921], 49). I suspect that this change was owing to the influence of Dilke, who became full-editor in 1830. For Cornwall's elegy, see *The Athenaeum,* no. 228 (1832), 162.

The compliment was to Keats whose *Ode to Psyche* and *Endymion* had inspired Hood's poem. As Rossetti noted,[30] a very large number of Hood's earlier poems are imitations of Keats. It may be added that the word "imitations" is not too strong in this case. That Hood knew Keats personally is unlikely,[31] but he had become well acquainted with his poetry some time before Keats died in 1821. This early acquaintance enabled Hood to become the first of a long line of poets who draw from Keats. In 1822 he published *Lycus, the Centaur* in *The London Magazine*. It is a narrative poem which has much in common with the story of Glaucus and Circe in book III of *Endymion*, and, as Douglas Bush notes, there are also occasional passages which recall *Lamia*.[32] Likewise published in 1822 was *The Two Peacocks of Bedfont*, a work in which Hood draws from *The Eve of St. Agnes*. In one of its stanzas we find the first of many attempts to capture the atmosphere of Keats's description of the stained-glass window:

> But youth looks upward to the window shine,
>   Warming with rose and purple and the swim
> Of gold, as if thought-tinted by the stains
> Of gorgeous light through many-colour'd panes. . . .

For about eight years after the publication of *Lycus, the Centaur*, the influence of Keats on Hood's poetry is striking. Especially is this true in the case of the odes. We find there an *Ode to Melancholy* and an *Ode: Autumn*. The latter is a rather charming attempt to expand some of the closely-packed lines of the original:

> Where are the songs of Summer?—With the sun,
> Oping the dusky eyelids of the south,
> Till shade and silence waken up as one,
> And Morning sings with a warm odorous mouth.[33]

The same process is followed in Hood's poem *Ruth* which opens with the line:

> She stood breast high amid the corn,

and then proceeds to develop the theme suggested by Keats's line describing Ruth who "stood in tears amid the alien corn."

---

30. T. Hall Caine, *Recollections of Dante Gabriel Rossetti*, London, 1882, pp. 179–80. Rossetti's love of Hood's poetry was partly conditioned by its resemblance to Keats's.

31. See Walter Jerrold, *Thomas Hood: His Life and Times*, New York, 1909, p. 124.

32. Douglas Bush, *Mythology and the Romantic Tradition*, Cambridge, 1937, p. 190. The author suggests that the first line of *Endymion* is reflected in lines 154–5 of *Lycus*, but it appears more definitely in *The Poet's Portion* (1830):

> So that what there is steeped shall perish never,
>   But live and bloom, and be a joy for ever!

33. Hood, stanza II. The fourth stanza describing the spirit of Autumn and the "luscious cells" of the bees, the brimming garners of grain and such like is not so well handled.

Hood's *Ode to Melancholy* is not nearly so successful in its imitation of Keats. Mlle. Villard notes that its author seems to have seen a copy of Keats's original version of the *Ode on Melancholy,* for he reproduces "almost word for word"[34] the grisly opening stanza which Keats had had the good sense to reject when the poem was sent to press. Hood may have undergone melancholy experiences enough during his lifetime (at least at a later date), but the melancholy cloak does not suit him. Indeed we may wonder whether, except in his thoroughly individual *Song of the Shirt* and such pieces, Hood was not usually on the wrong tack in his serious verse. Thackeray, another comic poet, had felt in his youth much as Hood did. His schoolmaster testified that Thackeray used to speak "in terms of homage to the genius of Keats that he would not have vouchsafed to the whole tribe of humorists."[35] Yet however much he might have aspired to follow in Keats's footsteps, Thackeray soon realized that his own bent was not in that direction. From the first he restricted his poetry to the comic. Hood attempted to excel in both veins. In the one his success is abundant: in the other it is rare.

Hood's debt to Keats is apparent in some other poems such as the long work *Lamia,* and in a few short pieces including *The Water Lady. The Water Lady* is one of several poems in which Hood follows Keats's versification, in this case using the stanza-form (and also the theme) of *La Belle Dame sans Merci:*

> Alas, the moon should ever beam
> To show what man should never see!—
> I saw a maiden on a stream,
> And fair was she!

The dramatic-romance *Lamia,* which was written in 1827, is of some interest to any student of Keats's poem. Hood's attempt to cast the Lamia story into dramatic form shows by comparison some of the flaws of the original. The opening incident in Keats's version, for example, is wisely rejected by the later poet. In other respects, he follows Keats more or less closely, securing some variety by the introduction of Mercutius into the tale and by the account of his murder at the hands of the sorceress.

Between 1821 and 1840, Hood was a well-known writer, yet his popularity can hardly be said to have rested on the poems to which I have referred. Nor would his borrowing from Keats have much effect

34. Léonie Villard, *The Influence of Keats on Tennyson and Rossetti,* Paris, 1914, p. 20. She refers, I presume, to lines 45 ff. of Hood's poem. The conjecture seems reasonable. Hood's friend Reynolds possessed a number of Keats manuscripts which he later gave to Lord Houghton. Mlle. Villard's study of Hood and Keats is the best account of the subject. It may be compared with an article by Frederic Olivero, "Hood and Keats," *MLN,* xxviii (1913), 233–5.
35. Lewis Melville, *William Makepeace Thackeray,* London, 1910, I, 31.

on the development of the earlier poet's reputation. These imitations are nevertheless of considerable interest. In the first place, they seem so obvious that one is tempted to wonder whether Hood imagined, in view of the neglect of Keats, that he could borrow openly without many readers becoming aware of it. Probably he did not consider such sides of the matter, although he did have that particular advantage over later poets who derive from Keats. Hood was the first who tried to profit from the example which Keats had set, and whether or not his imitations are of much intrinsic value, they give us some notion of the direction in which the wind would be blowing in the poetry of the Victorian age itself.

iii

FINALLY in this connection, there is Robert Browning. From the point of view of chronology, Browning hardly belongs to a discussion of the period 1821–40 and his view of Keats during those years would not have carried much weight. Yet for a number of reasons, he and his writings can best be considered here.

Browning was the first of the major Victorian poets to discover Keats. In his case, the discovery was not owing to a suggestion from one of Keats's friends but was made quite by accident. In 1826,[36] at the age of fourteen, he became a member of the slowly-growing band of Keats readers, and although he could hardly rank then as a "competent" judge, few were more ardently zealous than he was. Keats, together with Shelley (whose work he had discovered earlier), changed his whole conception of the function of poetry. Although his response to Shelley was more intense and had a much stronger effect on his own work, his liking for Keats was more lasting. Shelley paled for him in later years,[37] but Keats he praised to the end. In one of his *Parleyings* of 1887 he spoke of Christopher Smart as the only poet worth bothering about between Milton and Keats, "the superhuman poet-pair" as he called them.[38]

36. For an account of Browning's discovery of Shelley and Keats see Edmund Gosse, *Robert Browning: Personalia*, Cambridge, 1890, pp. 23–4. F. A. Pottle has shown that Shelley's work first came into Browning's hands in 1826 (*Shelley and Browning: A Myth and Some Facts*, Chicago, 1923, pp. 19 ff.). Keats seems to have been discovered shortly afterwards. Browning himself was rather vague on the point when he wrote to Wise in 1886: "I got at the same time nearly, *Endymion* and *Lamia*, &c., just as if they had been purchased a week before, and not years after the death of Keats!" (*Letters of Robert Browning*, New Haven, 1933, p. 246).

37. Cf. his letter to Furnival (1885) in Edward Dowden's *Robert Browning*, New York, 1915, p. 10 n.; also Alexander Carlyle, "Correspondence Between Carlyle and Browning," *Cornhill Magazine*, cxi (1915), 660 n. The decline of Shelley's influence was much earlier than the decline of Browning's love of his poetry. According to Pottle, Shelley's influence is not to be found after *Sordello* (Pottle, *op. cit.*, p. 32).

38. *Parleying with Christopher Smart*, section vi. See also Griffin and Minchin, *Robert Browning*, London, 1910, p. 262.

Browning's best-known tribute to Keats is his short poem *Popularity* written in the early Fifties when the influence of Keats on other poets was becoming marked. He very aptly describes how Keats's imitators had profited from the world of colour which his poetry had opened up:

> Hobbs hints blue,—straight he turtle eats:
>   Nobbs prints blue,—claret crowns his cup:
> Nokes outdares Stokes in azure feats,—
>   Both gorge. Who fished the murex up?
> What porridge had John Keats?

Perhaps the most interesting of his comments on Keats is one made in connection with the Carlyles. He told Allingham that he had little respect for the opinions of Carlyle and "his own little circle" and cited the case of their incapacity to recognize Keats:

One day I was talking of Keats, and Carlyle's opinion of him, to Mrs. Carlyle; she asked me to lend her something of Keats's, and I brought her *Isabella* and *The Eve of St. Agnes* (I was too knowing to try her with *Endymion*). She wrote me a letter—"Almost any young gentleman with a sweet tooth might be expected to write such things. *Isabella* might have been written by a seamstress who had eaten something too rich for supper and slept upon her back." Do you think (B. said) I cared about this more than for the barking of a little dog?[39]

This event occurred in 1845 and so irritated Browning that he actually remembered the "barking" quite distinctly many years later.[40]

In the light of Browning's own poetry, it is very difficult to account for his love of Keats. There are a few signs of Keatsian influence in the early poems, but by comparison with that of Shelley it is strictly limited. Browning spoke once of readers who "go grubbing among my old wardrobe of thirty years' accumulation, and, picking off here a quaint button, there a queer tag and tassel, exhibit them as my daily wear."[41] Although one can find occasional Keats-like buttons in several of the poems, they are certainly not his daily wear. Such, for example, is the following line in *Sordello:*

> I am to sing while ebbing day dies soft

which may recall Keats's "soft-dying day" in *To Autumn.* One critic, H. L. Hovelaque, considers that the influence of Keats on Browning was extensive, but I suspect that he overstates the case.[42] The place

39. *The Diary of William Allingham*, London, 1907, p. 310.
40. He told Allingham about the incident in 1881 but it seems to have occurred in 1845. Elizabeth Barrett mentions Mrs. Carlyle's letter (and also comments upon it herself) in that year. *Letters of Robert Browning and Elizabeth Barrett Barrett*, New York, 1899, I, 194.
41. G. F. Palgrave, *Francis Turner Palgrave*, London, 1899, p. 94.
42. Cf. H. L. Hovelaque, *La jeunesse de Browning*, Paris, 1932, pp. 128–30.

where Keats did leave some imprint on Browning's work was in his emphasis upon colour, to which Browning himself drew attention in *Popularity*. When it suits his purposes, Browning can be as vivid a painter as any of his contemporaries in poetry, and the flashing colours of *Pippa Passes* and other poems probably owe something to the general influence of Keats. There is some of Keats's richness, too, in the well-known lyric from *Paracelsus*:

> Heap cassia, sandal-buds and stripes
> Of labdanum, and aloe-balls . . .
> Or shredded perfume, like a cloud
> From closet long to quiet vowed,
> With mothed and dropping arras hung,
> Mouldering her lute and books among,
> As when a queen, long dead, was young.[43]

This general influence is of some importance, but by comparison with other Victorian poets, Browning owes very little to Keats. His own poetry represents a turning away from many of the things which Keats emphasized, and the whole temper of his genius is of a different cast. "My stress lay on the incidents in the development of a soul: little else is worth study." These words which he spoke with reference to *Sordello* are applicable to almost all his poems. His strong dramatic sense and his fondness for the grotesque enabled him to steer clear of the main line of Victorian poets who followed Keats.

To understand Browning's liking for Keats, one can turn to his essay on Shelley where he explains how poetry of a type essentially different from his own had, nevertheless, a great fascination for him. This eclecticism enabled him to do something which very few readers have ever been able to accomplish; that is, to retain, over a lengthy period, a love for both Shelley and Keats at the same time, without the one almost completely excluding the other. Browning contributed something to the revival of both poets, and neither could have asked for a more belligerent champion. He does not belong, however, to a Shelleyan "school," and even less to a Keatsian "school." He is the most original figure in Victorian poetry.

When Browning abandoned Byronism in 1826 and turned instead to Keats and Shelley, he was anticipating a tendency which in a few years was to become common among young men of his generation. Tennyson and his associates also represent the change. During the nineteen years in which Keats's poetry remained unpublished in England, the development of his reputation was aided not only by his friends such as Hunt, and by critics such as Landor, but by a negative

---

43. Cf. *The Shorter Poems of Robert Browning* (ed. W. C. DeVane), New York, 1934, p. 329. The editor suggests that Christopher Smart's *Song to David* might have been Browning's model for this passage.

factor of great importance: the general decline of Byron's popularity after 1830. While Byron's "muscular poetry" (as Harold Nicolson terms it) held the stage, there was little room for *Lamia* and *The Eve of St. Agnes*. The way was paved for their acceptance when Byron's mighty vogue finally collapsed a few years after his death.[44] Byron's decline seems to have been followed by a general confusion of standards on the part of the reading public. As Henry Taylor expressed it in 1834, ". . . the decline in popular estimation which he has suffered for these last few years, may be rather attributed to a satiated appetite on the part of the public than to a rectified taste."[45] New tastes were nevertheless being formed within this interregnum vacuum, and out of it, new names were emerging. At first the one to profit most was Wordsworth. Keats had to wait his turn, for as he said in his sonnet, "Fame, like a wayward girl," was still being coy. The further shift of taste which brings Keats's work definitely to the fore is not clearly developed until after 1850, and I have therefore left it for discussion in a later chapter. In such a development, the decline of Byron was the first essential step.

This account of the period 1821–40 may have given a misleading impression by the emphasis placed on those scattered writers and critics who early came under the spell of Keats's work. Together with Tennyson, they prepared the way for his acceptance by the Victorians, yet their number was necessarily very small. Like Taylor, many of Keats's friends seem to have had little hope of ever making any impression upon the prevailing indifference or hostility which his poetry had evoked. Some years after his death, Fanny Brawne herself had no inklings of her former lover's future renown. Writing to Brown in 1829, she said: "I fear the kindest act would be to let him rest for ever in the obscurity to which unhappy circumstances have condemned him."[46]

44. See S. C. Chew's excellent chapter in *Byron in England*, London, 1924, pp. 220–62.

45. Henry Taylor, *Philip van Artevelde*, London, 1834, Preface, p. xx.

46. *Letters of Keats*, p. lxiii. See Charles Dilke, *Papers of a Critic*, London, 1875, I, 11. In their introduction to Charles Brown's *Life of John Keats* (Oxford, 1937, pp. 13–14) Bodurtha and Pope discuss this letter but they do not explain why the remark was first printed in the papers of Dilke. Did Dilke receive a similar letter in 1831?

PART ONE

TENNYSON

"And so she throve and prosper'd; so three years
   She prosper'd; on the fourth she fell,
Like Herod, when the shout was in his ears,
   Struck thro' with pangs of hell."

The Palace of Art.

II

Keats's Debt to Tennyson

PERHAPS the most important single agency in effecting the revival of Keats was the famous group at Cambridge known as the Apostles.[1] It included Richard Monckton Milnes, Keats's first biographer, and Alfred Tennyson, his greatest follower in poetry. The development of Keats's reputation among the Victorians owed more to the enthusiasm of these two men than to that of any others. The contribution of Milnes is obvious enough, but the case of Tennyson is more subtle. His recognition of Keats involved, as we shall see, a direct influence on his own work. Thus Keats's poetry became familiar to many readers through the medium of a popular body of poetry modelled somewhat on his own. The questions of the reputation and influence of the earlier poet are hence intimately related. It will be found that Keats himself was deeply indebted to the success of his most eminent follower in the Victorian age.

The critics of the Thirties were not slow to seize on the similarities between the two poets. A writer in *The New Monthly Magazine*, reviewing the 1830 volume, observed:

It is full of precisely the kind of poetry for which Mr. Keats was assailed, and for which the world is already beginning to admire him. We do not mean that it contains anything equal . . . to the "Hyperion," the "Ode to the Nightingale," or the "Eve of St. Agnes." But it does contain many indications of a similar genius.[2]

So too Hallam's review in *The Englishman's Magazine* suggested the essential link between them. Was the coupling justified? If admiration is any clue to imitation, the asseveration was certainly well-founded. From the twentieth-century point of view, Tennyson's appreciation of Keats may seem somewhat limited, but his enthusiasm knew few bounds.

"There is something of the innermost soul of poetry in almost everything he ever wrote."[3] These words represent the prevailing tone of

1. For an account of the literary tastes of the group, see T. W. Reid, *Life of Richard Monckton Milnes*, I, 72 ff.

2. Thos. R. Lounsbury, *The Life and Times of Tennyson*, p. 224. As Lounsbury shows, the next review of Keats in *The New Monthly Magazine* (xxxvii [1833], 72) repeated the account of Tennyson's debt to Keats, but at this time disapproved of it. The reviewer (possibly Bulwer) states that *Oenone* and *The Hesperides* are "Keatesian [*sic*] to the marrow."

3. Hallam Tennyson, *Alfred Lord Tennyson: A Memoir*, London, 1898, II, 286. In notes hereafter this work is mentioned simply as *Memoir*.

Tennyson's references to Keats. In the *Memoir*, there are a considerable number of references, not merely general estimates but little "asides" which illustrate how thoroughly familiar the later poet was with all the writings of the earlier. Keats seems to have become part of his inner consciousness. In a letter urging Thackeray to visit him, he remarked that the country air "as Keats has it, is worth sixpence a pint." Tennyson's sister Mary early shared his appreciation. In 1834 she wrote to him, "Fred [Tennyson] has set off to quaff companionless a beaker full of the warm South."[4] And as Mlle. Villard notes, a consciousness of Keats frequently appeared during his travels. "One day as he was . . . admiring Alpine scenery near Mürren, his own enjoyment led him to think of what he aptly called Keats's 'keen physical imagination.' 'If he had been here' he added, 'he would in one line have given us a picture of that mountain.' "[5]

Tennyson's appreciation of Keats, unlike his early passion for Byron, was not a passing phase of his taste. Keats was Tennyson's favourite nineteenth-century poet. In discussing the Romantic poets with Allingham he exclaimed: "But the man I count greater than them all—Wordsworth, Coleridge, Byron, Shelley, every one of 'em —is Keats, who died at twenty-five—thousands of faults! . . . but he's wonderful!"[6] Shelley, by contrast, was too ethereal for him; some of his poems, he said, "seemed to go up, and burst."[7] The limits of Tennyson's appreciation of Shelley are best illustrated by the fact that it was his opposition which prevented Shelley's most characteristic lyric (*Life of Life*) from appearing in *The Golden Treasury*.[8] And even Wordsworth he could describe on occasion, to the horror of Palgrave, as "thick-ankled."[9] For parts of Coleridge he had great admiration. Like many Victorian poets, Tennyson was attracted to those features of Coleridge's poetry which anticipate the work of Keats, and he was unquestionably influenced by them. Yet Coleridge was not the master poet for Tennyson that Keats seemed to have been. He used to quote to his family the fragmentary *Eve of St. Mark* and the *Ode to a Nightingale* as illustrations of his conviction that "he would have been among the very greatest of us if he had lived."[10]

His choice of these two pieces is characteristic. Tennyson shared the limitations of his contemporaries in their approach to Keats. *Hyperion* did not please him so much as the odes and the pictorial narratives. Its sublime opening passage seemed to him somewhat

4. Léonie Villard, *The Influence of Keats on Tennyson and Rossetti*, p. 26.
5. *Ibid.*, p. 27.
6. *The Diary of William Allingham*, p. 295.
7. *Memoir*, II, 500.
8. B. Ifor Evans, "Tennyson and the Origins of the Golden Treasury," *TLS*, Dec. 8, 1932, p. 941.
9. *Memoir*, II, 505.
10. *Memoir*, II, 286.

superfluous and he remarked, oddly enough, that Keats's blank verse "lacked originality in movement."[11]

Yet on the basis of his other poems, Tennyson was prepared to say that Keats showed greater promise than any English poet since Milton.[12] It is highly significant that at the Keats Memorial celebrations of 1894, the words of Tennyson were repeated by more than one speaker. His stamp of approval had contributed much to the development of Keats's fame. As Sir Edmund Gosse said in his address:

Tennyson was more than once heard to assert that Keats, had his life been prolonged, would have been our greatest poet since Milton. . . . Fifty years ago to have made such a proposition in public would have been thought ridiculous, and sixty years ago almost wicked. . . . But all that is over now. Keats lives . . . among the English poets. Nor among them, merely, but in the first rank of them—among the very few of whom we instinctively think whenever the characteristic verse-men of our race are spoken of.[13]

Tennyson sometimes went beyond mere appreciation to link his own practice with Keats's. With reference to the "abominations" which he found in the poems of Jean Ingelow, he remarked in a letter: ". . . I myself in younger days have been guilty of the same, and so was Keats."[14] But such couplings are rare. Tennyson almost habitually denied the charge that his poetry had much in common with that of Keats, or of any other poet for that matter.

In spite of his protests, however, his name came to be inseparably linked with that of the author of *The Eve of St. Agnes*. It was almost as if he had caught the torch from the failing hands of Keats. In 1831, Hallam wrote confidently to Leigh Hunt that Keats had at last found a successor:

Since the death of John Keats, the last lineal descendant of Apollo, our English region of Parnassus has been domineered over by kings of shreds and patches. But, if I mistake not, the true heir is found.[15]

By the very nature of his poetry, Tennyson consciously or unconsciously prepared the way for the popularization of his predecessor.

11. *Memoir*, I, 152. See Douglas Bush: "Tennyson's deafness to Keats's blank verse seems curious and perverse, for his own is far closer to Keats than to Milton" (*Mythology and the Romantic Tradition*, p. 212 n.).

12. G. F. Palgrave, *Francis Turner Palgrave*, pp. 174–5. Palgrave elsewhere qualified Tennyson's statement (influenced perhaps by his own ardent feelings for Wordsworth): "That is, *potentially* above Wordsworth, whose *opus operatum* of eighty years gave him *actually* that place in Tennyson's mind" (*Landscape in Poetry*, London, 1897, p. 210 n.).

13. Edmund Gosse, *Critical Kit-Kats*, London, 1896, pp. 24–5.

14. *Memoir*, I, 287.

15. W. R. Nicoll and T. J. Wise, *Literary Anecdotes of the Nineteenth Century*, London, 1895, I, 24.

The reviewers seem to have taken for granted the kinship between the two poets. We have already noted how some of the more discerning reviews of the 1830 volume discovered in Tennyson the principal writer upon whom the Keatsian mantle had fallen. "We have seen" said Leigh Hunt, "no such poetical writing since the last volume of Mr. Keats."[16] This provocative comparison stimulated Lockhart's brilliantly biting review of 1833. He offers his readers, he says, "a new prodigy of genius—another and a brighter star of that galaxy or *milky way* of poetry of which the lamented Keats was the harbinger."[17] The union was again specified in a review of Monckton Milnes's poems in 1839, where the latter is chastised for paying homage to "the fantastic shrines of such baby idols as Mr. John Keats and Mr. Alfred Tennyson."[18] It is interesting that during these years, the worst stigma which some readers could attach to a poet's name was that he resembled Keats.

The bitterness of such censure was not to continue for long. In the Forties, Lockhart himself is said to have recanted and to have spoken (privately) in terms of highest praise of both Keats and Tennyson.[19] The Scorpion is even said to have played some part in bringing about the publication of one of the two editions of Keats's work issued in 1841.[20] Throughout the Fifties, the Keatsian stamp was already so manifest in a large number of Victorian poems that it was too late for critics to stem the tide. We find Clough in 1853 speaking of a recognizable "school of Keats." In the minds of most readers, there was no questioning Tennyson's importance in that "school."[21]

Tennyson's part in generating an awareness of Keats's place in English poetry was thus of the greatest significance. After the publication of his 1842 and 1847 volumes, the critics were grudgingly obliged to face the facts of slowly rising sales. And as Tennyson assumed his place as chief poet of the age, the revival of Keats was assured. Thackeray accurately represented the taste of his time when he pictured the surprise of Colonel Newcome when confronted with the new enthusiasms of the younger generation:

16. Lounsbury, *op. cit.*, p. 236.

17. *Quarterly Review*, XLIX (1833), 81. Much dispute has been waged concerning Lockhart's responsibility for the articles on Keats in *Blackwood's* (1818) and also for this review. The evidence to the contrary, especially in the instance of *The Quarterly*, seems rather vague to me, and I follow those who give Lockhart the credit for having written them. The whole question is reviewed by M. C. Hildyard, *Lockhart's Literary Criticism*, Oxford, 1931, pp. 6–12.

18. *Quarterly Review*, LXIV (1839), 60.

19. Andrew Lang, *Life and Letters of John Gibson Lockhart*, London, 1897, II, 400–01.

20. After 1840, editions became frequent: 1841, 1841, 1851, 1854, 1861, 1865, 1867, 1872, 1873, 1874, 1876, 1878, 1880, 1880, 1884, 1884, 1886.

21. See e.g., *Edinburgh Review*, XC (1849), 430; also Milnes's *Life and Letters of John Keats*, New York, 1848, pp. 253–4.

Lord Byron not one of the greatest poets of the world! Sir Walter a poet of the second order! . . . Mr. Keats and this young Mr. Tennyson of Cambridge, the chief of modern poetic literature![22]

In these ways, the reputation of Keats throughout the Victorian age owed more, perhaps, to Tennyson than to anyone else except Lord Houghton. As the name of Tennyson became increasingly more respected (and, in reality, more respectable) so too rose the reputation and influence of Keats. By 1872, even *The Quarterly* could see the handwriting on the wall and was prepared to admit that ". . . his writings have, we think, done more to determine the subsequent course of English poetry than those of any other poet."[23]

There were, however, some lingering reservations in the mind of this reviewer. He admitted Keats's importance, but he was not pleased with it. But as Keats's fame spread in succeeding decades, *The Quarterly* was obliged to back down all the way.[24] The whole history of Keats's reputation is told in the changing attitudes of that stalwart journal *The Quarterly*, and by 1893, the wheel had come full circle. What is significant in the lavish and unqualified praise finally accorded to Keats in the following review of Tennyson is that the success of Tennyson had secured the reputation, once and for all, of his young predecessor.

For Tennyson, as for many others,
> "The soul of Adonais, like a star,
> Beacons from the abode where the immortal are."

Keats's poems, steeped as they are in the purest essence of poetry, were peculiarly spiritual in their ideality. His mythological passion breathed a living soul into the divinities of Greece; his solitary wanderings in "faery lands forlorn" enabled him to throw the spell of enchantment over its dreams and legends; his gleanings from field and forest were fresh, sweet, and faithful; and his interpretation of the essential inner life of poetry was conveyed in language which was itself instinct with form and aglow with colour. *In all these four points Tennyson was the follower of Keats . . . and developed to the fruit what Keats had left in the bud.*[25]

The bodies of the early Quarterly reviewers were, no doubt, actually rotating in their graves.

22. Quoted by Sidney Colvin, *John Keats*, 1917, pp. 537–8.
23. *Quarterly Review*, cxxxii (1872), 60.
24. E.g., see the review of Arnold's essay on Keats (cliii [1882], 459–60), and of Colvin's biography of Keats (clxvi [1888], 308–38).
25. *Quarterly Review*, clxxvi (1893), 14. (Italics mine.)

III

Tennyson's Debt to Keats

i

UP to this point we have been working on an assumption made by the Victorians themselves that the coupling of Keats with Tennyson was entirely justified, that Tennyson was deeply influenced by Keats and even drew frequently from him not only in spirit but in phrasing. The assumption remains to be proved. It has been challenged, with considerable vigour, by J. F. A. Pyre in his excellent study of Tennyson's style.[1] Perhaps Mr. Pyre has been influenced by Tennyson's own dislike of the charge of imitation. In his Notes to *The Princess,* Tennyson complained that "a prosaic set" was growing up who believed that the poet "is forever poking his nose between the pages of some old volume in order to see what he can appropriate. They will not allow one to say 'Ring the Bell' without finding we have taken it from Sir P. Sidney. . . ."[2] Such complaints were several times reiterated.

We can sympathize with Tennyson's abhorrence of the stolid, axe-grinding source-hunter, but there is a tone about these declarations which is very revealing. As someone said in another connection: "Tennyson is indeed full of translations and reminiscences; he was a plagiarist, as Virgil and Spenser and Milton and Shelley were plagiarists, but *a plagiarist of less assurance*."[3] That is to say, he was very touchy on the point, and with some cause. Fausset speaks of the imitative nature of Tennyson's genius, and remarks that Bulwer Lytton's satirical lines of 1845 "contained a modicum of truth. . . ."

> Of borrowed notes, the mock-bird's modish tune,
> The jingling medley of purloined conceits,
> Out-babying Wordsworth and out-glittering Keats;
> Where all the airs of patchwork pastoral chime
> To drown the ears in Tennysonian rhyme![4]

A more kindly-expressed view is given by one of the most deeply sympathetic of Tennyson's readers, F. T. Palgrave, in a statement which should carry some weight:

1. J. F. A. Pyre, *The Formation of Tennyson's Style,* Madison, 1921, p. 21.
2. Notes by Tennyson to the Eversley edition of *The Princess,* p. 241.
3. W. M. Dixon, *A Primer of Tennyson,* London, 1902, p. 132.
4. Hugh I'Anson Fausset, *Tennyson,* London, 1923, p. 71.

It is among those poets with whom traceable references to their ancestors in art are frequent, allusions which, echo-like, multiply and sweeten their own strains . . . that Tennyson, all know, is to be classed.[5]

Palgrave's hint can be followed out in a number of directions. For example, W. P. Mustard has demonstrated one side of Tennyson's borrowings in his *Classical Echoes in Tennyson* (London, 1904). Leveloh, the German scholar, has traced and over-traced his debt to Spenser. Mlle. Villard has elaborated some aspects of his debt to Keats. Less successfully, Henry Van Dyke has written of his borrowings from Milton and the Bible.[6] Minor poems of the seventeenth century also find echoes in Tennyson, and his obligations to Wordsworth in his "pathetic" popular tales such as *Dora* or *Enoch Arden* should be sufficiently obvious.

I do not think that we need to be frightened by Tennyson's fervent protests against source-hunting. It is true enough that in drawing from Keats, he never went so far as some of his successors. We find no poems of his comparable to such direct imitations as Swinburne's *Hyperion* or Meredith's *Daphne*. Tennyson's borrowings are more subtle. Echoes of phrase appear and reappear in his verse and these give us some indication of the extent of the Keatsian influence. Keats himself has left us the best description of the process:

> How many bards gild the lapses of time!
> A few of them have ever been the food
> Of my delighted fancy,—I could brood
> Over their beauties, earthly, or sublime:
> And often, when I sit me down to rhyme,
> These will in throngs before my mind intrude. . . .

To trace out some of these echoes may give us a hint, first of all, of the time when Tennyson discovered Keats, and when his influence first made itself felt.

From what evidence we have, it seems probable that Tennyson had not discovered Keats before entering Cambridge in February, 1828. His father's library was well provided with collections of English poetry, but that of the neglected youth of the Cockney school does not seem to have been included. In Tennyson's first volume, *Poems of Two Brothers* (1827), there is ample evidence that he had been reading Byron and Ossian, but no sign of any acquaintance with Keats or, for that matter, Shelley.[7] If, as Palgrave says, the Apostles

5. *Memoir*, II, 497.
6. Henry Van Dyke, *The Poetry of Tennyson*, New York, 1915. Two of the chapters are entitled: "Milton and Tennyson" and "The Bible in Tennyson." It must be admitted that it is rather difficult to penetrate through the mists of pious and verbose homage of these chapters to discover what the influence really was.
7. The *Dell of E* is one of the few poems in the volume which seems to anticipate the Keatsian note.

introduced him to Shelley, it is quite probable that he made the acquaintance of Keats at the same time.

This brings us to the difficult question of *The Lover's Tale* (1828). Tennyson's own statements about the date of composition for the poem are somewhat confusing, and we do not know whether or not he had read Keats before writing it. There are only one or two lines in the early parts which show any possible direct imitation of Keats. Thus the passage

> All the west
> And even unto the middle south was ribb'd
> And barred with bloom on bloom, (1, 404–06)

seems to echo Keats's expression in *To Autumn:*

> While barred clouds bloom the soft-dying day. . . .

But as evidence on which to base a case, this is too flimsy. The interesting fact about the poem is that it is so Keatsian in tone. Here is Tennyson's first serious attempt to write a poem of any length (we may pass over the boyish *Devil and the Lady*), and it is remarkable how much *The Lover's Tale* does share in common with *Endymion*. There is a similar exuberance of words and descriptive details of landscape, and there is a similar emphasis on "panting" love. More than anything else, *The Lover's Tale* illustrates how in early manhood Tennyson was attracted to something which would develop into the Aesthetic Movement. Shelley began his career with a *Queen Mab*. But the youthful Tennyson, significantly enough, writes a poem in which philosophical and political issues have no place. It is a world of beauty and a world of a particular kind of passion. It is also the world of John Keats.

It was in these spheres that the youthful Tennyson's genius would flourish, as the volumes of 1830 and 1832 will illustrate. Whether or not he had actually discovered the author of *Endymion* before *The Lover's Tale* was written, remains an open question. What is certain, in the light of the trend of his own poetry, is that when he opened his first volume of Keats, he must have felt much like that young poet himself when, on a July evening of 1816, he first heard Chapman speak out loud and bold and a new planet swam into his ken. Tennyson's enthusiasm led, of course, to imitation, frequently of actual phrasing. Some of these imitations of phrasing may be traced out before considering the debt in what seem to me its more important, if less tangible, aspects.

If a Keatsian enthusiast of 1830 had come across a small volume marked *Poems Chiefly Lyrical* by A. Tennyson, he might have been struck, as he read, by a sense of familiarity with occasional expressions. A line in the *Leonine Elegiacs* for example,

Over the pools in the burn water-gnats murmur and mourn,

would have a familiar ring to it. A recollection of *To Autumn* would explain its familiarity, for Keats had written:

Then in a wailful choir the small gnats mourn. . . .

The word "rillets" in *Recollections of the Arabian Nights* might be less familiar, but a study of *Endymion* (II, 945) would disclose its probable source in the line:

In amorous rillets down her shrinking form![8]

Two years later, if he read through a second volume by the same author, he might have been much more forcibly impressed by other Keatsian echoes. In the little poem *Kate* for example, the rather striking expression in the line

Her heart is like a throbbing star,

would recall that Porphyro in *The Eve of St. Agnes* had arisen:

Ethereal, flush'd, and like a throbbing star
Seen mid the sapphire heaven's deep repose. . . .[9]

Or again, the dazzling picture of Lancelot in *The Lady of Shalott* might remind him not only of Spenser's Prince Arthur,[10] but of Keats's *Endymion*, beneath whose breast "was hung a silver bugle. . . ." (I, 173). Even the unfortunate prettiness of the following description would not affect him with the same sense of novelty as felt by a reader unfamiliar with Keats:

The shallop flitteth silken-sail'd. . . .

For Keats had used the same terms, fourteen years before, in his *Endymion*.[11]

8. Villard (*op. cit.*, p. 47) quotes William F. Arnold to the effect that Keats found the word in Browne's *Britannia's Pastorals*. As de Sélincourt shows in the glossary to his edition of Keats, the word becomes common after Keats used it.

9. Tennyson's penchant for such peculiar stellar images seems to have been modelled on that of Keats. Compare, e.g., *Lancelot and Elaine*, 1234-5:
Whereon the lily-maid of Astolat
Lay smiling, like a star in blackest night,
with *Endymion*, I, 990-1:
This said, he rose, faint-smiling like a star
Through autumn mists. . . .

10. Cf. *The Faerie Queene*, I, VII, 29, 30. The passages clearly demonstrate that Tennyson sometimes drew directly from other poets. See W. S. Kennedy, "Tennyson and Other Debtors to Spenser's Faerie Queene," *Poet Lore*, x (1898), 493.

11. Paul Leveloh discusses the use of "shallop" in his *Tennyson und Spenser . . .* , Marburg, 1909, p. 27. Keats used it several times, e.g., *Endymion*, I, 423. In *Endymion* we also find the expression "silken sail" (IV, 249).

Such echoes persist in the later volumes of Tennyson's verse. Although he seems to make a break away from the *spirit* of Keats, he retains his habit of imitating isolated passages. Sometimes the imitation seems to be conscious. Keats had written:

> Where swarms of minnows show their little heads. . . .
> If you but scantily hold out the hand,
> That very instant not one will remain. . . .
>   (*I Stood Tip-toe*, 72 ff.)

Tennyson in *Geraint and Enid* (467 ff.) provides a parallel:

>   . . . like a shoal
> Of darting fish, that on a summer morn . . .
> Come slipping o'er their shadows on the sand,
> But if a man who stands upon the brink
> But lift a shining hand against the sun,
> There is not left the twinkle of a fin. . . .

On the other hand, the imitation is often, no doubt, unconscious. The phrase has settled in Tennyson's mind and reappears without any definite realization of source. Thus when in *Guinevere* (line 281) the young nun describes to the Queen the spirits of the hills,

> With all their dewy hair blown back like flame,

we may be reminded of the carved angels in *The Eve of St. Agnes,*

> With hair blown back, and wings put cross-wise on their breasts.[12]

Similarly, perhaps, with the parallel passages in *The Gardener's Daughter* and the *Ode to a Nightingale:*

> The lime a summer home of murmurous wings,

and

> The coming musk-rose, full of dewy wine,
> The murmurous haunt of flies on summer eves.

One could multiply such examples of this phase of Tennyson's debt to Keats. They are of interest not only in their own right as a comment on Tennyson's methods of writing, but because they show how deeply steeped the poet was in the entire body of Keats's work from *I Stood Tip-toe* to the ode, *To Autumn*. In all Keats's poetry he seems to have

---

12. Villard (*op. cit.,* p. 51) asserts that Tennyson uses the description of the angels in a passage other than the one I have noted. She suggests that Tennyson had in mind the "eager-eyed" angels who "stared" from the cornice when he described the gargoyles in *Godiva:*

> The little wide-mouth'd heads upon the spout
> Had cunning eyes to see . . .
> Fantastic gables, crowding, stared. . . .

appreciated, to the point of actual imitation, Keats's power of expression, the fact that here was a poet who, like himself, looked on fine phrases like a lover.[13] Here was a poet in whom he found, as he himself beautifully said of Virgil,

> All the chosen coin of fancy
> flashing out from many a golden phrase. . . .
> All the charm of all the Muses
> often flowering in a lonely word.

Like Swinburne, he could appreciate the fact that here was a poet with an immense vocabulary of 8,700 words (exclusive of inflected forms), "more than Milton and as many as the Odyssey and the Iliad together."[14] And this side of his appreciation and imitation seems to have remained with him always.

But there were many other aspects of Keats which, although they at first attracted him strongly, he seems to have outgrown. It is in these more general aspects that we find the real stamp of Keats, much more than in actual imitation of lines.[15] To follow them out involves, first of all, some understanding of what Keats stood for in the minds of Tennyson and the Victorian public at large. We cannot be in a position to understand the exact nature of Keats's influence on the early Tennyson until we can appreciate in what manner Keats was read by Tennyson's generation. The halo of twentieth-century Keatsian study must be gently but firmly removed.

ii

WHEN A. J. Farmer asserts that Keats is the father of English decadence, that in his statements on beauty "on croit entendre Gautier,"[16] the twentieth-century reader is very likely to object in strong terms. Keats seems to us, at his best, closer to Shakespeare than to Gautier in France or the aesthetes of English decadence. Yet Mr. Farmer is probably right, at least from the historical point of view. The confusion is owing to the different interpretations which can be made of Keats's theory of beauty. When Keats says, for example, that "with a great poet the sense of Beauty overcomes every other consideration, or rather obliterates all consideration," he is leaving us a wide margin

---

13. *Letters of Keats*, p. 368.
14. Georges Lafourcade, *Swinburne's Hyperion . . . With an Essay on Swinburne and Keats*, London, 1927, p. 71.
15. For example, Tennyson drew expressions not infrequently from such poets as Carew, Marvell, and Shelley. But it would be a hazardous task to prove from this that his own poetry resembles theirs in spirit. Imitation of details suggests artistic interest, not necessarily anything more.
16. Albert J. Farmer, *Le mouvement esthétique et "décadent" en Angleterre (1873–1900)*, Paris, 1931, p. 5.

of possible interpretation. His theory of "negative capability" can apply equally well to *King Lear* or to the *Emaux et Camées* depending on the twist which we give to the word "Beauty," a word which was to be the rallying cry for a number of his poetic successors and around which a cult was to develop.

The fact is that Keats's views of beauty seem to have passed through two, possibly three, stages.

"If I should die" he wrote in 1820, "I have left no immortal work behind me—nothing to make my friends proud of my memory—but I have lov'd the principle of beauty in all things. . . ."[17] Keats's letters and poems are replete with such references to beauty. He conceived of poetry as the creation of beauty. But upon examination, it will be found that his conception of poetry as the creation of beauty is not a static one. It undergoes several changes during the course of his career. These changes, as it happens, do not evolve in simple chronological order, for as early as *Sleep and Poetry* he had caught glimpses of his final position. But they may serve as recognizable points of reference.

In the first stage, he seems to maintain that the proper subject for poetry is simply the sensuousness of nature in what might be termed its "happier" aspects. When he charts out his career in *Sleep and Poetry*, he realizes that he must pass through the elementary stage of simple awareness:

> First the realm I'll pass
> Of Flora, and old Pan. . . .

There are several passages in the letters praising the virtues of pure sensation, chiefly the frequently quoted "O for a Life of Sensations rather than of Thoughts!"[18] Professor Garrod maintains, in fact, that it is only on this level that Keats attains any true success in his poetry.[19] Stress on sensuous beauty itself is not, however, the only characteristic of this stage in Keats's theory of poetry. It involves a rejection not simply of any form of thought, but of the tragic sides of nature. Poetry is to deal with the pleasant only, and the ideal will be achieved, says Keats, when

> . . . they shall be accounted poet kings
> Who simply tell the most heart-easing things.
> (*Sleep and Poetry*, 267–8)

Again:

> —It is a flaw
> In happiness to see beyond our bourn—

17. *Letters of Keats*, p. 468.
18. *Letters of Keats*, p. 68.
19. H. W. Garrod, *Keats*, Oxford, 1926, p. 30. Garrod's reading of Keats represents a revival of the usual Victorian view.

> It forces us in Summer skies to mourn:
> It spoils the singing of the Nightingale.
>> (*To J. H. Reynolds*)

Wordsworth's eyes, said Matthew Arnold, avert their ken from half of human fate. The same charge can be laid against Keats in this early stage. He seems to stand, as he describes himself in the Ben Nevis sonnet, with the mists above him and below him. He makes no effort to penetrate the mists, but concerns himself solely with the beauties of the natural phenomena perceptible to his senses. "Nothing startles me beyond the Moment,"[20] he writes. This theory of art leads to the work of Pater, and in its extremes to the decadents of the Nineties.

A second stage in Keats's concept of beauty (really bound up with the first) may be passed over quickly as Keats himself does not deal with it at much length. The beauty which the poet describes should be suggestive as well as sensuous. It should be described so that the reader's mind will be stimulated to imaginative reverie. "When Man has arrived at a certain ripeness in intellect" writes Keats, "any one grand and spiritual passage [of poetry] serves him as a starting-post towards all 'the two-and-thirty Palaces.' " It must have been on some such basis that Keats wrote *La Belle Dame* and much of *The Eve of St. Agnes.* It is obvious enough how deeply Tennyson was attracted to this side of Keats, a matter to which I shall return shortly.

What might be termed the third and final stage of Keats's conception brings us to the very core of his theory of poetry: his ideas of the poetic character, poetic truth, and the effects of poetry on the "soul." At this stage, Keats asserts that the materials of great poetry must be all life. The poet must be cognizant of a world in which evil forces are at work. As he writes in lines which anticipate Tennyson in *In Memoriam:*

> The greater on the less feeds evermore. . . .
> Still do I that most fierce destruction see,
> The Shark at savage prey—the hawk at pounce,
> The gentle Robin, like a pard or ounce,
> Ravening a worm—
>> (*To J. H. Reynolds*)

He must also be cognizant of the world of men, with its sorrows and its strife. "Scenery is fine" writes Keats in 1818, "but human nature is finer."[21] The poet's picture of the world therefore must be all-inclusive. Until he "faces the facts" (as Shakespeare faced them in *King Lear*) his picture of life will be incomplete and immature, and also his concept of beauty.

20. *Letters of Keats*, p. 69.
21. *Ibid.*, p. 111.

According to the maturing Keats, the poet must arrive at this higher stage, in which he can appreciate "the agonies, the strife of human hearts," before he can penetrate to what Keats calls the "dark passages" of the "Mansion of Many Apartments" which is life.[22] Such penetration, based on a comprehension of all experience, is achieved, as Keats says many times, by the imagination, not by the reason. In *The Fall of Hyperion* he was struggling to express these mature conceptions of the poet's role.

And it is on this basis that his conception of the poetic character is built up. Here the reader may be referred, with a few reservations, to Middleton Murry's *Keats and Shakespeare* or to the more conservative study by Mr. Thorpe, *The Mind of Keats*. We find, I think, that what Keats was aiming at was a certain objectivity not to be confused with escapism. If the poet's statements about beauty and poetry are examined in their context, we find not the note of Gautier but that of Shakespeare.[23] His greatest wish was to succeed as a dramatist,[24] and he felt that great drama could never be written by anyone who adopted the prophetic robes, as Wordsworth had done in *The Excursion*.

It is this remarkable awareness of the final end of poetry which contributes so much to the attractiveness of Keats today. As T. S. Eliot says, "There is hardly one statement of Keats about poetry, which, when considered carefully . . . will not be found to be true; and what is more, true for greater and more mature poetry than anything that Keats ever wrote. . . ."[25]

The last phrase may serve to remind us that Keats's theory of the "third stage" remained, for the most part, as theory. He did not live to write his *King Lear*, yet the usual twentieth-century study of his work is inevitably coloured by our recognition that he was moving in that direction.

The twentieth-century reader often fails to realize how recent this interpretation of Keats is. Generally speaking, Tennyson and other Victorians had not discovered what seems to us to have been the real direction of Keats's efforts. There were good reasons why this should have been so. Much of our present-day information is based on the second *Hyperion*, a poem which was not printed until 1856 and then at a private press with a very restricted circulation. Keats's letters were not published until 1848. The Victorian attitude to Keats was seriously conditioned by these facts.

22. *Letters of Keats*, pp. 141–2.
23. For example: "The only means of strengthening ones intellect is to make up ones mind about nothing—to let the mind be a thoroughfare for all thought. Not a select party" (*Letters of Keats*, p. 426).
24. *Letters of Keats*, pp. 368, 439–40.
25. T. S. Eliot, *The Use of Poetry and the Use of Criticism*, London, 1934, p. 101.

I referred earlier to a remark by Landor in which he compares Keats to Shakespeare. If his remark is examined closely, it will be found that he meant Keats had a Shakespearean command of words. Nothing more than this is suggested. And this is also exactly what Matthew Arnold meant when he spoke of the resemblance between Keats and Shakespeare in his well-known essay of 1880. As far as I have been able to determine, the first writer who saw beyond Landor's conception of the case and recognized that Keats had developed a Shakespearean *attitude* to poetry was David Masson. In 1860, Masson published an essay on Keats in *Macmillan's Magazine* and offered a sound defence of the poet's "lack of fixed principles,"[26] which he compared to that of Shakespeare. On the same basis he pointed out the real differences between Keats and Shelley. Although badly written, the essay shows remarkable critical insight and deserves more attention than it has received.[27] It was decades ahead of its time. If Arnold read it, he must have missed its point, for although he too links Keats and Shakespeare, he has in mind only the power of phrase which the two poets share in common.

In brief, Arnold, like Tennyson and all his Victorian readers, saw Keats without the benefit of Mr. Murry. They saw the poet who had developed to a marked degree his conception of poetry on the first two planes. They were unaware, except in a vague sort of way, of his gropings towards the third. As a result, in spite of their many sentimentalizings of his early death, they read and appreciated Keats for what he had written, not what he might have written. They read and loved a poetry of richly sensuous beauty, and they appreciated it for that without worrying too much about those penetrating little asides in *Sleep and Poetry* and *Endymion* or in the letters (after their publication in 1848). It represented, for many, the Bible of the Aesthetic Movement, with all the associations which that phrase implies. We must not look for any more than this in Tennyson's approach to Keats.

Critics today, such as Fausset, complain that the Victorian poets misunderstood Keats by seizing on one quality of his poetry, its sensuousness, and disregarding all else.[28] I have taken some pains to show, historically, why his Shakespearean potentialities eluded them. Beyond this, their reading of Keats had one advantage. They did not

26. David Masson, "The Life and Poetry of Keats," *Macmillan's Magazine*, III (1860), 1–16. On page 9 we find this sentence, remarkable both for its bad construction and its truth: "Unlike the feminine and ethereal Shelley, whose whole life was a shrill supernatural shriek in behalf of certain principles, Keats was a slack, slouching youth, with a thick torso, a deep grave voice, and no fixed principles."

27. Georg Brandes was one of the few influenced by Masson's views. He quotes from Masson's article freely in his study of Keats, and says at one point: "Keats's poetical indifference to theories and principles was . . . in itself a theory and a principle." (*Main Currents in Nineteenth Century Literature*, London, 1916, IV, 138).

28. Hugh I'Anson Fausset, *Keats*, London, 1922, p. 9.

lose themselves in mazes of speculation stimulated by the poetic theory found in the letters. They kept their eyes on the poems themselves.

With that evidence before them, and that evidence alone, Keats appeared to them as a poet who had succeeded in escaping the sordid and disturbing environment of nineteenth-century life, a poet who had evolved in its place a picturesque world of the past, a world painted in lavish colours and felt intensely through the senses.

Tennyson was one of the earliest to come under the spell of Keats's world. As I have suggested, we may imagine his reaction at Cambridge when he opened his first volume and discovered a poet whose awareness of experiences, painted with such breath-taking richness of image and suggestiveness of overtone, had so much to attract his admiration. The event was to leave a strong stamp on his poetry. He had lingered just outside the Temple of Beauty before, but his reading of Keats led him to the very steps of the altar and encouraged him to accept a creed seemingly thoroughly congenial to him. For a number of years he was to remain something of a faithful ministrant. Looking back on the volumes of 1830 and 1832 now, it is possible for us to isolate the seeds of his later apostasy. But the dominant note of those volumes was one of faith, faith in what seemed to be the message of Keats's *Ode on a Grecian Urn*—the self-sufficiency of beauty. Lockhart was perfectly justified in coupling the two poets.

iii

ONE of the greatest dangers in any study of Tennyson lies in seeking a single label for his poetry. Variety of genres and diversity of moods are among its most curious and most important features. The author of *In Memoriam* may have been simple enough, but he was by no means single-minded. Generalizations about his cult of the beautiful in the volume of 1832 must be qualified by a realization that side by side with *The Lady of Shalott* we find such a piece as *The Two Voices*. But we can speak, nevertheless, of general tendencies. And the general tendency of the young Cambridge graduate was certainly Keatsian.

The cult of beauty as practised by Keats and Tennyson may be conveniently considered from two points of view. On the negative side, it involved an exclusion of certain subjects (such as political or philosophical theories) as unfit for poetic treatment. On the positive side, it involved an emphasis on the pictorial beauties of the past or of landscape, on vivid sensation, on suggestiveness, on art itself. From both points of view, the similarities between Keats and Tennyson are striking. It is here that one may trace the all-important kinship of spirit between the two poets.

It would lie beyond the scope of this study to attempt to motivate further Keats's extraordinary break from the practice of his fellow romantic poets who had employed so much of their verse for political ends, whether reactionary or radical. After a study of Shelley or Byron or Wordsworth, it always seems strange to enter the world of Keats and find the complete dearth of political theories or aspirations in his writing. We know that he was a warm liberal, but he did not seem to consider politics a fit subject for poetry. A sonnet to Kosciusko and a few stray references to the activities of Leigh Hunt are all he has left us. In the same year that Shelley was embodying his faith in progress into his *Prometheus Unbound,* Keats was luxuriating in the love-myth of *Endymion.* It was an aspect of Keats's poetry that Rossetti would appreciate, but we do not often think of Tennyson in connection with it.

Speaking of Tennyson's treatment of politics, Stopford Brooke makes the rather startling assertion that the poet was here very close to Keats:

He was much more, on this side, the true successor of Keats, to whom all these political and social questions were . . . repulsive; and who took refuge from them in the stories of the Greeks and of the Renaissance out of which time had withdrawn the coarse and left the beautiful.[29]

The statement seems, at first, preposterous. We think of the poet whose verses were distributed among the troops before Sebastopol or quoted by Tory Imperialists in the House of Parliament. Yet, while certain political ideals were very dear to Tennyson, it will be found that Brooke's statement contains a certain modicum of truth. It might be more strictly accurate to say that while Keats was a revolutionary by sentiment and Tennyson a reactionary, both poets could steer entirely clear of political issues and centre their poetry in the past. When Tennyson did so he was closest to Keats. The fact is that Keats set Tennyson an example of inestimable value. He showed him that it was possible to write mythological poems and legends without imposing upon them a superstructure of political ideology. Most of Tennyson's finest poetry was written when he was content to forget such issues as the feminist movement, the dangers of trade unions, the future of the Empire and "The red fool-fury of the Seine."

So too with matters philosophical. Keats was as strongly convinced as Jeffrey that such a poem as *The Excursion* "will never do." On the mistakes of his contemporary poets, he states in lines which he might have applied to much of Tennyson's later work had he lived to read it:

29. Stopford A. Brooke, *Tennyson,* London, 1894, p. 38.

> . . . the themes
> Are ugly clubs, the Poets Polyphemes
> Disturbing the grand sea. A drainless shower
> Of light is poesy; 'tis the supreme of power;
> Tis might half slumb'ring on its own right arm.
> (*Sleep and Poetry*, 233–7)

He wavered, perhaps, in the second *Hyperion,* but almost the entire body of his verse illustrates his conviction that systematized thought has no place in poetry. There is no more "philosophy" in that beautiful piece which closes his career, *To Autumn,* than there is in *Mariana* or *The Lady of Shalott.* Keats would have approved of Tennyson's defence of his *Day Dream* (1842):

> So, Lady Flora, take my lay,
>   And if you find no moral there,
> Go, look in any glass and say,
>   What moral is in being fair.
> O, to what uses shall we put
>   The wildweed-flower that simply blows?
> And is there any moral shut
>   Within the bosom of the rose?

One of the most interesting of Tennyson's earlier poems in this connection is a little piece called *The Poet's Mind.* His editors do not appear to have observed that he seems to be drawing here on the final scene in *Lamia.* Critics differ on the real meaning of *Lamia,*[30] but Tennyson apparently took it in its most obvious sense, that the world of reasoned philosophy destroys the world of beauty:

> Do not all charms fly
> At the mere touch of cold philosophy?
> There was an awful rainbow once in heaven. . . .
>   (*Lamia,* II, 229–31)

Seemingly taking over from Keats the picture of the "sophist" Apollonius with his withering eye,[31] Tennyson expands the contrast between his world and the world of poetry:

> Dark-brow'd sophist, come not anear;
>   All the place is holy ground. . . .
>   Holy water will I pour
>   Into every spicy flower. . . .
> The flowers would faint at your cruel cheer.
>   In your eye there is death,
>   There is frost in your breath. . . .

30. See J. H. Roberts, "The Significance of Lamia," *PMLA,* L (1935), 550–61.
31. Keats refers to Apollonius as the "sophist" in lines 172 and 291 of Book II. The references to his withering eye are numerous. See also Wordsworth's *A Poet's Epitaph.*

In few poems does Tennyson so openly insist on the sanctity of the beautiful.

Finally, to follow beauty tended to involve, in practice, a minimization of realistic human interest. Tennyson's innumerable shadowy "moonshine maidens" (as Lockhart called them) find their counterpart in the stock figures of Isabella or Madeline. Poetry written according to these standards is not only at the opposite pole from that of Chaucer and Browning but even from Wordsworth at his best, for Wordsworth could declare with some justice: "I have wished to keep the Reader in the company of flesh and blood."[32] When Christopher North reviewed the volume of 1830, he justly observed that *"At present Tennyson has small power over the common feelings and thoughts of men."*[33]

These precepts might be considered as the basic Commandments which Keats's poetry embodies, the *Thou Shalt Nots* for a poet who wished to follow his lead in developing verse devoted to beauty itself, unsullied by any extraneous considerations.

Such *Thou Shalt Nots* were no particular hardship for the author of *The Lotos-Eaters* and of *Fatima*. Indeed, they must have been genuinely congenial to his taste. Tennyson's pretensions to the role of political or philosophical poet were somewhat late in maturing. In the volumes of 1830 and 1832 and, to a considerable extent of 1842, he was largely content to transmute experience in terms of sensation and mood, as Keats had done. The desire to escape the issues, issues with which so much of his later poetry is concerned, was a fundamental trait of his character. Hallam's death, together with many other factors, forced him to struggle with problems which, on many occasions, he was only too glad to disregard. When the struggle was real to him, he reached, as Mr. Nicolson emphasizes, perhaps the highest notes in all his poetry:

> Be near me when my light is low,
>   When the blood creeps, and the nerves prick
>   And tingle; and the heart is sick,
> And all the wheels of being slow.
>
> (*In Memoriam*, L)

But all too often there is no struggle. Insufficiently equipped intellectually to cope with the issues, Tennyson falls back on compromises which, when he is most honest with us, he himself feels to be inadequate. The desire to escape such questions was hence a very real part of his nature. Keats provided the means for him. He offered an example of a sort of poetry which made such an escape not only permissible but desirable.

---

32. *Observations Prefixed to "Lyrical Ballads"* (1800).
33. Quoted by H. I. Fausset, *Tennyson*, p. 36.

So much for the negative side of the matter. On the positive side, Keats's cult of the beautiful served to show Tennyson what alternative spheres are open for the emphasis of a poet who prefers to leave aside the issues with which Shelley, Wordsworth, and Byron had been so deeply concerned. One fruitful alternative is an emphasis on the pictorial. Both Keats and Tennyson attempted to make words serve the function of pigments.

One of the cardinal sins of modern art, according to Irving Babbitt, is the confusion which results when an artist strives to secure effects not proper to the medium in which he is working. Measured by the doctrine of *The New Laokoon,* Keats is certainly one of the great sinners of all time, worthy to rank with Amy Lowell and her Imagist followers. What is the fragmentary *Eve of St. Mark* if not pure word-painting? It is significant that Tennyson considered as one of Keats's finest pieces a poem which consists exclusively of a succession of pictures such as these:

> Down she sat, poor cheated soul!
> And struck a lamp from the dismal coal;
> Leaned forward, with bright drooping hair
> And slant book, full against the glare.
> Her shadow, in uneasy guise,
> Hover'd about, a giant size,
> On ceiling-beam and old oak chair. . . .

As one writer states, "If Spenser is often referred to as the 'poets' poet' it seems that Keats might with good reason be described as the painters' poet."[34]

In few things is Tennyson closer to Keats than in this. With an acutely developed sense for visual details, he elaborates his pictures, as in *The Lady of Shalott:*

> Sometimes a troop of damsels glad,
> An abbot on an ambling pad,
> Sometimes a curly shepherd-lad,
> Or long-hair'd page in crimson clad,
>   Goes by to tower'd Camelot. . . .

In *The Palace of Art,* where he was ostensibly signing his declaration of independence from the cult of the beautiful, he nevertheless lingers over picture after picture:

> For some were hung with arras green and blue,
> Showing a gaudy summer-morn,
> Where with puff'd cheek the belted hunter blew
> His wreathed bugle-horn.[35]

34. Georges Lafourcade, *op. cit.,* p. 27.
35. *The Palace of Art,* 61–4. See *The Eve of St. Agnes:*
> A chain-droop'd lamp was flickering by each door;
> *The arras, rich with horseman, hawk, and hound.* . . .
>   (Italics mine.)

In his study of *Keats's Epithets,* D. W. Rannie suggests that all poets may be classed into three groups: "those who paint (or carve), those who sing, and those who prophesy."[36] Until his prophetic consciousness became dominant, Tennyson can be grouped in the first class almost as readily as Keats. With them, of course, is Spenser, or to be more specific, the Spenser of Legouis.[37]

It is the peculiar quality of Tennyson's pictures which links them to those of Keats rather than to those of his predecessors such as Thomson and the pictorial school of the eighteenth century. The opening passage of *St. Agnes' Eve* may be noted in this connection, a passage influenced, obviously enough, by Keats's picture of the beadsman:

> Deep on the convent-roof the snows
> Are sparkling to the moon;
> My breath to heaven like vapour goes;
> May my soul follow soon![38]

The delight which both poets shared in such vignettes left a strong stamp on their work. Of *Endymion* Keats wrote: ". . . I must make 4000 Lines of one bare circumstance and fill them with Poetry. . . ."[39] He filled them, of course, with beautiful pictures. The youthful Tennyson never attempted anything so extensive, but his shorter poems show the same trait. Diffuseness was inevitable. Even when his pictures were purely redundant, he was loath to pass them by. In 1832, he had been foolish enough to print some of these, with apologies, and Lockhart pounced on them with manifest delight. "Mr. Tennyson . . . says with great candour and simplicity, 'If this poem were not already too long, *I should have* added the following stanzas,' and *then he adds them. . . .*"

The concentration which we find in the images of *La Belle Dame* or *Hyperion* or *In Memoriam* was something which both poets slowly mastered. We find the same difficulty in tracing out Endymion's feelings for Diana amidst the luxuriant settings of Keats's poem as we do in following Oenone's lament against the background of the vale of Ida. Both are suffused in the pictorial, "like bees in their own sweetness drown'd." Tennyson was seldom more successful than in *The Lotos-Eaters,* a poem in which all the lavishly pictured details of setting are entirely appropriate to his theme.

Allied with the pictorial is an emphasis on sensuousness, on sensa-

---

36. *Essays and Studies by Members of the English Association,* 1912, III, 112.

37. Paul Leveloh (*op. cit.,* p. 16) regards Keats's use of Spenser as an important factor in bringing Tennyson into the same tradition.

38. J. C. Collins points out that the original title was *St. Agnes.* In 1857, it was changed to *St. Agnes' Eve,* "thus bringing it near to Keats' poem, which certainly influenced Tennyson in writing it. . ." (*The Early Poems of Tennyson,* London, 1900, p. 238).

39. *Letters of Keats,* p. 52.

tion itself. "Du reste, avant Gautier, avant Flaubert, il [Keats] fait de la sensation le centre même de la vie de l'artiste."[40] The song of a nightingale, the sight of the Grecian urn stimulated Keats to soaring ecstasies of sensation. Tennyson tried to follow suit in *Eleanore* and *Fatima:*

> I roll'd among the tender flowers;
> I crush'd them on my breast, my mouth;
> I look'd athwart the burning drouth
> Of that long desert to the south.

But the sensational plunges in which Keats revelled were really not suited to Tennyson's more subdued taste. What did appeal to him was one aspect of the earlier poet's sensationalism, the penchant for rich sensuous details. Tennyson's genius seldom soars. It was a genius essentially elegiac. In his sea of doubts, he clings to things material like a drowning sailor to a raft. And so, if he could not participate entirely in Keats's sensations on hearing the nightingale, he could nevertheless relish to the full the sensuous beauty of the lines:

> I cannot see what flowers are at my feet,
> Nor what soft incense hangs upon the boughs,
> But, in embalmed darkness, guess each sweet. . . .

Or:

> O for a beaker full of the warm South,
> Full of the true, the blushful Hippocrene. . . .

Obvious traces of his appreciation are to be found in *The Palace of Art,* in the 1832 version at least. The following passage in which the "Soul" delights herself with a rich banquet recalls the marmalady description in *The Eve of St. Agnes.* It is significant that in 1842 Tennyson chose to excise it:

> With piles of flavorous fruits in basket-twine
>   Of gold, *upheapèd,* crushing down
> *Muskscented* blooms—all taste—grape, *gourd* or pine— . . .
> *Ambrosial pulps and juices,* sweets from sweets
>   *Sunchanged,* when sea winds sleep.
> With graceful *chalices of curious wine,*
>   Wonders of art—and *costly jars,*
> And bossèd *salvers.*[41]

---

40. Albert J. Farmer, *op. cit.,* p. 5.
41. (Italics mine.) Tennyson tried his hand again at a similar scene in part IV of *The Lover's Tale.* Keats's delight in the carvings of the Grecian Urn and in his picture of the wine that had "been cool'd a long age in the deep-delved earth" reappears here:
> . . . wines that, heaven knows when,
> Had suck'd the fire of some forgotten sun,
> And kept it thro' a hundred years of gloom,
> Yet glowing in a heart of ruby—cups
> Where nymph and god ran ever round in gold. . . .
>   (*The Lover's Tale,* IV, 192–6)

So too the spirit of Keats reappears in descriptions of the female body. Tennyson never quite descended to the "slippery blisses"[42] of *Endymion*, but he does not stint, in the earlier poems, to linger over descriptions of "Idalian Aphrodite beautiful" or of the sea-fairies:

> White limbs unrobèd in the crystal air,[43]
> Sweet faces, rounded arms, and bosoms prest
> To little harps of gold. . . .

The later Tennyson seldom took such liberties. "Tennyson's sensuousness" says Fausset, "was not as deep, avid or vulgar as that of the young Keats often was. It was more decorous and less true."[44] Hence it represents something of a passing phase in his writing. Furthermore, to break from Keats meant, among other things, to bowdlerize.

Finally, in this connection, besides an emphasis on the pictorial and the sensuous, the cult of the beautiful involved a certain approach to Nature which the two poets held in common.

Among his major contemporaries, Keats's attitude to Nature was distinct enough. The great Shaftesburian tradition which had come to flower in the *Lyrical Ballads,* in *Childe Harold,* and in *Queen Mab,* left scarcely a trace on his work. Acutely conscious of the destructive forces of Nature (which were to disturb the Victorians so deeply), he turned aside from the prevailing romantic concept to one where the out-of-doors world is regarded merely as a beautiful *spectacle.* He never speaks of it as the key to the universe or as the reflecting pattern of the poet's soul. A beautiful landscape was for him a joy for ever, but nothing more, certainly not something with which spiritual union can be achieved.

Keats's attitude anticipated Tennyson's famous description of Nature as "red in tooth and claw." Much as the latter might admire the author of *Tintern Abbey,* Wordsworth's nature-worship left him cold.[45] As Palgrave noted: "Tennyson's general rendering of Nature might therefore be defined . . . as nearer the manner of Keats than any other, at least of our more recent poets. Landscape with him is mainly regarded as the source of the pure pleasure of the eye. . . ."[46] We shall look in vain either in *To Autumn* or *The Lotos-Eaters* for anything beyond this.

But objectivity of attitude by no means precludes an extensive treatment of landscape. Indeed, both poets turned to beautiful ren-

42. *Endymion,* II, 758.
43. *The Sea-Fairies* first appeared in 1830 and was not reprinted until 1853. This line was then omitted.
44. H. I. Fausset, *Tennyson,* p. 56.
45. See J. W. Beach, *The Concept of Nature in Nineteenth Century English Poetry,* New York, 1936, p. 406.
46. F. T. Palgrave, *Landscape in Poetry,* p. 285.

derings of landscape as they turned to the past and to art. In all three they found the roots of beauty.

One would suspect that Tennyson's debt to Keats in the matter of landscape painting was not so extensive as in some other respects.[47] On the whole, it would seem that Keats's nature-poetry served primarily to *confirm* a bent of Tennyson's own nature towards objectivity and stress on minutely-rendered details of natural setting. In his literal exactness he went far beyond Keats, but much of his concern with such matters had been anticipated in the younger poet's pictures of sea and forest and sky. To consider only one example, Keats's picture of the Argonauts in *Endymion:*

> Until, from the horizon's vaulted side,
> There shot a golden splendour far and wide,
> Spangling those million poutings of the brine
> With quivering ore.
>
> (*Endymion*, I, 349–52)

So too Tennyson delights in descriptions of vivid light on water:

> A sudden splendor from behind
> Flush'd all the leaves with rich gold-green,
> And, flowing rapidly between
> Their interspaces, counterchanged
> The level lake with diamond-plots
> Of dark and bright.
>
> (*Recollections of the Arabian Nights*, 81–6)

But to turn to other aspects of Tennyson's kinship with Keats, we might briefly consider his use of romantic overtone. I have suggested previously that Keats's theory of poetic beauty developed on three planes. The second was one in which, by building up an aura of suggestiveness in a poem, he secures a remarkable effect of something beyond actuality. Perhaps the best example is the famous passage which Tennyson himself called "the last perfection, . . . the wild and wonderful—

> Charm'd magic casements, opening on the foam
> Of perilous seas, in faery lands forlorn."[48]

We find notes of it again in the haunting lines:

> And they are gone: ay, ages long ago
> These lovers fled away into the storm.

Here is romantic imagery at its best, an imagery which, as Fausset says, "conveys to us hints of an infinite world beyond human experi-

47. Mlle. Villard (cf. *op. cit.,* p. 33) states that the influence is particularly marked in the *Leonine Elegiacs, A Dream of Fair Women,* and other poems.
48. *The Diary of William Allingham,* p. 327.

ence. . . . It is an unconscious confusion of vivid images under the stress of powerful emotion. . . ."[49] Or best of all, we find this peculiar type of beauty in *La Belle Dame sans Merci*, a poem which Tennyson and Palgrave included in *The Golden Treasury*. It is the beauty of Turner's painting at its best: it is the beauty of *Kubla Khan*.

"Natural magic" Arnold called it. The term suggests not only its evocative beauty but its elusiveness. We cannot offer tangible evidence to show that when Tennyson wrote *The Lady of Shalott* he was drawing on either Keats or Coleridge. Yet seldom is the debt so patent. For he has learned from their example the singular beauty which can be achieved by romantic overtones. He has learned a peculiar effect. We find it again in that weirdly beautiful stanza of the *Palace of Art*:

> One seem'd all dark and red—a tract of sand,
>   And some one pacing there alone,
> Who paced for ever in a glimmering land,
>   Lit with a low large moon.

Romantic colourings of this kind are usually associated with mediaeval subjects in both Keats and Tennyson. The *Idylls of the King* is an interesting illustration of what Tennyson sacrificed when he parted company with Keats. When we compare *The Lady of Shalott* with *Guinevere* we feel the absence in the latter of that strange Keatsian suggestiveness which the younger Tennyson had been able to emulate. "Poetry" he had said, "is like shot silk with many glancing colours. . . ." *The Lady of Shalott* creates just such an impression. But from *Guinevere* one carries away instead the picture of a self-righteous Victorian husband (disguised in armour) who, with many remarks of self-congratulation, offers his forgiveness on a platter. The note of "Celtic" or Natural magic is gone.

The mediaeval poems illustrate only one aspect of Tennyson's fondness for the past. It appears likewise in the poems written against a classical background—poems which represent perhaps his highest achievement.

In the verse of classical inspiration—and that includes hundreds of scattered lines and phrases—we have less of Tennyson's weakness and more of his strength . . . except . . . the small body of perfect lyrics. For the classical themes generally banished from his mind what was timid, parochial, sentimental, inadequately philosophical, and evoked his special gifts and his most authentic emotions, his rich and wistful sense of the past, his love of nature, and his power of style.[50]

How much does Tennyson's use of classical myth owe to Keats? Douglas Bush's study *Mythology and the Romantic Tradition* indicates that

49. H. I. Fausset, *Keats*, pp. 71, 73.
50. Douglas Bush, *Mythology and the Romantic Tradition*, p. 202.

the debt was considerable. In discussing that debt, we need not become involved in the vexed issues of which of the two was the more "classical."[51] Keats's sense of mythology seems to have been more intuitive and fresh, Tennyson's more learned and solid, but both drew deeply from the realms of "Flora and old Pan."

The enthusiasm which the beauty of Greek legend aroused in the younger poet permeates all his work. To Psyche he writes:

> . . . I will be thy priest, and build a fane
> In some untrodden region of my mind. . . .

His enthusiastic and extensive treatment of gods and goddesses served to put new life into the dry bones of mythology. He, more than any other romantic poet, confirmed and established a tradition which runs through the entire nineteenth century, a tradition first developed, as Professor Bush shows, by Wordsworth in such pieces as Laodamia.[52] Tennyson was in a position to profit from this tradition, and Keats's pioneering fostered his own use of myth by illustrating its rich possibilities. In Endymion and Hyperion, the poet had demonstrated how a classical fable "forbids anything in the nature of modern realism, and compels concentration on the universal and more or less symbolic aspects of the theme."[53] The example was of invaluable assistance to Tennyson and contributed much to his conception of the self-sufficiency of Beauty which we have been tracing. It is unnecessary to suggest anything much beyond the general influence. Oenone or Ulysses or Tithonus are fables readily distinguishable from those of Keats.

The final aspect of the cult of the beautiful which should be considered is the emphasis which both poets place on art. I have referred earlier to A. J. Farmer's tracing the "art for art's sake" credo back to Keats. "En effet, l'art a été pour lui, comme pour Baudelaire et Flaubert, un moyen d'évasion, le suprême alibi."[54] To be exact, much of Tennyson's extreme concern for style comes very much closer to a dilettantish escapism than Keats ever came. The implications behind Emerson's contemptuous dismissal of Poe as "the jingle man" apply equally well to a considerable body of Tennyson's writings. But whatever the degree of unhealthiness which underlies their mutual concern with art, it was certainly one of the most important links in the bond which unites Keats with Tennyson.

51. Professor Bush's cardinal principle here comes to our aid. "In the history of English poetry," he writes, "there is no absolute classicism, there are only conceptions —perhaps misconceptions—of classicism" (Mythology and the Renaissance Tradition, Minneapolis, 1932, p. 6).

52. Douglas Bush, Mythology and the Romantic Tradition, p. 70.

53. Ibid., p. 210.

54. A. J. Farmer, op. cit., p. 7.

The young Cambridge graduate, with tastes inclining to the *pré-cieux*, was no doubt aware that among his romantic predecessors there was a general tendency towards carelessness in expression, exemplified in the work of Byron and almost advocated by Shelley. He turned instinctively to the poet who had at least striven to "load every rift of his subject with ore."[55] Tennyson was many things, a prig, a prophet, and a poet-laureate. But he was also, before all else perhaps, an artist. And it was as an artist that he turned to the poetry of Keats for inspiration and example. Inasmuch as illustrations have already been cited to show the extent to which the younger poet's style affected Tennyson's, I shall not expand the analogies further at this point.[56]

In all these ways, Tennyson seems to have been influenced by the example of Keats. Sometimes, as in the imitation of lines and phrases, his debt is obvious enough. Elsewhere, as in matters of a general approach to mythology or to nature, it is a more subtle process. Suffice it to say that while he remained the poet of "beauty for beauty's sake" so to speak, the Keatsian note is a very significant aspect of his writing. This is not to assert that Tennyson was merely derivative, but that he knew how to profit from the example of a body of poetry which he admired very deeply. In his own way, he remained independent enough. What is more, he grew progressively more independent as time went on.

iv

"In regard to published criticism" Palgrave tells us, "more than once he remarked that it was his misfortune . . . to be little moved by praise, but long to remember points of censure."[57]

We may wonder sometimes how Tennyson felt about one point of censure stressed so heavily by Lockhart and other critics that his early poetry was simply an attempt to "out-glitter Keats." His own statement refuting the charge that he had written under the aegis of Keats is strongly indignant. Always touchy when charged with imitation, Tennyson seems to have been especially displeased when he found himself coupled with the Cockney poet. I have a strong suspicion that the accusation made by his critics was an important factor goading him on to independence.

We have considerable evidence that during the period from 1832 to 1842 he was making an effort, conscious or unconscious, to minimize the links which bound him to Keats and to develop a note more

55. *Letters of Keats*, p. 507.
56. Keats's influence on Tennyson's versification is difficult to estimate. See Villard, *op. cit.*, p. 40.
57. *Memoir*, ii, 496.

entirely his own. At least he was slowly moving in that direction over
the period, and continued to do so in after years.

There are some signs of it in the revisions to which he subjected
the 1832 poems which were republished in 1842. Some of the more
obvious Keatsian stanzas were removed altogether as in the case of
The Palace of Art, to which I have referred. Elsewhere revision pro-
duces a different note. Thus a stanza of *Mariana in the South* appeared in 1832 as:

> She moved her lips, she pray'd alone,
> She praying, disarray'd and warm
> From slumber, deep her wavy form
> In the dark lustrous mirror shone.

In 1842, we find instead:

> Complaining, "Mother, give me grace
> To help me of my weary load"
> And on the liquid mirror glow'd
> The clear perfection of her face.

The concretely sensuous picture has given place to one more abstract
and remote. Maud has been substituted for Madeline. There is also
a certain bowdlerizing tendency here which continues in Tennyson's
later work.[58]

The real extent of Tennyson's gradual breaking away from Keats is
found in the new poems of the 1842 volume. Several of them do not fit
the requirements of Keats's dislike of the didactic. Collins says of
them:

The serious poet now speaks. . . . The sensuous is subordinated to the
spiritual and moral. . . . It is interesting to note how many of these poems
have direct didactic purpose. How solemn is the message delivered in such
poems as *The Palace of Art* and *The Vision of Sin* . . . in *Godiva,* in
Ulysses.[59]

58. Sometimes there were reversions. Harold Nicolson suggests that when the
middle-aged Tennyson added the following lines to *Lucretius,* it was under the stimulus
of Swinburne:
> . . . how the sun delights
> To glance and shift about her slippery sides,
> And rosy knees and supple roundedness,
> And budded bosom-peaks. . . .
Actually, Tennyson was drawing from a passage in *Endymion* (II, 943–5) in which the
water is described as delighting to caress her "kissing breasts" and "lily shoulders":
> O that her shining hair was in the sun,
> And I distilling from it thence to run
> In amorous rillets down her shrinking form!
In any case, such *Endymion*-like passages are comparatively rare in the mature
Tennyson.

59. Collins, *op. cit.,* Introduction, p. xix.

In other words, these poems represent a disregard of one of the chief *Thou Shalt Nots* of the poets who follow Keats. The appeal to "thought" rather than to pure sense places Tennyson in a different world. "One must" he said, "distinguish Keats, Shelley, and Byron from the great sage poets . . . who are both great thinkers and great artists, like Aeschylus, Shakespeare, Dante, and Goethe."[60] Several of the poems of the 1842 volume represent his first bid to secure a place among these "great sage poets."

This statement requires qualifications. Accounts of Tennyson's development frequently misfire when they make out that the change from his earlier to his later style was brought about overnight. Actually, he combined the painter and philosopher at all stages of his career. It is a matter of emphasis. Generally speaking, after 1842, the Keatsian is subordinated to other elements whereas in the earlier poems it had tended to predominate. In 1842 the two are generally balanced against each other. In the final version of *Oenone,* for example, we find indeed an edifying "moral." "The sound and prosaic wisdom of the goddess [Pallas] is" says Bush, "so very Victorian that we become embarrassingly aware that she is undressed, apart from a spear, and it seems . . . as if the Queen herself had started up in her bath and begun to address the Duke of Argyll."[61] I suspect that Bush is overemphasizing its place in the poem. The moral is there, certainly. But it is balanced by many other things—the lavishly pictured setting and the delineation of the mood of Oenone herself. As someone said of Spenser's allegory, we might say of Tennyson's moralizing at this stage: "it won't bite you." We are still a long way from that stage of Tennyson's writing when the "moral" fairly loads every line to the exclusion of almost everything else, as in *The Ancient Sage* (275–7):

> An evil thought may soil thy children's blood;
> But curb the beast would cast thee in the mire,
> And leave the hot swamp of voluptuousness. . . .

One may wonder if, to the mind of the Ancient Sage, *Endymion* was somehow associated with the ape and tiger.

This general tendency in Tennyson's writings effects a considerable change in the basic colouring of his verse. The rich brilliance of the earlier poems is subdued.

> All in the blue unclouded weather
> Thick-jewell'd shone the saddle-leather,
> The helmet and the helmet-feather
> Burn'd like one burning flame together. . . .

60. *Memoir*, II, 287.
61. Douglas Bush, *Mythology and the Romantic Tradition*, p. 205.

There are passages comparable with this in *Gareth and Lynette* and elsewhere, but the general note after 1842 is more sombre. Tennyson passes, as Palgrave puts it, "from Titian to Rembrandt."[62]

Perhaps the most interesting poem in this connection is *The Palace of Art*. It is a curious piece. As Spenser does when he paints his Bower of Bliss, Tennyson seems to take away with his left hand what he gives with his right. The beautiful Keats-like pictures almost stifle the allegory. But the latter is there nevertheless, and it shows how the young poet was already concerned with the dangers of the Cult of Beauty. In the introductory section he states his theme: "an allegory . . . of a soul, a sinful soul possess'd of many gifts . . . that did love beauty only . . . seeing not that Beauty, Good, and Knowledge are three sisters. . . ." And in picturing the fate of the isolated artist's soul, he prophesies his own development:

> And so she throve and prosper'd; so three years
> She prosper'd; on the fourth she fell,
> Like Herod, when the shout was in his ears,
> Struck thro' with pangs of hell.

For in spite of all the similarities which can be traced between Keats and the early Tennyson, an essential difference of temperament divides them. With Tennyson, the desire for beauty was one trait only of a complex personality. It was not complete enough to prevent his apostasy from the Keatsian attitude to poetry. To Tennyson, as Mlle. Villard notes, ". . . beauty was not . . . the very essence and heart of life but its adornment. . . ."[63] In this attitude of mind we find one of the several causes for the breakdown of an influence which had predominated in the earlier writing of Tennyson.

In the process of becoming independent Tennyson lost, of course, a great deal. For Fitzgerald and others, the disappearance of the Keatsian influence after 1842 marked the decline of his poetry. "A wretched waste of power" Fitzgerald called *The Princess,* and added, "I feel almost hopeless about Alfred now, I mean about his doing what he was born to."[64] Succeeding Tennyson volumes made Fitzgerald even more unhappy. He had wished that Tennyson might succeed Keats (his own favourite poet), but by 1872 he had given up hope. A letter of that year (full of characteristic prejudices) indicates the place where he finally ranked Tennyson:

I wonder Messrs. Browning, Morris, Rossetti &c., can read Keats's hastiest doggerel and not be ashamed at being trumpeted as great poets in the *Athenaeum* and elsewhere. Only to mention Tennyson alone, to compare themselves with; who *used not* to think himself equal to Keats at all. I

62. *Memoir,* II, 497.
63. Léonie Villard, *op. cit.,* p. 44.
64. *Letters of Edward Fitzgerald,* London, 1889, I, 188. See also pp. 30–1 and p. 454.

don't know what he thinks now after so much worship has been offered him. To Keats he is not equal in invention and strength of continued flight, at any rate; but certainly farther above Browning & Co. than below his predecessor.[65]

Fitzgerald set the decline of Tennyson too early when he attacked everything after 1842. Probably Palgrave was nearer the truth when he traced the decline to a later date and treated *Maud* as the climax of Tennyson's powers.[66] Yet Fitzgerald's assertions are not without point. Under the sway of Keats, Tennyson's best endowments came to flower. When he entered the arena of Victorian controversy, he was entering into something for which he was inadequately equipped. *Ulysses* represents one poem which secures the effect that "thought is felt" as Herbert Read describes it.[67] But the effect is all too rare. More often it is one of bare and prosaic moralizing.

In growing away from the influence of Keats, Tennyson developed, it will be noted, not along the path which Keats himself had plotted out, but along the path which he specifically set out to avoid. "We hate poetry that has a palpable design upon us" Keats wrote.[68] Tennyson all too often sets out with a palpable design upon us. The great tragedy of Victorian literature is that so many of its poets either lacked the capacity to pass beyond the stage of *Venus and Adonis*, or, in the act of passing beyond it, reached only a state of spurious philosophizing. As Keats was well aware, Shakespeare had restricted his youthful exuberance in the interests of character. Tennyson, lacking the dramatic faculty, substituted for his early Keatsianisms something which, in his hands, was far less palatable.

Yet one could hardly have expected him to have remained within the strict precincts of the Cult of Beauty (as the Victorians understood it). In the first place, his Keatsianisms had been held up to heavy ridicule. In *Merlin and the Gleam* he looks back to his early career and describes his struggles (in lines which might have applied equally well to Keats):

> Once at the croak of a Raven who crost it
> A barbarous people,
> Blind to the magic
> And deaf to the melody,
> Snarl'd at and cursed me.

But what was more important, Tennyson had a prophetic soul as *The Vision of Sin* shows. He there had a startling vision of a wrinkled little man (a curious anticipation of T. S. Eliot's *Gerontion*) who seemed to

65. T. W. Reid, *Life of Richard Monckton Milnes*, II, 263–4.
66. F. T. Palgrave, *Landscape in Poetry*, p. 289.
67. Herbert Read, *Wordsworth*, Toronto, 1932, p. 173.
68. *Letters of Keats*, p. 96.

him to represent the final end of one who had lived by the senses only. And when he gazed into the future far as human eye could see, he saw something more than

> . . . the heavens fill with commerce, argosies of magic sails,
> Pilots of the purple twilight, dropping down with costly bales. . . .

As *The Palace of Art* also seems to indicate, he may sometimes have caught a prophetic glimpse of what the Keatsian strain in poetry would become, in its perverted form, during the course of his own lifetime. Perhaps the figure of Oscar Wilde rose before him, as Gilbert pictured him:

> With a poppy or a lily
> In his med-i-ae-val hand.

One may imagine his righteous middle-class shudder. And so, in Arnoldian phrase, his "other self" asserted itself. In words once applied to *Punch*, Tennyson skirted the seacoast of Bohemia, but he never actually landed there. A revealing illustration is to be found in Max Nordau's *Degeneration* (1895) in which the English "Aesthetic School" is severely attacked. Nordau is careful to draw a firm line of distinction between such "graphomaniacs" as Rossetti and Morris on the one hand, and Tennyson on the other. Tennyson, he says, is a "sound" poet.[69] *Nomen bonum instar unguenti fragrantis.*

In his determination to be "sound," Tennyson gradually parted company with Keats. The imitation of Keats he left to other more receptive hands, which were not lacking in the Victorian age. He himself turned away, with considerable reluctance perhaps, from a model which had left such a strong stamp on much of his writing and encouraged him along lines in which some of his finest poetry was written.

69. Max Nordau, *Degeneration*, New York, 1895, p. 99.

PART TWO

ARNOLD

They still think that the object of poetry is to produce exquisite bits and images—such as Shelley's . . . and Keats passim: whereas modern poetry can only subsist by its contents: *by becoming a complete magister vitae as the poetry of the ancients did: by including, as theirs did, religion with poetry, instead of existing as poetry only. . . .*

Arnold's letter to Clough, Oct. 28, 1852

HUGH STEPHENS LIBRARY
STEPHENS COLLEGE
COLUMBIA, MISSOURI

IV

Criticism: High Seriousness and Natural Magic

i

HOWEVER slow was the growth of Keats's fame among the Victorian general public, it was rapid and far-reaching among the poets. When Arnold's friend Clough was reviewing a volume of poems by Alexander Smith in 1853, he spoke of its author as "the latest disciple of the school of Keats, who was no well of English undefiled, though doubtless the fountain-head of a true poetic stream."[1] Tennyson and others who represented that poetic stream were, from the first, extremely enthusiastic about Keats. Rossetti and his associates drew from him extensively and were unstinted in their praise. And even Browning, whose debt to Keats was comparatively small, placed his poetry on a pedestal not far removed from that of his beloved Shelley. By the end of the century, as Maurice Baring shows, Keats was "beyond discussion" in literary circles.[2]

In the midst of this progressively swelling chorus of praise, the voice of Matthew Arnold sounds strangely discordant, like the croak of the bad fairy at the christening party for the little princess. Paeans to popular literary idols were seldom of much concern to him. As was his fashion in such matters, he went his own way:

> The solemn peaks but to the stars are known,
> But to the stars, and the cold lunar beams:
> Alone the sun arises, and alone
> Spring the great streams.

The object of this chapter and the two following is to trace out Arnold's reaction to Keats in three spheres, each closely linked with the others in Arnold's mind, but more conveniently discussed under separate heads. The present chapter aims to show that in the light of Arnold's criteria for modern poetry, Keats represented a writer of the second order. In the next, I deal with his view of Keats as a man, and finally, with his estimate of Keatsian style and its effect on his own poetry.

Arnold's first recorded reference to Keats strikes the note of dissatisfaction which is to persist in much of what he later says of him.

1. *Poems and Prose Remains of Arthur Hugh Clough,* London, 1869, I, 360.
2. Maurice Baring, *Lost Lectures,* London, 1932, p. 102.

113733

After reading Monckton Milnes's biography of the poet in 1848, he writes to Clough:

What harm he has done in English Poetry. As Browning is a man with a moderate gift passionately desiring movement and fulness, and obtaining but a confused multitudinousness, so Keats with a very high gift, is yet also consumed by this desire: and cannot produce the truly living and moving, as his conscience keeps telling him.[3]

The objections here stated reappear in many Arnoldian references to Keats and culminate, of course, in his well-known essay of 1880. The latter is sometimes regarded as his most unsatisfactory contribution to literary criticism. It is an essay based on an "heretical" assumption that Keats is inferior not only to Wordsworth but to Byron.

What are the bases of his objections? One obvious answer is that Arnold was simply a very strict critic. "We must accustom ourselves" he writes, "to a high standard and to a strict judgment."[4] Arnold is very hard to satisfy, that is, completely satisfy. With the possible exception of Homer and Dante, no writer on whom he touches, not even Shakespeare, is spared the probe of adverse criticism.[5] It may be fairly urged, in fact, that his critical standards are *too* high. "Poor Arnold!" exclaimed one of his friends on hearing of his death, "he won't like God."[6]

Such considerations serve only to warn us not to regard his harsh treatment of Keats as unique in his criticism. The real answer, however, must go beyond this. To treat with the problem may bring us to the core of Arnold's criticism and poetry. For Arnold measured Keats by the same standards with which he measured his own work, and he found both wanting. But first let us examine the standards themselves.

A thorough study of the author of *Essays in Criticism* reveals him as perhaps the most complex figure in the Victorian scene. This complexity arises from the fact that it was his life-long habit to superimpose upon what might be called his "natural" bent, a pattern, an objective, devised in accordance with what he considered to be needful. Because of this habitual tendency of his mind, a note of conflict develops, a note which is the key to much of his own poetry. It also results in the many seeming inconsistencies in his criticism, his curi-

3. *The Letters of Matthew Arnold to Arthur Hugh Clough* (ed. Howard Foster Lowry), London, 1932, p. 97. Further references to this work appear in the footnotes under the name of the editor only.

4. "The Study of Poetry," *Essays in Criticism, Second Series*, Macmillan, 1935, p. 3. A saying of George Herbert's sets the tone of all his criticism. See *Fortnightly Review*, xxv (1879), 240.

5. On Shakespeare's noddings, see "A Guide to English Literature," in *The Works of Matthew Arnold*, London, 1904, x, 186. In subsequent references to the collected works, essays will be cited followed by the number of the volume in which they appear. (See bibliographical note in my Preface.)

6. Quoted by Stuart P. Sherman, *Matthew Arnold*, New York, 1932, p. 274.

ous juggling feats, for example, with "natural magic" and the "Grand Style." Thus, while he was himself something of a Puritan,[7] he had insight enough to see that Puritanism (as it had evolved after the English Civil War) was the force in English society most in need of reform, and hence all his life he fought this many-headed "wild beast" as he once called it in fun.[8] So too, he was something of a romantic. But he discerned in much of the poetry of his contemporaries whither romanticism was leading, and he made strenuous efforts to channel the tide by the application of certain standards. As a result, when he speaks of Keats, conflicting sides of his taste come into play.

This feature of Arnold's thought must seriously condition any rounded study of his writing. As a poet and critic, what he felt about Keats and what he felt to be *needful* were not always quite the same thing. To follow out what Trilling aptly styles the "subtle critical dialectic"[9] of Arnold's thinking, one must be prepared to balance one block of clauses with another block of qualifying clauses. I have therefore been obliged to follow the method which Arnold himself employs in *The New Sirens,* that is, of ode followed by palinode.

Finally, I am aware that the real danger of such a study, as mentioned in the preface, applies here especially. In research, unless we are very careful, we always find what we are seeking. I am not eager to prove the hazardous proposition that Arnold was a Keatsian in disguise. It will be enough if I can show that his Keats essay in itself does not tell quite the whole story; and further, that as a poet he was, as Lowry says, "closer than he knew to much that he disparaged in Keats."[10]

But I do not wish to go beyond this to lose sight of the essential differences. Arnold serves, after all, as one of the best examples of the reaction against many of the things for which Keats had come to stand in the latter half of the century. To compare the two writers is sometimes illuminating, for, to employ a homely figure, the attempt to place square pegs into round holes is not such a fruitless procedure as it is often made out to be. One learns something of the nature of both the peg and the hole in the process.

ii

"A MAN's theory of the place of poetry" says Mr. Eliot, "is not independent of his view of life in general."[11] It will be found that Arnold's

---

7. A. W. Benn draws attention to some of the misunderstandings which "arose from the Puritan associations which, in spite of vehement disclaimers, clung to Arnold through life" (*The History of English Rationalism,* London, 1906, II, 311)

8. *Letters,* I, 273.

9. Lionel Trilling, *Matthew Arnold,* New York, 1939, p. IX.

10. H. F. Lowry, *op. cit.,* Introduction, p. 32.

11. T. S. Eliot, *The Use of Poetry and The Use of Criticism,* p. 119.

literary estimates are related to an underlying social and moral ideal, an ideal which he evolved early in life. Even at Oxford, as we now know, his foppishness was only a mask to conceal an underlying seriousness. In 1844, during what is considered his most "aesthetic" period, being a poet meant for him struggling hard to get clear on the great questions.[12]

The young man who looms up before us in the Clough letters is one seeking desperately to orientate himself to the world at large, to develop for himself some unified *Weltanschauung* in place of a lost orthodoxy. As early as 1848 we find him writing to his friend on the failure of Keats and Browning to achieve unity. "They will not be patient" he complains, "neither understand that they must begin with an Idea of the world in order not to be prevailed over by the world's multitudinousness: or if they cannot get that, at least with isolated ideas: and all other things shall (perhaps) be added unto them."[13] Five years later he warns Clough against the same tendency.[14] During these five years, Arnold appears to have matured his own methods of facing the "multitudinous" forces in the life of his own day, to which he was so sensitive. On the moral plane, he strove for a balanced and harmonized organization of life: on the intellectual, for a critical state of mind which would enable him to deal with these forces objectively. We find both in the oft-quoted lines on Sophocles:

> . . . whose even-balanc'd soul,
> From first youth tested up to extreme old age,
> Business could not make dull, nor Passion wild:
> Who saw life steadily, and saw it whole. . . .

The quest for these ideals colours not only Arnold's poetry but much of his literary criticism, where we find him in search of models who approximate to them, models who inspire the reader to rise above the "sick hurry" and "divided aims." "I hate all over-preponderance of single elements" he writes, in a sentence which Irving Babbitt cites as the key to his writings.[15] Arnold valued writers such as Joubert, who, in his eyes, stands for balance and calm.

The attitude of mind which he felt must serve as a basis for the modern poet he found at its best, however, not in the French writer of *pensées* but in Goethe.[16] He defined this attitude of mind as "the

---

12. Alan Harris, "Matthew Arnold: The Unknown Years," *Nineteenth Century and After*, CXIII (1933), 503.

13. H. F. Lowry, *op. cit.*, p. 97.

14. See *ibid.*, p. 130.

15. Irving Babbitt, "Matthew Arnold," *The Nation*, CV (1917), 118.

16. For Arnold's estimate of Goethe, see *Discourses in America*, London, 1885, p. 145; also his Preface to *Literature and Dogma*, VII, xxiv. He seems to have fought shy of giving any rounded critical estimate of Goethe beyond his *A French Critic on Goethe* (cf. *Letters*, III, 30).

intellectual maturity of man himself; the tendency to observe facts with a critical spirit . . . to judge by the rule of reason, not by the impulse of prejudice or caprice."[17] Matthew Arnold was misunderstood by his contemporaries, says Babbitt, "not because he was less modern, but because he was more modern than they. . . . The modern spirit [for which he stood] is synonymous with the positive and critical spirit, the refusal to take things on authority."[18]

For Arnold the poet, the attainment of these objectives was an individual and personal problem. His reflective verse records a humanist's strivings to preserve the identity of his own soul, and to attain personal perfection. By the late eighteen fifties, however, he had come to realize that individual salvation (if we may secularize the term) was not enough, that his problem was a social problem, and that to stabilize his own position he must make his standards operative in society as a whole. *Rugby Chapel* is a statement of his own ideal as well as a tribute to Dr. Arnold. "The study of perfection" he writes, "leads us . . . to conceive of true human perfection as a *harmonious* perfection, developing all sides of our humanity; and as a *general* perfection, developing all parts of our society."[19] This realization, together with several other factors, led Arnold into the field of criticism. His personal ideals become "socialized" into critical standards.

I have dwelt on this matter at some length to show why it is that Arnold came to expect so much from literature, why he laid such stress on that over-worked phrase of his, "a criticism of life." For while he was prepared to throw in his lot with what he termed "the main movement of mind of the last quarter of a century,"[20] he nevertheless felt the need for some sustaining forces to replace the crumbling masonry of the old order. To poetry itself he looked for one of the vital cornerstones of support for the foundations of a new world, a world in which God could be defined only as *"The Eternal, not ourselves, that makes for righteousness."* [21] Thus he asserts in *The Study of Poetry:* ". . . most of what now passes with us for religion and philosophy will be replaced by poetry."[22] The greatest part of Arnold's poetics is loaded with this conception. If, as Fra Lippo expressed it, poetry was something

17. "On the Modern Element in Literature," *Essays in Criticism* (the so-called *Third Series*), Boston, 1910, pp. 48–9.
18. Irving Babbitt, *op. cit.*, p. 117.
19. *Culture and Anarchy*, Cambridge, 1935, p. 11. For an interesting account of Arnold's "social conscience," see H. V. Routh, *Towards the Twentieth Century*, Cambridge, 1937, pp. 167–209.
20. *Letters*, II, 195.
21. *God and the Bible*, VIII, 26.
22. *Essays in Criticism, Second Series*, p. 2.

That were to take the Prior's pulpit-place
Interpret God to all of you,

then poetry, Arnold maintains, must demonstrate what he calls "high seriousness." What is perhaps his clearest statement of this objective occurs in his study of *Celtic Literature.* Comparing the Keats-like Celtic poetry with that of Goethe, he says:

. . . Goethe's task was,—the inevitable task for the modern poet henceforth is,—as it was for the Greek poet in the days of Pericles, not to preach a sublime sermon on a given text like Dante, not to exhibit all the kingdoms of human life . . . like Shakespeare, but to interpret life afresh, and to supply a new spiritual basis to it.

And he adds, in words which might well have been directed against Keats:

This is not only a work for style, eloquence, charm, poetry; it is a work for science; and the scientific, serious German spirit, not carried away by this and that intoxication of ear, and eye, and self-will, has peculiar aptitudes for it.[23]

Now how does *To Autumn* measure up in the light of such demands as these? Arnold, as we shall see, makes for that poem certain provisions on a lower plane. But it is obvious that however successfully Keats has rendered the mood inspired by a beautiful September day, he has made no attempt here to fulfil the exacting requirements which Arnold makes for the modern poet. The poem is lacking in the very thing which Arnold professed to seek in all modern literature, "high seriousness." The obvious answer is that the poem has a high seriousness of its own, though in the light of the standards which Arnold applied, it remains inadequate.

We have here what must have been Arnold's basic objection not only to the ode, *To Autumn,* but to all of Keats's writings. As the Clough correspondence shows, Keats represented to him an artist who had failed to cope with modern life, who had merely responded to its sensations and made little or no attempt to unify his impressions into a whole. "Keats" as he says in his essay on Heine, "passionately gave himself up to a sensuous genius. . . ."[24] His Victorian contemporaries were content for the most part to accept the work of the young romantic on that level, but not so Arnold. Of Scott, Wordsworth, and Keats, he affirms: ". . . they do not belong to that which is the main current of the literature of modern epochs, they do not apply modern ideas to life; they constitute therefore, *minor currents.* . . ."[25] When Arnold is thinking along these lines he has a good

23. *On the Study of Celtic Literature,* New York, 1883, pp. 130–1.
24. *Essays in Criticism, First Series,* London, 1935, p. 177.
25. *Ibid.,* pp. 177–8.

word (perhaps his only good word) for Shelley. Shelley and Byron, he says, at least made a "bold attempt" to face the issues of modern life. They failed because, in the words of his famous pronouncement, they "did not know enough."[26] But Keats, in his eyes, seems to have missed the issues altogether. He lacked, as we find it stated in the *Essays in Criticism*, the "matured power of moral interpretation."[27]

As I shall attempt to show in a later connection, throughout his formal essay on Keats Arnold confuses the issues by claiming for him something more than sensuousness. Upon careful examination, this "something more" turns out to be a certain healthiness which Arnold finds in Keats's sensuousness, but little beyond that. He never thinks of Keats as an adequate interpreter of the modern world. He never thinks of him as capable of "the noble and profound application of ideas to life," a virtue which he sometimes praised in Wordsworth.[28] He confuses the issues further by comparing Keats to Shakespeare, for he is thinking only of the power of expression which the two poets share in common, not of any similarity beyond this.[29] If his statements are considered in the light of Arnold's basic standards, it will be clear that he thinks of Keats "at bottom" as he would say, as simply the poet of sensuous beauty, the best of his kind, but little more. "Keats" as Robert Lynd expresses it, "is great among the pagans, not among the prophets."[30]

In the previous chapter, I discussed some of the reasons why the Victorians passed over Keats's concern with what I termed the "third stage" of his concept of beauty. Arnold did not rise beyond the interpretation of his contemporaries. On Clough's suggestion he had read the letters, but he did not seem to have been aware that Keats was groping in directions not dissimilar to those he himself projected.[31] Professor Bush, with his unfailing shrewdness of observation, has drawn attention to this fact, although he does not indicate the para-

26. *Essays in Criticism, First Series*, London, 1935, p. 7.

27. *Essays in Criticism, Second Series*, p. 85.

28. *Ibid.*, p. 100. The confusion in the Wordsworth essay itself is a matter to which I refer later. (See J. Dover Wilson, *Leslie Stephen and Matthew Arnold as Critics of Wordsworth*, Cambridge, 1939.)

29. Keats's work is "Shakespearean, because its expression has that rounded perfection and felicity of loveliness of which Shakespeare is the great master" (*Essays in Criticism, Second Series*, p. 86).

30. Robert Lynd, "Keats: The Matthew Arnold View," in *Old and New Masters*, London, 1919, p. 64. This essay itself seems to me weak on the question of what Arnold really thought of Keats. Lynd assumes Arnold actually considered Keats a great moral force.

31. Arnold's first remark after reading the letters is curious. He writes to Clough: "What a brute you were to tell me to read Keats' Letters. However it is over now: and reflexion resumes her power over agitation" (H. F. Lowry, *op. cit.*, p. 96). Does the word "agitation" mean that he is angered by Keats's sensuousness, or does it suggest that he has merely been disturbed by the references to Keats's death, or, a third alternative, excited by Keats's discussions of poetry?

doxical aspects of his comparison.[32] The significance of Keats's concern with the highest functions of literature was something which Arnold sensed only vaguely on a few occasions, as when he noted that the young poet was unable to "produce the truly living and moving, as his conscience keeps telling him."[33] These words sum up the essence of his own struggle as a writer of poetry. Such observations are rare, very rare.

In short, measured by the standards of high seriousness, of "modernity" we might say, Keats failed to satisfy Arnold's tastes. He was drawn to the earlier poet, as we shall see, under certain conditions. But in the light of his basic ideal, Keats was inadequate and failed to arouse his whole-hearted interest. In his private writings, except in the letters to Clough, he never mentions the name of Keats.[34] While many of his contemporaries rejoiced in the fact that their romantic idol was a pagan rather than a prophet,[35] Arnold considered the work of such an artist on a lower, less significant plane. Tennyson he treated as "deficient in intellectual power,"[36] and his criticism applies with equal force to the work of Tennyson's favourite model.

Finally, "high seriousness" in art meant for Arnold not merely the ability to deal with modern ideas, but the ability to deal with them objectively and dramatically, in such a way as to produce a certain desired effect. In the Preface of 1853 he defines the functions of the poet in these terms:

He will esteem himself fortunate if he can succeed in banishing from his mind all feelings of contradiction, and irritation, and impatience; in order to delight himself with the contemplation of some noble action of a heroic

32. Douglas Bush, *Mythology and the Romantic Tradition*, p. 253. An interesting parallel between *The Strayed Reveller* and the second *Hyperion* (published in 1857) gives additional evidence. Lines 207–60 of Arnold's poem develop Keats's thesis that:

> None can usurp this height . . .
> But those to whom the miseries of the world
> Are misery, and will not let them rest.
> (*The Fall of Hyperion*, I, 147–9)

33. H. F. Lowry, *op. cit.*, p. 97.

34. It is true, of course, that Arnold seldom discusses any literature whatever in his letters. However, he refers to Wordsworth, Sophocles, Milton, Goethe, Byron and Homer on occasion, while there is only one passing reference to Keats. When writing to his sister on May 15, 1880, he announces that he is preparing his essay on that poet (*Letters*, III, 64).

35. I employ the word "pagan" as Arnold used it. Concerning the distinction which he draws between the "Greek" of the age of Pericles and the purely "pagan," see *Essays in Criticism, First Series*, pp. 194–222.

36. *Letters*, I, 168. Again, he writes to Campbell (*Letters*, I, 316) comparing Tennyson with Goethe, Byron and Wordsworth and remarking ". . . my interest in him is only slight, and my conviction that he will not finally stand high is firm." For a general discussion of Arnold's attitude towards his fellow Victorian poets, cf. Stanley T. Williams, *Studies in Victorian Literature*, New York, 1923, pp. 97–108.

time, and to enable others, through his representation of it, to delight in it also.[37]

Arnold valued writers of the past such as Homer who gave him this effect whether they dealt with "modern" ideas or not. This was his classical yardstick, and measured by it, such a poem as *The Eve of St. Agnes* again falls short. I shall return to this topic in another connection.

It might be more accurate to shift our metaphor and say that when Arnold came to literature, he wielded a two-pronged fork. He made certain demands as a "modernist" (as I have used the word) and he made certain demands as a classicist. Keats was impaled on both points.

iii

IN a letter of December 17, 1860, written to his sister, the author who had recently completed his strictly "classical" *Merope* makes some revealing comments on the Middle Ages:

I have a strong sense of the irrationality of that period, and of the utter folly of those who take it seriously, and play at restoring it; still, it has poetically the greatest charm and refreshment possible for me. The fault I find with Tennyson in his *Idylls of the King* is that the peculiar charm and aroma of the Middle Age he does not give in them. There is something magical about it, and I will do something with it before I have done.[38]

These words were written while Arnold was engaged in the preparation of his lectures on Homer. They should serve to remind us that the attempt to fit his criticism into a single all-inclusive formula is a difficult task at best. His emphasis on classical standards would give the impression that he had much more in common with the eighteenth century than with his own. In the Preface of 1853 the resemblance is especially noticeable. But as a recent article illustrates, he felt very little sympathy for the world of "our excellent and indispensable eighteenth century,"[39] and, indeed, the great body of his criticism betrays the fact that his principal interest lay with the writers of the romantic age. In some respects, his criticism gives him away much as his poetry will be found to do.[40] With the romantics in general he

37. *The Poems of Matthew Arnold* (ed. Sir Arthur T. Quiller-Couch), London, 1926, p. 15.
38. The last sentence is of some interest. Perhaps Arnold was projecting another *Tristram and Iseult*, or, what is more likely, he was thinking ahead to a prose study such as his *Maurice de Guérin* (1863) or *On the Study of Celtic Literature* (1867).
39. E. K. Brown, "Matthew Arnold and the Eighteenth Century," *University of Toronto Quarterly*, IX (1940), 202–13. See also Paul Elmer More, *Shelburne Essays, Seventh Series*, New York, 1910, pp. 223–8.
40. Stuart P. Sherman (*op. cit.*, p. 162) draws attention to one rather glaring example of this tendency in Arnold's literary criticism, his honour roll of what he considered

had more in common than he himself, perhaps, was aware. With Keats in particular he found more to admire than his basic standards would allow. Arnold was something more than a pure "message-hunter." He provided a place for Keats.

The essay on Joubert was originally entitled *A French Coleridge*. With more justice, perhaps, the essay on Maurice de Guérin might have appeared as *A French Keats*. It is here, at any rate, that Arnold elaborates his distinction between poetry as "the interpretress of the natural world" and as "interpretress of the moral world," a distinction which, as he employs it again in the Keats essay itself, constitutes for the earlier poet the open sesame to some realm of Arnoldian poetic respectability.

Never did the most influential of Victorian critics make a more happy attempt to define poetry than in this study of an obscure French writer. For once he offers a definition devoid of his usual catchwords:

The grand power of poetry is its interpretative power; by which I mean, not a power of drawing out in black and white an explanation of the mystery of the universe, but the power of so dealing with things as to awaken in us a wonderfully full, new, and intimate sense of them, and of our relations with them.[41]

To illustrate this "magical power of poetry" he selects from Keats the lines:

> moving waters at their priestlike task
> Of pure ablution round Earth's human shores.[42]

And in the *Study of Celtic Literature* he cites two other "touchstones," here from the *Ode to a Nightingale:*

> White hawthorn and the pastoral eglantine,
> Fast-fading violets covered up in leaves—

and

> . . . magic casements, opening on the foam
> Of perilous seas, in fairy lands forlorn—[43]

In this sphere of naturalistic interpretation, of "natural magic," Arnold rates Keats very highly. "No one else in English poetry, save Shakespeare," he says, "has in expression quite the fascinating felicity of Keats, his perfection of loveliness. . . . He is; he is with Shakespeare."[44]

---

to be the "chief poetical names" in English poetry besides Shakespeare and Milton: "Spenser, Dryden, Pope, Gray, Goldsmith, Cowper, Burns, Coleridge, Scott, Campbell, Moore, Byron, Shelley, Keats, [and Wordsworth]."
41. *Essays in Criticism, First Series*, p. 81.
42. *Ibid.*, p. 82.
43. *On the Study of Celtic Literature*, p. 126.
44. *Essays in Criticism, Second Series*, p. 85.

It would be almost an impertinence to dwell on the felicity of the prose statement itself. When we find Arnold dismounted from his classical hobby-horse, we discover that he has left us some of the finest lines of criticism ever penned on Keats's poetry.

Such passages of criticism provide a clue to the nature of Arnold's appreciation of Keats's accomplishment, and his own poetry offers additional evidence. In holiday mood, he found enjoyment and consolation from the "Celtic" type of poetry in which he regarded the work of Keats as supreme. His lectures on Celtic literature were evolved almost entirely from this mood, and that book enables us to discern why, in spite of his basic standards, he yet had some good things to say for poetry of the *Ode to a Nightingale* variety.

"The Celtic" says Mr. Trilling, "is synonymous with the romantic." I suspect that he is overstating the matter, but a logomachy would be unavoidable if one attempted to follow the issue further.[45] In general, what Arnold meant by the "Celtic" in poetry was, on the one hand, a lack of concern for the sphere of man's thoughts and for his attempts to orientate his life into a pattern; on the other, a strong concern for style, for the rendering of Nature, "her weird power and her fairy charm,"[46] and finally, an abundance of "sentiment," of melancholy turn for the most part, such as is to be sensed in Gray's *Elegy Written in a Country Churchyard.*

And what connection have such things, so characteristic of Keats's poetry, with the standards of "high seriousness"? There is a conflict here which appears many times in Arnold's writings. It underlies the curious twists of argument in his study of *Wordsworth,* an essay which embodies what appears to be, as Dover Wilson calls it, "the most audacious *non sequitur* in the annals of English criticism."[47] Arnold has, as we shall see, an answer. But what he says does not wholly reconcile the difficulty. He asserts, in effect, that the Celtic has a seriousness of its own, that while its function is by no means so high as that of the ideal poetry he sought to inculcate, it yet may serve as a

45. Cf. Lionel Trilling, *op. cit.,* p. 239. I myself have not troubled to quibble over the word "Celtic" for Arnold's use of labels is always loose enough, and always open to challenge from the historians. J. M. Robertson, for example, objects strenuously to the terms "Hellenism" and "Hebraism" on the grounds that historically speaking, the Hebrews were not, as Arnold styles them, a great force for morality but an immoral race (*Modern Humanists,* London, 1901, pp. 137 ff.). Actually, Arnold was not very much concerned with the historical associations of such an epithet as "Celtic," and the term serves his purpose well enough.

46. *On the Study of Celtic Literature,* p. 121.

47. John Dover Wilson, *op. cit.,* p. 36. It seems to me that Arnold's selections from Wordsworth demonstrate clearly enough that he really thought of the poet as a superior sort of Celt and was genuinely moved by his work on that plane. But characteristically enough, he was not content to defend Wordsworth on only these grounds, and in the essay treats him as a sage. In the process, as Mr. Wilson puts it, he tries to eat his cake and have it too. As I have pointed out, something of the same tendency appears in the *John Keats* essay.

sort of substitute. Mr. Trilling has defined this function very neatly. "Celtic style" he writes, "has for Arnold a moral content—the refusal to accept the despotism of fact and of the merely practical world." It has, he continues:

. . . the delicate melancholy, the tone of old, unhappy, far-off things . . . of magic casements, of lost causes and impossible loyalties. It is, in short, the style of . . . all that is the opposite of getting and spending, the Philistine activities which have laid waste the powers of England.[48]

iv

THAT Matthew Arnold could be deeply moved by Celtic effects in poetry we have no cause to doubt. "The life of the senses" he once admitted "has its deep poetry . . . ,"[49] and he could respond with enthusiasm to the matured sensuousness of:

Hedge-crickets sing; and now with treble soft
The red-breast whistles from a garden-croft;
And gathering swallows twitter in the skies.

But when we recall Arnold's basic demands for poetry, we can see how these lines would remain for him, ultimately, insufficiently adequate. In the light of his strong sense of what was needed in Victorian life, it is clear enough why such poetry seldom received the fullest stamp of his approval. He hardly considered it a desirable model for his age.

In *Maurice de Guérin* we find a strikingly acute analysis of what is termed the "peculiar temperament" of a poet of Keats's stamp. Such a poet:

. . . is in a great degree passive . . . he aspires to be a sort of human Aeolian harp, catching and rendering every rustle of Nature. . . . He goes into religion and out of religion, into society and out of society, not from the motives which impel men in general, but to feel what it is all like; he is thus hardly a moral agent, and, like the passive and ineffectual Uranus of Keats's poem, he may say:
          ". . . I am but a voice;
          My life is but the life of winds and tides;
          No more than winds and tides can I avail."
He hovers over the tumult of life, but does not really put his hand to it.[50]

I have quoted the passage in full because it represents the best example of Arnold's ability to understand what Keats, in practice, had accomplished: the artistic transmutation of experience for its own

48. Lionel Trilling, *op. cit.*, pp. 238–9.
49. *Essays in Criticism, First Series*, p. 215.
50. *Ibid.*, pp. 107–8.

sake, not for any extraneous considerations. "What matters in Keats" as Albert Guérard writes, "is not theory but performance."

Art for art's sake, as a creative impulse, not as a doctrine, had no more perfect exponent. Not once, but at least half a dozen times, he gave us a vision of unsurpassable beauty. And his greatest poems are wholly free from partisan blight. *La Belle Dame sans Merci* is the very essence of Romantic mediaevalism, but without a hint of Tory sentimentality.[51]

Arnold's capacity to analyse this fundamental trait does not imply, of course, a capacity to admire it whole-heartedly. For him, great poetry combines what he calls "the faculty of naturalistic interpretation" with "the faculty of moral interpretation;" and the "moral," he adds, "usually ends by making itself the master."[52] In words which embody his final judgment: "For the second great half of poetic interpretation, for that faculty of moral interpretation which is in Shakespeare . . . Keats was not ripe."[53] On this basis, Arnold refused to rate Keats with what Tennyson called "the great sage poets." His work remains, for him, a minor stream.

One might well ask, in fact, what distinction Arnold would draw between John Keats and Théophile Gautier? The extent of the English poet's influence in the development of the concept "art for art's sake" is a matter which I propose to develop in a later chapter and I shall therefore avoid it here. But to employ an expression of Saintsbury's, Arnold must have sensed the decadent snake in the wavingly Celtic grass of Keats's writings and realized its importance. Nowhere, so far as I know, does Arnold refer directly to Rossetti or Morris, either publicly or privately,[54] but his reference to Gautier makes clear where he stood in the question of art for art's sake. In the *Wordsworth* essay, after offering a plea for morals in art, he observes that sometimes,

. . . we find attractions in a poetry indifferent to them [morals]; in a poetry where the contents may be what they will, but where the form is studied and exquisite. We delude ourselves. . . . A poetry of revolt against moral ideas is a poetry of revolt against *life;* a poetry of indifference towards moral ideas is a poetry of indifference towards *life.*[55]

By way of illustration Arnold suggests the *Emaux et Camées,* pointing out the fallacy of making art an end in itself. "Now, when we come across a poet like Théophile Gautier, we have a poet who has taken up his abode at an inn, and never got farther."[56]

51. Albert Guérard, *Art for Art's Sake,* New York, 1936, p. 42.
52. *Essays in Criticism, First Series,* p. 111.
53. *Essays in Criticism, Second Series,* p. 85.
54. He mentions Swinburne occasionally and once speaks of William Rossetti (*Letters,* I, 30). On the whole, however, he spares comment on the growing "aesthetic" group among Victorian poets.
55. *Essays in Criticism, Second Series,* p. 102.
56. *Ibid.,* p. 103.

One wonders if Arnold thought Keats had got any farther. Apparently he did. As we have seen, his reasons for so thinking were not quite the same as those of the twentieth-century reader of Keats of the stamp of Mr. Middleton Murry. The Shakespearean direction of Keats's efforts was something which was little recognized in 1880, and Arnold missed most of it. But from the letters he attained some realization that Keats's "yearning passion for the Beautiful" meant, ultimately, something more than a yearning for mere sensuous indulgence.[57] This in itself was enough to distinguish the English lover of the beautiful from Gautier. So, too, Arnold found some "signs of character and virtue"[58] in Keats's biography. Finally, in his reading of Keats's poetry, Arnold concentrated attention on his "healthiest" productions, and this may also have influenced his opinion. It is a significant comment on the difference of tastes between Arnold and the majority of his fellow-poets such as Rossetti, Morris, and Tennyson. The Pre-Raphaelites revered the author of *The Eve of St. Mark, La Belle Dame sans Merci, The Eve of St. Agnes,* and *Lamia.* Arnold does not choose to refer to these poems in his published criticism. A letter written to Colvin after reading his *Life of John Keats* contains a very revealing sentence: "But the value you assign to the 'Belle Dame sans Merci' is simply amazing to me." In this same letter, he makes mincemeat of *Endymion,* and for *Hyperion* he has little more than a passing pat of approval:

What is good in *Endymion* is not, to my mind, so good as you say, and the poem as a whole I could wish to have been suppressed and lost. I really resent the space it occupies in the volume of Keats's poetry. The *Hyperion* is not a poetic success, a *work,* as Keats saw, and it was well he did not make ten books of it; but that, of course, deserves nevertheless the strongest admiration, and its loss would have been a signal loss to poetry; not so as regards the *Endymion.*[59]

In his essays, Arnold seldom refers to *Hyperion* and then only to dismiss it as a failure.[60] The poems to which he does refer, and from which he draws almost all his illustrations, are the three great odes, the sonnets and a few fragments. If, like the Pre-Raphaelites, he seems to have missed much of the great power of *Hyperion,* he at least limited his attention to those poems in which both the morbid

57. *Essays in Criticism, Second Series,* p. 82.
58. *Ibid.,* p. 74.
59. Letter to Sidney Colvin, June 26, 1887. Quoted by E. V. Lucas, *The Colvins and Their Friends,* p. 193. Cf. Sidney Colvin, *John Keats,* 1917, p. 543 n.
60. *Essays in Criticism, Second Series,* p. 85. In chapter VI, I have pointed out that Arnold's poetry itself owes not a little to those poems favoured by the Pre-Raphaelites, but as a critic he recommends only those poems which I have listed. *To Autumn* seems to have been his favourite. He refers to it several times; e.g., *Essays in Criticism, First Series,* p. 112 n.

and the excessively sensuous and pictorial sides of Keats are minimized. The mediaevalized narratives affect his poetry, but they do
not appear in his criticism.

It was the healthy note in Keats's work that Arnold uses as a basis
on which to compare Keats with Maurice de Guérin, a writer more
"morbid and excessive"[61] in his eyes:

Even between Keats and Guérin, however, there is a distinction to be
drawn. Keats has, above all, a sense of what is pleasurable and open in
the life of nature; for him she is the *Alma Parens:* his expression has, therefore, more than Guérin's, something genial, outward, and sensuous.[62]

Arnold's best appreciations of Keats's poetry rest on the fact that he
was able to read it in this manner. The distinction between his taste
for Keats and that of Rossetti is of considerable importance in any
general consideration of the impact of Keats on Victorian readers.
Arnold's liking for Keats in no way equalled Rossetti's, but he had,
nevertheless, an appreciation of the saner and healthier side of his
writing which Rossetti might have done well to emulate.

These things seem to me to underlie the distinction which Arnold
would draw between Keats and Gautier. Yet, to draw to a close our
discussion of Arnold's basic estimate of Keats's poetry, such a distinction would not be strong enough, in the last analysis, to warrant a truly
high rank for Keats's achievement. The latter remained, in Arnold's
eyes, one of the second order. To this conclusion he was driven not
only by his own tastes but because he was so deeply concerned with
what was the right kind of poetry for the social needs of his own day.
He demanded a certain high seriousness, and he looked for a certain
chastened style. Keats, in the long run, supplied neither. His writing
did not serve the function of exemplifying the things which Arnold
felt it was his mission to inculcate upon the Victorian age.

The criticism of Matthew Arnold, largely because of its style,
achieves an air of "disinterestedness," an air which is really very
deceptive. Underlying the surface of urbane detachment is, as Brownell notes, a predominating missionary spirit:

Never has the missionary spirit . . . been exhibited with more charm and
more distinction—less associated with its customary concomitants. But
never, also, has it been more mistakably [*sic*] illustrated.[63]

Arnold's evaluation of the Romantic Poets is conditioned in no small
part by missionary considerations. It is "tinged" as Mr. Eliot says,
with "his own view of what it was best that his own time should
believe."[64]

61. *Essays in Criticism, First Series,* p. 109.
62. *Ibid.,* p. 112.
63. W. C. Brownell, *Victorian Prose Masters,* New York, 1901, p. 159.
64. T. S. Eliot, *op. cit.,* p. 110.

No praise would have pleased the ear of the Prophet of Culture more than to hear said of him the words which he applied to Goethe in his *Memorial Verses*. Indeed, his chief aspiration seems to have been to fulfil in England the role of Physician of the Iron Age. It was in this capacity that he diagnosed the maladies of Victorian England and Victorian poetry and prescribed the application of certain standards. His usual remedies were the writings of the Greeks or of Goethe, or, in some cases, those of Milton. Wordsworth, he found, had also his peculiar healing power, and Byron was a sort of tonic. But the poetry of Keats is not very often recommended for its remedial qualities. Arnold treats the Celtic, as Keats represented it, as a sort of antidote, an excellent one in its way, but one of the second order. Moreover, he felt that his age was suffering from a surfeit of the Keatsian, and its value was therefore strictly limited.

"The misapprehensiveness of his age is exactly what a poet is sent to remedy"[65] writes Browning, and in this sense of the word, Arnold remained a poet long after he had abandoned the writing of verse. He recommended types of poetry with a view to pulling out "a few more stops" as he said, "in that powerful but at present somewhat narrow-toned organ, the modern Englishman."[66] At the time when he turned his hand to his essay on Keats, the enlightened sections of the Victorian reading public were not suffering, on the whole, from much misapprehensiveness to the Keatsian in poetry, and, as was his manner, Matthew Arnold therefore directed the greatest part of his attention in other directions.

65. Robert Browning, *Shelley*, Hull, n.d., p. 17.
66. *Essays in Criticism, First Series*, Preface, pp. vii–viii.

V

Johnny Keats

Right stately sat Arnold—his black gown adjusted
Genteelly, his Rhine wine deliciously iced,—
With puddingish England serenely disgusted,
And looking in vain (in the mirror) for "Geist." . . .
Robert Buchanan, *The Session of the Poets.*

WRITING in 1867, Frederic Harrison laid his oft-repeated charge that Matthew Arnold was lacking in "principles . . . coherent . . . interdependent, subordinate and derivative."[1] With respect to his knowledge of abstract philosophy, Arnold was quite prepared to admit the truth of the charge, but, on other levels, his thought has a certain unity which Harrison could not see. He too has his coherent principles.

One such principle exemplified throughout his literary criticism concerns the extreme importance to be placed on biography. As E. K. Brown remarks: "Much as Arnold has to say of the strictly literary merits of the men he writes about, his fundamental interest is in their character, as exhibited in their lives and as expressed in their works."[2] This predilection for dwelling on a poet's character has serious effects on Arnold's estimate of the poetry itself. In the case of Keats it is exceptionally important, especially as it emerges in his final study of that poet, which appeared in 1880. About four-fifths of the essay *John Keats* are devoted to a consideration of the poet's character and conduct.

Arnold's statements should be related not only to his own standards but to the history of Keats's reputation throughout the Victorian age as well.

In the opening chapter it was suggested that the evolution of Keats's reputation and influence was largely fostered by four factors. Not the least important of these was the resurrection of his personality by his biographers, Lord Houghton and Sir Sidney Colvin.

In an essay attacking Keats (published in 1846), Thomas De Quincey quoted with approval the stanza from *Don Juan* in which Byron spoke of Keats's death at the hands of *the Quarterly.*[3] De

---

1. Frederic Harrison, "Culture, A Dialogue," *Fortnightly Review,* viii (1867), 608.
2. *Representative Essays of Matthew Arnold* (ed. E. K. Brown), Toronto, 1936, Introduction, p. xx.
3. Thomas De Quincey, "John Keats," *Tait's Magazine,* xiii (1846), 252.

Quincey's action was characteristic, for Byron's mockery was not for his own age merely; it served as testimony for later generations of Keats's critics. For over sixty years after Keats's death, the lingering conception of his character was that he had been a puny weakling and an ignorant, badly-bred surgeon's apprentice.

In the reputation of no other English poet has the question of personality played such a significant role in its development. More than almost any other factor, the "Keats legend," that is the story of his death being attributable to the adverse criticism his poetry had received, retarded it. A complete appreciation of his writing demanded the disproving of the commonly-accepted picture of what Arnold calls "Johnny Keats."[4]

One half of the legend could not, of course, be disproved. As Arnold was only too well aware, Keats did not attend Eton or Winchester. But on the other hand, Shelley's representation of him in *Adonais* and the *Quarterly* articles after his death both served to stamp on the public mind the impression of a milksop sort of youth, lacking any form of courage whatsoever. Facts concerning this side of his character would rectify the impression and his masculinity was gradually recognized after 1848. It was, however, a long struggle. For some women readers, the story of Keats's supposed extreme weakness had a sort of attraction with which they were loath to part. A "lady-reviewer" of 1870, although admitting that she might be wrong, speaks nevertheless of Keats in these terms:

We gather how tenderly sensitive a soul was doomed to struggle awhile in life's trying vortex, to struggle awhile despairingly, and to sink. The harsh, stern stuff which genius cannot dispense with . . . was notably absent.[5]

Among men, but for different reasons, the impression also lingered. As late as 1885, so discerning a critic as Courthope refers to his "effeminacy," his "physical disability," his "contented materialism."[6]

In another country, even if Keats's character had really been what it was supposed to have been, the damage to his reputation might not have remained so extensive. But in England, it was almost irreparable. A French reviewer writing in 1867 had the good sense to seize on this fact: "Keats est peut-être le moins Anglais des poètes que la Grande-Bretagne a produits dans notre siècle. Il manque de cette *manliness*. . . ."[7]

---

4. *Essays in Criticism, Second Series*, p. 75. He takes over the term, of course, from the *Blackwood's* review of Keats (1818).

5. *Victoria Magazine*, xv (1870), 56.

6. W. J. Courthope, *The Liberal Movement in English Literature*, London, 1885, pp. 182–3. Two years later Courthope again attacked Keats's lack of the masculine when he reviewed Colvin's life of Keats (*National Review*, x [1887], 11–24).

7. Louis Etienne, "La poésie païenne en Angleterre," *Revue des Deux Mondes*, LXIX (1867), 298.

The first great attempt to repair the damage and to see Keats's character in its true light was Monckton Milnes's *Life and Letters of Keats* which appeared in 1848. Up to this time, except for a few sentences by Leigh Hunt, practically nothing had been published to rectify the conventional notions of his character. Milnes's biography may be said to mark the turning point in the reputation of Keats. It seems to have received considerable attention and was widely reviewed.[8] Keats was at last brought before the public in a favourable manner. It is significant that when Arnold wishes to qualify his sharp criticism of Keats's character, he refers at once to the evidence which Milnes had presented thirty-two years before.[9]

It may seem surprising that the biography was so long delayed, and one's first guess might be that the fault would lie with the dilettante Milnes. Actually the delay was occasioned by a series of accidents. Keats's friend Charles Brown was to have been his biographer, but Brown, after quarrelling with George Keats, found that he lacked valuable materials which were in the hands of the latter. He did eventually prepare a *Life of Keats* which he delivered as a lecture in 1836, but he was unable to find a publisher for it. Five years later, he abandoned his scheme and turned over his materials to Milnes.[10] In 1842, George Keats died and Milnes was able to purchase the documents which had been in his possession and then begin a biography of Keats in real earnest.

If we are to believe Hall Caine, Milnes's undertaking to write about Keats was itself an accident, and the person ultimately responsible for his doing so was Walter Savage Landor. Milnes had originally planned to write a life of Shelley, but Landor, says Caine, "threw cold water on Houghton's enthusiasm, and then said: 'But a young fellow named Keats died at Rome a while ago, and he was a real poet —why not get up a life of him?' "[11] The story is not improbable. Although Landor did not dislike Shelley,[12] we have seen how keen was his enthusiasm for Keats, and furthermore, he was acutely aware of his neglect. "There is nothing in the ruins of Rome" he remarked, "which throws so chilling a shadow over the heart as the monument of Keats."[13] Landor would be aware of the desirability of a biography, and, with his encouragement, it was finally published.

As a biography, the book does not belong in the same rank with

8. For examples of its warm reception, see the *Westminster Review*, L (1894), 346–71; and *Sharpe's London Magazine*, VIII (1849), 55–60. Others are mentioned in the bibliography appended to W. M. Rossetti's *Life of John Keats*, London, 1887. See also the *Letters of Edward Fitzgerald*, I, 195.

9. *Essays in Criticism, Second Series*, p. 75.

10. Charles Brown's *Life of Keats* was finally published in 1937 by the Oxford University Press.

11. Hall Caine, *My Story*, New York, 1909, pp. 52–3.

12. See *The Works of Walter Savage Landor*, v, 287.

13. *Ibid.*, VI, 34.

that published in 1887 by Sidney Colvin.[14] But it achieved its purpose and Keats was slowly popularized as a result of the efforts of a very effective champion. Milnes's zeal was equalled only by his confidence. "Contrary to the expectation of Mr. Shelley" he boldly proclaimed in 1848, "the appreciation of Keats by men of thought and sensibility gradually rose after his death, until he attained the place he now holds among the poets of his country."[15]

In reality, this "place" was still rather vulnerable, but yearly, throughout the latter half of the nineteenth century, it became more and more secure. Reviews and essays, such as James Russell Lowell's highly appreciative memoir of 1851, indicate the shift in opinion, and steady praise continued throughout the Sixties and Seventies. Joseph Severn tells us that by 1863 Keats's grave had become a pilgrimage point for visitors from all over the world.[16]

If Arnold had written his study of Keats before 1878, it is likely that the tone of his comments on Keats's character would have been considerably different. The sympathetic analysis which he made of Keats's personality in the *Maurice de Guérin* essay gives us some clue to what he might have written had not an event occurred which offended his taste very deeply. For in 1878 an old sore was reopened. Buxton Forman published the letters to Fanny Brawne, and in the outburst which followed this publication, it is apparent that the High Victorian snake had been scotch'd, but by no means killed by the combined efforts of poets, essayists, and biographers during the previous forty years. It looked for a while, in fact, as if all Milnes's strivings to establish the character of Keats were to come to naught as a result of the disclosures which these letters made.[17]

From the time of the first *Blackwood's* review to R. H. Hutton's essay of 1887, the associations of "surgeon's apprentice" were apt to be latent in the minds of Keats's more sophisticated readers. Such people objected to the rather *uncultivated* manner in which he had

14. In Colvin's second biography of Keats (the revised and enlarged study published in 1917) he himself draws attention to some of the errors which Milnes had made (*John Keats*, New York, 1917, pp. 531–7).

15. Richard Monckton Milnes, *Life and Letters of John Keats*, New York, 1848, p. 253.

16. Joseph Severn, "On the Vicissitudes of Keats' Fame," *Atlantic Monthly*, xi (1863), 406.

17. Among those who objected to the letters in strong terms were Colvin, Arnold, Swinburne, Charles Eliot Norton, William Watson, Frederick Tennyson and many others. Edward Fitzgerald's comments make a refreshing contrast: ". . . I for one, am glad of them. I had just been hammering out some notes on Catullus. . . . Well, when Keats came, I scarce felt a change from Catullus: both such fiery Souls as wore out their Bodies early; and I can even imagine Keats writing such filthy Libels against any one he had a spite against . . . had Keats lived two thousand years ago" (*Letters of Edward Fitzgerald*, i, 413). Fitzgerald's friends, however, later forced him to retract. See *ibid.*, p. 426, and also *More Letters of Edward Fitzgerald*, London, 1901, p. 199.

met death. The Fanny Brawne letters simply re-crystallized this reaction. When it was seen, as Lafourcade expresses it, that Keats not only did not die like a gentleman but did not make love like a gentleman, it was too much.[18] Even Swinburne could comment: ". . . a manful kind of man or even a manly sort of boy, in his love-making or in his suffering, will not howl and snivel after such a lamentable fashion."[19]

It is in the light of this background that Matthew Arnold's condemnations must be considered. If the author of *Poems and Ballads* could cast such stones, it is hardly surprising that the author of *Literature and Dogma* would have had some harsh things to say. His essay sums up an important stage in the evolution of Keats's biography. It also gives us some insight into the author's criteria.

As a rule (except in the *Shelley* essay) Arnold attempts to strike a balance in his biographical estimates, to play off virtues against shortcomings. A large part of his study of Keats is devoted to illustrating what he calls the "signs of character and virtue"[20] in his subject. Thus he draws attention to certain manifestations of Keats's "manliness,"[21] his sound attitude towards friendship, and his ability to criticize his own writings. On the other side of the scale, however, Arnold's remarks are of a nature to destroy the balance completely. They represent a tone which appears again in his estimates of Burns, Shelley and Chaucer, but never so offensively as here. The fine adjustment of estimate disappears, and we are left with an impression which none of his qualifications will ever dispel.

At the very outset of his essay, we find such comments as these:

. . . Keats's love-letter is the love-letter of a surgeon's apprentice. It has in its relaxed self-abandonment something underbred and ignoble, as of a youth ill brought up. . . .

and again:

It is the sort of love-letter of a surgeon's apprentice which one might hear read out in a breach of promise case, or in the Divorce Court. The sensuous man speaks in it, and the sensuous man of a badly bred and badly trained sort.

Any palliatives which Arnold offers elsewhere in the essay never can efface the impression which these sentences give. He was once tagged with the title of "High Priest of the kid glove persuasion," but

18. Georges Lafourcade, *Swinburne's Hyperion with an Essay on Swinburne and Keats,* p. 57.
19. *The Complete Works of Swinburne* (Bonchurch edition), London, 1925–27, XIV, 297.
20. *Essays in Criticism, Second Series,* p. 74.
21. *Ibid.,* p. 79. "His attitude towards the public is that of a strong man, not of a weakling avid of praise, and made to 'be snuff'd out by an article.'"

in these remarks, the kid glove seems to have worn very thin. The mailed fist of the Victorian moralist is all too apparent beneath it. The Brawne letters seem to have offended Arnold so much that for additional charges of Keats's lack of "character and self-control,"[22] he goes back to the very highly questionable evidence of Haydon's *Autobiography*. In 1853, Arnold had hesitated over the validity of Haydon's pictures of Keats's drunkenness and weakness, but, in 1880, he is prepared to give them a prominent place.[23] The disclosure of Keats's career as a lover had been too much for him.

It is interesting to compare his reaction in this respect with a comment he made in 1859 on the correspondence of George Sand and Alfred de Musset (which Sainte-Beuve had allowed him to examine). "De Musset's letters were, I must say, those of a *gentleman* of the very first water."[24] The difference suggests one of the two mainsprings of Arnold's attack on Keats's character, that is, the poet's shortcomings on the social plane. The other mainspring is related to larger issues of morality, where, as Trilling notes, "the sexual concern is [for Arnold] almost central. . . ."[25] "Conduct" said the author of *Literature and Dogma,* is "three-fourths of human life."[26]

In earlier years, Arnold had not taken the question of sensuality quite so seriously. Thomas Arnold leaves us a remarkable picture of his brother as a young man: "The name of Voltaire coming to be discussed, my brother said, with a wave of his hand, 'as to the coarseness or sensuality of some of his writings, that is a matter to which I attach little importance.' "[27]

Such tolerance gradually disappeared. In this we have one of the few instances of a change in Arnold's thought over the course of his lifetime. His writings show a progressive distrust of the France which read *Nana* and worshipped at the shrine of the *Goddess of Lubricity.* Swinburne's famous description of him as "David, the son of Goliath"[28] contains a hint of the veiled Puritanism of the son of Rugby's headmaster. It was Arnold's habit to carry an occasional coal to Newcastle himself, and the Keats essay certainly gives him away. He

---

22. *Essays in Criticism, Second Series,* p. 72.

23. On August 3, 1853, he wrote to Clough: "Read the details about poor Keats at the end of Haydon's first and the beginning of his second vol. Haydon himself is a false *butcher*—revolting" (H. F. Lowry, *op. cit.,* p. 139). Arnold seems to me here to be questioning seriously the truth of Haydon's account, although his words are open to other interpretations.

24. *Letters,* I, 140.

25. Lionel Trilling, *op. cit.,* p. 344. In this connection see also Trilling's interesting analysis of why Arnold chose to disregard Byron's conduct (p. 372).

26. *Literature and Dogma,* VII, 15.

27. Quoted by Hugh Walker, *The Literature of the Victorian Age,* Cambridge, 1931, p. 456.

28. A. C. Swinburne, "Mr. Arnold's New Poems," *The Fortnightly Review,* VIII (1867), 425.

condemned much of Keats because he sensed in his life and work the seeds of a moral breakdown. The predominant note of the essay is that "beauty" is not enough, for "beauty," as Arnold employs the word throughout most of the essay, has for him the smack of what Buchanan had called "The Fleshly School of Poetry."

Readers of Arnold's essay throughout the Eighties received a variety of impressions from it. Some felt (as Swinburne did) that he had been extremely kind to Keats's character.[29] Others were influenced more by his strictures. For example, his then widely-known disciple, R. H. Hutton, followed out a similar line of attack in a *Spectator* article of 1887.[30] But on the whole, Arnold's censure does not seem to have held ground for long. The strong objections to the Brawne letters gradually disappeared, and in Colvin's excellent biography of 1887, the controversial aspects of Keats's personality seem to have been cleared up once and for all. Among the essayists of the Nineties, the question of his character is no longer a sore point. Arnold's reading of him represented only a temporary phase, the last stand, perhaps, of the stricter views of an older day. Indeed, the following sentence written by Robert Bridges in 1895 closes not merely his own book but a whole chapter in the evolution of the reputation of a poet born one hundred years before:

And if I have read him rightly, he would be pleased, could he see it, at the universal recognition of his genius, and the utter rout of his traducers: but much more moved, stirred he would be to the depth of his great nature to know that he was understood, and that for the nobility of his character his name was loved and esteemed.[31]

29. "As a man, the two admirers who have done best service to his memory are, first . . . Lord Houghton, and secondly Mr. Matthew Arnold" (*The Complete Works of Swinburne*, XIV, 301).

30. R. H. Hutton, *Brief Literary Criticisms,* London, 1906, pp. 81–7.

31. Robert Bridges, *John Keats* (privately printed), 1895, p. 97.

VI

Poetry and Poetics

I N his excellent study of Byron, Professor Grierson draws attention to the decline of that poet's reputation in nineteenth-century
England and by contrast, to the enormous influence of Keats:

Keats has been, without any exception, the greatest influence in English
poetry for a whole century. To his example and inspiration are due all
the wonderful sensuous felicity, the splendour of exotic phrasing and harmony of Tennyson's 1842 volumes; the bold and varied experiments of
Browning's *Bells and Pomegranates;* the curious subtleties of *The Blessed
Damozel* and the *House of Life; The Defence of Guenevere* and *The
Earthly Paradise; Poems and Ballads,* and *Atalanta in Calydon.*[1]

In this impressive list, no poem of Matthew Arnold's is mentioned.
For Arnold's work represents, on the whole, a conscious reaction
against the Keats tradition as it had evolved in Victorian poetry. To
consider the nature of his reaction and some qualifications of its
success in Arnold's own poetry will round out this study of Arnold
and Keats.

We have already considered some of Arnold's standards of excellence in poetry and his dissatisfaction with Keats's work in the light
of them: the younger poet's excess of "multitudinousness," his lack
of knowledge, restraint, and "modernity," his failure to achieve the
proper effects in poetry of nobility and animation. Arnold was not
averse to testing his own work on the same basis. He cancelled his
Empedocles on Etna from the edition of 1853 on the ground that he
had failed to do what he felt the poet must do, that is, "to delight
himself with the contemplation of some noble action of a heroic
time." So too, in the same year, we find him writing to Clough:

I am glad you like the Gipsy Scholar—but what does it *do* for you? Homer
animates—Shakespeare *animates*—in its poor way I think Sohrab and
Rustum *animates*—the Gipsy Scholar at best awakens a pleasing melancholy. But this is not what we want. The complaining millions of men
. . . what they want is something to *animate* and *ennoble* them—not
merely to add zest to their melancholy or grace to their dreams.—I believe
a feeling of this kind is the basis of my nature—and of my poetics.[2]

The conflict between Arnold's poetics and his most characteristic
poetry is striking enough. His struggle to free his poetry from Keatsian

1. H. J. C. Grierson, *The Background of English Literature,* London, 1925, p. 109.
2. H. F. Lowry, *op. cit.,* p. 146.

style is very similar to his deeper struggle to eliminate romantic melancholy. In the latter sphere, three poems represent his principal attempts to put his critical precepts into practice: *Sohrab and Rustum, Balder Dead,* and *Merope,* but the greatest part of his verse is essentially romantic in character. The unity which he sought seems to have eluded him,[3] and his poetry records his disillusionment, his cry of pain:

> No, thou art come too late, Empedocles!
> And the world hath the day, and must break thee,
> Not thou the world.
> *(Empedocles on Etna,* ii, 16–18)

The mood of disillusionment is expressed in poems which are deeply intimate, honest, and sincere, but hardly meeting the requirements which their author demanded. On the other hand, that part of his work in verse which satisfied his critical sense fails to satisfy us as poetry. *Sohrab and Rustum* is an interesting effort, but *Balder Dead* and *Merope,* however admirable their objectivity, fall flat as poetry. "The mind in creation" writes Shelley in his *Defence of Poetry,* "is as a fading coal, which some invisible influence, like an inconstant wind, awakens to transitory brightness. . . ." The coal only faintly glimmers in *Balder Dead;* in *Merope* it is quite extinct.

For when Arnold sought to exclude from his verse the things which truly moved him, the "inconstant wind" deserted him. He was deeply moved by a sense of wandering between two worlds, one dead, the other powerless to be born, and *Dover Beach* and the *Obermann* stanzas successfully record his nostalgia for a lost faith. He was moved by a sense of frustrated isolation in love which appears in the series of lyrics written to the shadowy "Marguerite," and (in veiled form) in *Tristram and Iseult* and *The Forsaken Merman.* Finally, as *The Scholar Gipsy* and *Thyrsis* show, he was inspired by a quest for an ideal which seems forever to escape him:

> I cannot reach the Signal-Tree to-night,
> Yet, happy omen, hail!

There is an overtone to the word "to-night" which is suggestive. It was in such moods that Arnold's finest and most representative poetry was written. Only then, and not when he was trying to write according to the recipe of his poetics, do we find that

> A bolt is shot back somewhere in our breast
> And a lost pulse of feeling stirs again. . . .
> *(The Buried Life,* 84–5)

3. See C. B. Tinker, "Arnold's Poetic Plans," *Yale Review,* xxii (1933), 782.

Matthew Arnold's desertion of the muses at an early stage in his career was prompted by several causes. Not the least important must have been his realization that the situations which touched him strongly were personal not dramatic, and that he had failed to write poetry of the type which he regarded as worthwhile.

It is in this sphere of desired effects that we find the major conflict between Arnold's poetry and his poetics. A parallel conflict of somewhat minor proportions exists in the sphere of style. The discrepancy here between theory and practice is not nearly so marked, for Arnold succeeded, more often than not, in achieving the chastened forms of expression which he regarded as desirable. As we shall see, Keats is singled out from the romantic poets to serve as his principal whipping-boy in matters of style, and his criticism voices a strong reaction against Keats's influence. It must be noted at the outset that this reaction against Keatsian phrasing was, on the whole, much more adequately put into force in Arnold's poetry than his reaction against the romantic writers in general, and to the nostalgic effects common to most or all of them.

The height of popularity attained by Tennyson's Keats-like poetry throughout the Forties produced, inevitably, a certain reaction in the following decade. A school of writers known as the "Spasmodics" attempted to break away from the growing convention of smoothness and liquidity represented by those who followed Keats, and sought to substitute in its place a certain harshness and vigour.[4] Arnold himself regarded the Spasmodics as "provincial,"[5] but from one point of view his own attitude to questions of style had something in common with theirs. In place of the Keatsian and Tennysonian he wanted, however, not intensity so much as restraint, simplicity, the "grand style" as he calls it in his lectures *On Translating Homer*. As early as 1848 he had taken this stand. Writing to Clough he exclaims: "But what perplexity Keats Tennyson et id genus omne must occasion to young writers . . . yes and those d—d Elizabethan poets generally. Those who cannot read G[ree]k sh[ou]ld read nothing but Milton and parts of Wordsworth: the state should see to it."[6]

These words were not written merely for effect. They represent a

---

4. Although the Spasmodics reacted against Tennyson, they did not react against Keats directly. They objected to Tennyson's habit of softening the intensity of Keats, for Keats himself placed high value on intensity. Both Sidney Dobell and Alexander Smith were influenced by Keats. Dobell's *Keith of Ravelston* certainly harks back to *La Belle Dame sans Merci* and in his prefatory note to *Balder*, he asserts that he was influenced by "memorable passages in the letters of Keats." Smith's debt to Keats is more noticeable. A reviewer said of his *Life Drama* that here was "a finer poet than Keats was in the very qualities in which Keats was finest" (William Sinclair's Introduction to *Poems of Alexander Smith*, Edinburgh, 1909, p. xxxiv).

5. H. F. Lowry, *op. cit.*, p. 147.

6. *Ibid.*, p. 97.

conviction which Arnold reiterates on numerous occasions. Many years later, when he came across a phrase in Keats which Rossetti loved, the phrase in which Keats spoke of "loading every rift of the subject with ore," Arnold wrote emphatically in the margin, "*dangerous.*"[7] He felt that a certain plainness was desirable in modern poetry. In the first place, its absence implied for him a lack of concern for the truly serious. It represented a mere "dawdling with the painted shell" of the universe, as he said of Tennyson:[8]

More and more I feel that the difference between a mature and a youthful age of the world compels the poetry of the former to use great plainness of speech . . . and that Keats and Shelley were on a false track when they set themselves to reproduce the exuberance of expression, the charm, the richness of images, and the felicity, of the Elizabethan poets.[9]

And in an earlier letter he gives his opinion that had Shakespeare and Milton lived in the nineteenth century, "I think it likely" that the style of each would have been far less *curious* and exquisite."[10]

The over-simplified school-boy account of Matthew Arnold always pictures him as concerned only with what things are said, not how they are said. The account is not strictly accurate. He was profoundly interested in matters of style and had a strong sense of its value.[11] What he did object to was not a concern for style but a concern for a certain *kind* of style. "We have poems which seem to exist merely for the sake of single lines and passages; not for the sake of producing any total impression."[12] It was this tendency which drew down his condemnation on the Elizabethans.[13] Style for Arnold is a moral problem rather than an aesthetic one. In terms of the effects he sought, the Elizabethans represented bad models. That is why, in the 1853 Preface, we find him advocating "the subordinate character of expression."

In this same Preface, it is significant that Arnold draws his principal example of the dangers of such a style from Keats's *Isabella*, one of the poems which aroused the delighted admiration of the Pre-Raphaelites. He admits that it is "a perfect treasure house of felicitous words and images; and almost in every stanza there occurs one of

7. E. V. Lucas, *The Colvins and Their Friends*, p. 193.
8. H. F. Lowry, *op. cit.*, p. 63.
9. *Ibid.*, p. 124.
10. *Ibid.*, p. 65.
11. See *On Translating Homer, passim,* and also his description of Keats as a "form seeker" (H. F. Lowry, *op. cit.*, p. 101).
12. Preface to the *Poems* of 1853, in *The Poems of Matthew Arnold* (ed. Sir A. T. Quiller-Couch), p. 7.
13. On his general dislike of the Elizabethan Age see E. K. Brown, "Matthew Arnold and the Elizabethans," *University of Toronto Quarterly*, 1 (1932), 333–51. See in addition Arnold's letter to Colvin in which he contrasts his own "first love" in poetry (Virgil) with Keats's early enthusiasm for Spenser (E. V. Lucas, *op. cit.*, p. 193).

those vivid and picturesque turns of expression . . . which thrill the reader with a sudden delight." But such an effect, however pleasing to his contemporaries, is inadequate for Matthew Arnold:

This one short poem contains, perhaps, a greater number of happy single expressions which one could quote than all the extant tragedies of Sophocles. But the action, the story?[14]

It might be noted that in our own century, when Irving Babbitt launched his attack on "confusion in the arts," he quoted with approbation these words of Arnold's to prove his contention that the harmful influence of Keats's power of suggestiveness has been to break down the barriers between poetry, painting, and music.[15] Arnold could well recommend a reconsideration of the theories of the *Laocoön* to an age which witnessed the occurrence of this breakdown.[16]

A large part of Arnold's verse exemplifies the theory of style which he expounded to Clough and to the English public at large. I do not mean that he ever achieved the "grand style" (in the sense which he used that phrase), although he made strong efforts to do so in *Sohrab and Rustum*, an Homeric imitation of which he was very proud.[17] But in many poems he did achieve what we might call an anti-Keatsian style, a style from which Keatsian exuberance has been almost entirely chastened. We may consider such poems before passing on to those which are much closer to Keats.

Perhaps the most outstanding feature of Arnold's chastening of style is his minimization of sensuousness. Not only is there a complete dearth of tactile and olfactory sensations (which his contemporary, Baudelaire,[18] was exploiting in every possible direction), but colour itself is almost entirely absent. Lafcadio Hearn goes so far as to say that the poems are simply "colorless."[19] In such typical pieces as *Memorial Verses* or *To Marguerite*, one is a long way from the world of dazzling colours which Keats had employed so lavishly. As

14. Preface to the *Poems* of 1853, p. 10.
15. Irving Babbitt, *The New Laokoon*, New York, 1910, pp. 129–30.
16. In 1848 he advises Clough to follow up the Keats letters with the *Laocoön* of Lessing (see H. F. Lowry, *op. cit.*, p. 97) and in the poems of 1867 appears his *Epilogue to Lessing's Laocoön*. Although one of the clumsiest of his pieces as a poem, it gives us an insight into his interest in the problems of the proper spheres of the various arts.
17. For Arnold's comparison of *Sohrab and Rustum* with Tennyson's *Morte d'Arthur*, see H. F. Lowry, *op. cit.*, p. 145. On the un-Homeric features of the poem, see Douglas Bush, *op. cit.*, pp. 262–3.
18. For example, Baudelaire speaks thus of the blended charms of his mistress:
O métamorphose mystique
De tous mes sens fondus en un!
Son haleine fait la musique,
Comme sa voix fait le parfum!
(*Tout Entière*)
19. Quoted by Lionel Trilling, *op. cit.*, p. 144.

Trilling notes, Arnold does achieve a certain warm gray tone at times, and he is often successful with moonlight effects, as in *Mycerinus:*

> While the deep-burnish'd foliage overhead
> Splinter'd the silver arrows of the moon.[20]

But the great world of colour, as we find it in *The Eve of St. Mark* or the *Ode to a Nightingale* is one upon which Matthew Arnold seldom draws. Many of the poems, especially those of the 1867 volume, will illustrate F. L. Lucas' remark that Arnold "tended to prefer sackcloth to satin," and that often his "bareness becomes threadbare."[21] Such jerky pieces as the *Epilogue to Lessing's Laocoön* or *Heine's Grave,* whatever their virtues as criticism, are of a baldness which makes even the style of Wordsworth seem blazing with colours by comparison.

One hardly needs to quote from these poems to illustrate the point. Any lines selected at random will serve. A better example is such a piece as *The Strayed Reveller* where certain concessions are made to the pictorial sense:

> See, how glows,
> Through the delicate flush'd marble,
> The red creaming liquor,
> Strown with dark seeds!

Arnold seems almost Keatsian here, but if the poem is more closely examined, a striking difference is to be noted. The short line (of which he was so fond) eliminates the tendency to develop metaphor and simile. I have referred earlier to some resemblance between the theme of this poem and Keats's *Hyperion.* We may note also a certain similarity in details. Keats had written:

> As when, upon a tranced summer-night,
> Those green-rob'd senators of mighty woods,
> Tall oaks, branch-charmed by the earnest stars,
> Dream, and so dream all night without a stir. . . .[22]

Arnold's lines are:

> Ah cool night-wind, tremulous stars!
> Ah glimmering water—

---

20. *Mycerinus*, 98–9. The entire poem is an excellent example of how Arnold subordinates his descriptive digressions, far more so, it may be added, than *Sohrab and Rustum.* For example, he has the opportunity to describe a banquet scene. Instead of dwelling over it as Keats would have done, he disposes of it in eight lines and then passes on to issues which seem of more consequence to him.

21. F. L. Lucas, *Eight Victorian Poets*, Cambridge, 1930, p. 50.

22. *Hyperion*, I, 72–5. Keats may have been influenced by Milton's *Arcades:*
> Under the shady roof
> Of branching elm star-proof.

Fitful earth-murmur—
Dreaming woods!
(*The Strayed Reveller*, 282–5)

The two passages are more interesting in their divergencies than in any likeness which they share. Arnold chooses to do without the richness of imagery, and here as elsewhere in such poems, subordinates his colours as he advocated in the 1853 Preface. It is, in fact, much closer to sculpture than to painting, and a type of sculpture very different from that sometimes employed by Keats. In *Hyperion* the delineation of the great figures of the fallen Titans has all the massiveness of Michelangelo. Arnold's sculpture is on a different scale. As Quiller-Couch observes, his poetry leaves the impression of something done in "low relief."[23]

The theme of *The New Sirens* confirms, I think, this general impression. Arnold could be tempted, as the Obermann poems show, by the world of the romantic retreat. And *The New Sirens* demonstrates that he was sometimes attracted to an indulgence of the passions *à la Byron*. But he does not speak in his poems of the Lotosland of sensuousness as an alternative worthy to sway him from the paths of a dedicated life. The comparative plainness of style in most of his poetry corroborates what seems to have been a bent of his own nature.

If, in the sphere of word-painting Arnold seems to be in reaction against Keats, in that of verse-music he seems to be in reaction against Tennyson. Keats's charming smoothness of style had been extensively developed by the poet-laureate. The success of such a poem as *The Lotos-Eaters* in its manipulation of dulcet sounds into perfect harmony became, for the Victorian reader, the very standard of excellence. Matthew Arnold refused to conform. Through all his experiments with metrical forms he was working along his own lines, not in the direction of smoother melodies but towards a simpler, more intellectualized conversational style, and, it may be added, away from Keats and Tennyson. As Trilling remarks, his poetry has certain affinities with the "iron harmonies," the dissonance of John Donne, rather than with the "golden singers" of the stamp of Keats.[24] The comparative absence of melody, together with the want of suggestiveness in pictorial image, gives his style an air of asceticism which is at the opposite pole from that of *The Eve of St. Agnes*.

In view of the Keatsian vogue in the later Victorian age, it was not unnatural that Arnold's stylistic methods would be little understood by his contemporaries. A reviewer of 1867, in comparing Arnold with Tennyson, grants the palm to the latter for the following reasons:

23. *The Poems of Matthew Arnold* (ed. Sir A. T. Quiller-Couch), Introduction, p. xii.
24. Lionel Trilling, *op. cit.*, p. 145.

. . . in variation of softly brilliant, exquisitely appropriate imagery, picture after picture of breathing, ruddy-tinted life, each picture speaking
forth the argument in glow of noblest colour, each picture moving on as
in rhythmic starry dance to the music of the whole,—the . . . poetry of
Tennyson has the everlasting and incomparable superiority.[25]

Each one of these epithets is revealing. Keats's lessons had been
learned only too well by the generations which succeeded his own,
and Arnold's efforts to rectify the convention would hardly be appreciated. If that stylistic reformer had read the review, however, he
would merely have shrugged. He was content to rest his case in another court. "My poems" he said, "represent . . . the main movement of mind of the last quarter of a century, and thus they will
probably have their day. . . ."[26]

On the other hand, if Arnold had chosen to reply to the review, taking examples from a restricted group of his own poems, he might have
been able to challenge comparison with the followers of Keats on
their own ground. He might, for example, have cited the case of his
Scholar Gipsy with its succession of striking vignettes and its Keatsian
stanza form:

> Shepherds had met him on the Hurst in spring;
> At some lone alehouse in the Berkshire moors,
> On the warm ingle bench, the smock-frock'd boors
> Had found him seated at their entering. . . .

For Arnold, in spite of all his protests against the influence of Keats's
style, did not succeed in remaining completely immune himself. A
group of his poems bear the unmistakable stamp of the earlier artist.
This group includes some of his very finest work: *Thyrsis, The Scholar
Gipsy* and *Tristram and Iseult*. We have already seen how, in his
criticism, he provided a place for Keats. So too in his poetry. On
some important occasions he was content to relax his customary
ascetic standards of style (which he only half-relaxed in *Sohrab and
Rustum*) and to indulge fully in a sort of Keatsian holiday. It was in
some such mood that several of his most attractive pieces of poetry
were written.

Furthermore, in these same poems there are signs of an even more
important form of influence than that of style. It seems likely that one
of Arnold's favourite themes was considerably modified by the influence of Keats's *Ode on a Grecian Urn* and *Ode to a Nightingale*. One
of the central ideas of *The Scholar Gipsy* is the contrast between the
reality and immortality of the scholar as opposed to the mutability
of the ordinary life which surrounds the poet:

25. Peter Bayne, "Mr. Arnold and Mr. Swinburne," *The Contemporary Review*, vi
(1867), 356. The reviewer significantly enough declares himself a Keats enthusiast
as well as a Tennysonian, and rates Keats above both Arnold and Swinburne (pp. 338
and 356).
26. *Letters*, ii, 195.

No, no, thou hast not felt the lapse of hours.
For what wears out the lot of mortal men?
　'Tis that from change to change their being rolls . . .
The generations of thy peers are fled,
　And we ourselves shall go;
But thou possessest an immortal lot. . . .

We find this theme used again in *Thyrsis* and also in *Tristram and Iseult*. In each case we may be reminded of Keats's odes:

Thou wast not born for death, immortal Bird!
No hungry generations tread thee down;
The voice I hear this passing night was heard
In ancient days by emperor and clown.

Arnold has made his Gipsy Scholar into a symbol very much his own, but his underlying conception owes much to Keats for whom the voice of the nightingale and the image of the Grecian urn were likewise symbols of permanence in a world of flux. Both *The Scholar Gipsy* and the *Ode to a Nightingale* are open to the same pedestrian query around which endless disputes have waged. How can the nightingale's song be immortal, for it is obviously only transitory? How can the dead gipsy scholar still roam the Oxford countryside? Keats's answer is that the song had beauty: Arnold's that the scholar had knowledge. The difference of ideals is significant, but not more so than Arnold's sharing with the earlier poet this romantic desire for something which will have the permanence of the Grecian urn:

When old age shall this generation waste,
Thou shalt remain, in midst of other woe
Than ours, a friend to man. . . .

Without the example of Keats, *The Scholar Gipsy* and *Thyrsis* would have been very different poems, not only in style but in the very conception of a theme which is of great importance in Arnold's best poetry. *Tristram and Iseult*, as we shall see, also provides examples.

　To return to the question of style. John Keats speaks in his letters of looking upon fine phrases like a lover. Arnold, with his notion of the subordinate place of suggestiveness in style, seldom leaves that impression. Nor does he seem to have been much given to Tennyson's habit of searching the work of his predecessors for details to incorporate into his poems. He remains, on the whole, an independent, and not a derivative poet of Tennyson's class. Yet he did borrow on occasions. He borrowed even from Tennyson as he grumblingly admitted. "One has [Tennyson] so in one's head" he told J. D. Coleridge, "one cannot help imitating him sometimes."[27] The debt to Keats is similar.

---

27. *Life and Correspondence of John Duke Coleridge*, London, 1904, I, 210. Arnold is referring specifically here to the last two lines of *Sohrab and Rustum*.

If Arnold was influenced by the Nightingale and Grecian urn odes in the general conception of his *Scholar Gipsy*, in the matter of style he seems to have drawn rather from a third poem, *To Autumn. To Autumn* represented to Arnold Keats's most satisfactory poem, and, in all probability, he had learned it by heart. In any case, when he commenced to write his *Scholar Gipsy*, echoes of the style of the earlier piece seem to have risen to mind. His picture of the Cumnor hill country owed not a little to Keats's account of an autumn day in Winchester. Thus (italics mine):

> While to my ear from uplands far away
> *The bleating of the folded flocks is borne,*
> With distant cries of reapers in the corn—
> All the *live murmur* of a summer's day.
> Screen'd is this nook o'er the high, *half-reap'd* field,
> And here till sun-down, Shepherd, will I be.
> Through the thick corn *the scarlet poppies peep,*
> And round green roots and yellowing stalks I see
> Pale blue convolvulus in tendrils creep.

Keats had described his personified Autumn as asleep on a "half-reap'd furrow" and "drows'd with the fume of poppies." And in his descriptions of the sounds of evening he mentions that "full-grown lambs loud bleat from hilly bourn" (which is not the only case where the rhyme-ending itself seems to have influenced Arnold). What is more important than such details, however, is the picture of Autumn herself. When Keats wrote:

> Who hath not seen thee oft amid thy store?
> Sometimes whoever seeks abroad may find
> Thee sitting careless on a granary floor,

he gave to the later poet a hint for the whole scheme of *The Scholar Gipsy*, the succession of pictures of the heaven-seeking wanderer:

> At some lone homestead in the Cumner hills,
> Where at her open door the housewife darns,
> Thou hast been seen, or hanging on a gate
> To watch the threshers in the mossy barns.

Finally, as H. W. Garrod has shown in his excellent study of Keats's versification, Arnold was largely indebted to that poet's experiments in the odes for the very stanza form of *The Scholar Gipsy*. He attempted to modify Keats's patterns somewhat, but not, in Garrod's opinion, with much success.[28]

Arnold's other great Oxford poem, *Thyrsis*, also shows the stamp of Keats. Indeed, when the Victorian poet stated in a letter that the

28. H. W. Garrod, *Keats*, pp. 95-7.

diction of *Thyrsis* was modelled on the example of Theocritus, and that "the images are all from actual observation,"[29] he was neglecting to mention a third source for the poem but one which should be obvious enough. As Swinburne wrote, "No countryman of ours since Keats died has made . . . words fall into such faultless folds and forms of harmonious line."[30] We sense the inspiration of Keats in such delightful descriptive lines as these:

> Soon will the high Midsummer pomp come on,
>   Soon will the musk carnations break and swell,
> Soon shall we have gold-dusted snapdragon,
>   Sweet-William with its homely cottage-smell,
>   And stocks in fragrant blow;
> Roses that down the alleys shine afar,
>   And open, jasmine-muffled lattices,
>   And groups under the dreaming garden-trees,
> And the full moon, and the white evening-star.

It is difficult to isolate the specifically Keatsian element here. The phrases "jasmine-muffled lattices" and "gold-dusted snapdragon" give us a hint of it, but there is something more. It is an attitude to nature which the two poets share in common.

As I have indicated in an earlier chapter, the more enlightened Victorians such as Arnold and Tennyson could appreciate the difference between Keats's treatment of nature and that of the other romantics, his capacity to regard it as a spectacle rather than as the key to the universe. In an early poem Arnold had written:

> Know, man hath all which Nature hath, but more
> And in that *more* lie all his hopes of good.

At the same time, Keats's poetry embodies a keen delight in the beauties of that soulless spectacle, the beauties of quiet English landscapes and gardens which Arnold too loved so well:

> I cannot see what flowers are at my feet,
>   Nor what soft incense hangs upon the boughs,
> But, in embalmed darkness, guess each sweet
>   Wherewith the seasonable month endows
> The grass, the thicket, and the fruit-tree wild;
>   White hawthorn, and the pastoral eglantine;
>   Fast fading violets cover'd up in leaves;
>   And mid-May's eldest child,
>   The coming musk-rose, full of dewy wine. . . .

In one of his last letters Keats remarks: "How astonishingly does the chance of leaving the world impress a sense of its natural beauties on us. Like poor Falstaff, though I do not babble, I think of green fields. I muse with the greatest affection on every flower I have known from my infancy. . . ."[31] In *Early Death and Fame*, Arnold described such a mood of heightened intensity, but on the whole he never really experienced to the full the "fine rapture" of Keats's delight in the beauties of nature as we find it in *Endymion* or *I Stood Tip-toe*. He had, however, a sense for the beauties which, if less intense, is equally exquisite at times:

> Say, has some wet bird-haunted English lawn
> Lent it the music of its trees at dawn?
> (*Parting*, 18–19)

In a superb line of *Sohrab and Rustum* the spirit of the dying young warrior is described:

> Regretting the warm mansion which it left,
> And youth and bloom, and this delightful world.

Arnold himself had a love for the bloom of this "delightful world" which has many affinities with that of Keats. The earlier poet can hardly be said to have been responsible for the love in itself, but it is unquestionable that his example conditioned Arnold's expression of it in verse. One can only regret that the author of *Thyrsis* did not profit from the example more often. When he is willing to do so, his style takes on a warmth which it badly needs, and his metre itself profits from a certain softening. To many readers, Arnold's best work as a poet is that written under the aegis of Keatsian inspiration:

There, in that lament for the lost Thyrsis, Arnold, it seems to me, truly and finally found himself. At last he was content, following Keats, to be, for moments at least, simply beautiful.[32]

There are touches of richness in some of the other elegies, in *A Southern Night* for example or in *Stanzas Composed at Carnac*. But by far the most striking instances of the Keatsian note are the two poems with mediaeval settings: *Tristram and Iseult* and *The Church of Brou*. The latter is a very uneven piece of work, but the final section makes it worthy to rank with Arnold's best. Part II is rather obviously modelled on Tennyson's *Lady of Shalott*, and part III, although the influence is not quite so easily traced, is certainly Keatsian. Generally speaking, the picture of the blazing colouring of the stained-glass owes not a little to Keats's stanzas in *The Eve of St. Agnes* describing the "stains and splendid dyes" of Madeline's chamber window with its "twilight saints and dim emblazonings." In any case, we are a long way from the Arnold of the Preface of 1853:

31. *Letters of Keats*, p. 465.
32. F. L. Lucas, *Eight Victorian Poets*, p. 51.

> . . . a flood of light
> Streams from the setting sun, and colours bright
> Prophets, transfigur'd Saints, and Martyrs brave,
> In the vast western window of the nave;
> And on the pavement round the Tomb there glints
> A chequer-work of glowing sapphire tints,
> And amethyst, and ruby. . . .[33]

What is perhaps more important, the basic theme of the lines echoes that of the *Ode on a Grecian Urn*. Keats addresses the marble lover in these words:

> Bold Lover, never, never canst thou kiss,
> Though winning near the goal—yet, do not grieve;
> She cannot fade, though thou hast not thy bliss,
> For ever wilt thou love, and she be fair!

and Arnold picks up the note of the last line and adapts it to his own uses:

> So rest, for ever rest, O Princely Pair!
> In your high Church, 'mid the still mountain air. . . .

Arnold's niece, Mrs. Humphry Ward, has suggested that her uncle had a strain of the "Celtic" in his ancestry[34] (much as Arnold had put forward that claim for Keats). *The Church of Brou* might well be cited to substantiate her suggestion. So too might *Tristram and Iseult*.

Tristram and Iseult is also a very uneven piece utilizing a great variety of verse forms. The most successful sections, as Saintsbury notes, are those in loose rhymed heroics, a form which Arnold probably acquired from Keats.[35] It is in these sections that the influence of Keats is most strongly marked.

I have remarked earlier on the fact that Arnold's criticism makes no mention of *The Eve of St. Mark*. He seems, nevertheless, to have been familiar enough with it, as this poem tends to show. In two descriptive sketches of Iseult of Brittany we find Arnold indulging himself to the full in the very kinds of word-painting to which he had objected in the writings of Keats:

> What Lady is this, whose silk attire
> Gleams so rich in the light of the fire?

In the lines following and in later passages, he dwells over the details of her widowed evenings, the "silver lamp" which she places in her window, the "rosary beads of ebony tipp'd with gold" with which she

---

33. The passage offers many striking parallels with Hérédia's sonnet *Vitrail*, a remarkable piece which packs the whole story of *The Church of Brou* into fourteen lines.
34. Mrs. Humphry Ward, *A Writer's Recollections*, London, 1919, pp. 40–1.
35. George Saintsbury, *Matthew Arnold*, London, 1902, p. 25.

prays at her prie-dieu.[36] The precision with which Iseult the Fair is presented, together with the careful rendering of the settings in which she appears, give to her figure a striking pictorial quality which rivals that of Bertha in *The Eve of St. Mark.* When Arnold was seeking pictorial effects he knew as well as Rossetti where to go for inspiration and example.

Best of all in this connection, however, is the unforgettable description of the huntsman of the tapestry who gazes down on the bodies of the dead lovers. A few lines from *The Eve of St. Agnes* (or their echo in Tennyson's *Palace of Art*) seem to have served to stimulate Arnold's extended picture. Keats had written (italics mine):

> The *arras,* rich with *horseman,* hawk, and hound,
> *Flutter'd* in the besieging wind's uproar;
> And *the long carpets rose* along the *gusty floor.*

Arnold speaks of the December air in which

> *Flaps* the ghostlike tapestry.
> And on the *arras* wrought you see
> A stately *Huntsman,* clad in green. . . .
> And those *blown rushes* on the *floor.*[37]

Keats's anachronistic "carpets" have been changed to "rushes," but the general idea remains the same. The passage is a fine sample of the way in which the concentrated images of Keats could serve the purposes of a poet in quest for "natural magic."

Furthermore, as in *The Church of Brou,* Arnold draws not only from *The Eve of St. Agnes* but from the *Ode on a Grecian Urn* as well. As we have seen, he was very fond of the latter poem and its central idea of permanence in the midst of the mutability of man had a certain fascination for him. Arnold endows his huntsman on the tapestry with the same kind of reality which Keats gave to the figures on the urn, but, after establishing his contrast, he adds to his ending a dramatic twist of a different variety. One cannot refrain from quoting:

> Cheer, cheer thy dogs into the brake,
> O Hunter! and without a fear
> Thy golden-tassell'd bugle blow,
> And through the glades thy pastime take!
> For thou wilt rouse no sleepers here.
> For these thou seest are unmov'd;
> Cold, cold as those who liv'd and lov'd
> A thousand years ago.

36. *Tristram and Iseult,* III, 78–93.
37. Arnold may possibly have drawn from Tennyson's *Palace of Art* as well, but the emphasis on the wind-blown quality of the tapestry suggests that the principal source was Keats. Tinker and Lowry regard Byron's *Siege of Corinth* as the model. Cf. *The Poetry of Matthew Arnold: A Commentary,* Oxford, 1940, pp. 114–5.

It need only be said that this passage deserves to rank beside that which probably suggested the theme which it expresses. The last two lines, especially, have that same quality of haunting overtone which Keats achieved in another poem:

> And they are gone: ay, ages long ago
> These lovers fled away into the storm.

The style of such passages as we have been examining represents what I have called Arnold's "holidays" from his more usual restrained, ascetic form of expression. When one thinks of his work as a whole, the Keatsian element seems rather subordinate. But to speak qualitatively rather than quantitatively, it is of the utmost importance. For it is in a series of some of Arnold's finest poems that the stamp of Keats is most marked, whereas in the great bulk of his minor work it is conspicuous by its absence. What is more, the influence of Keats was, in Arnold's case, almost entirely beneficial. In theme, it contributed much to his most attractive (if most romantic) poems. In style it gave to his poetry a warmth of life and a glow of colour which, at best, constitute some of its most exquisite qualities. One can only wish that Arnold had relaxed his objections to the Keatsian more often than he did, and that he had been more content to allow free play to what Mrs. Ward termed the "Celtic element" in his own nature. When the style of *The Ode to a Nightingale* or *The Eve of St. Agnes* finds its way into the poetry of Matthew Arnold his verse becomes, as F. L. Lucas nicely says, "as lovely as sincere."[38]

It has been the contention of these chapters that the author of *Essays in Criticism* was considerably dissatisfied with Keats and with his influence on Victorian poetry, that he attempted to qualify the popularity of Keats's achievement (in spite of his own admiration of it on certain levels), and that he sought to stem the tide of his influence by setting up standards of excellence, such as those stated in the 1853 Preface, contrary to the main practice of Keats and his Victorian successors. By ranking Keats below Byron and Wordsworth he was exemplifying his own conviction that such poetry as *Lamia* represented a "minor current." Of Keats's importance he must have been aware, but whole-hearted recognition he was not prepared to offer.

In *The Function of Criticism at the Present Time* Arnold has high praise for Edmund Burke because, in his last years, Burke had questioned the validity of his own stand on the French Revolution and hence returned "upon himself."[39] One wonders whether, in his approach to Keats, Arnold ever returned upon himself. The praise which he was willing to grant to Keats on certain levels, the defence of his

38. F. L. Lucas, *Eight Victorian Poets*, p. 51.
39. *Essays in Criticism, First Series*, p. 15.

poetry in terms of "natural magic" are indeed indicative of a certain return upon himself. But by far the best example of Arnold's quali- fication of his basic stand is to be found not in his criticism but in the volumes of poetry he published from 1849 to 1867. However much he might badger and quarrel with the Keatsian current in Victorian poetry, he himself failed to remain outside it. His words on the influ- ence of Tennyson apply even more to Tennyson's influential pred- ecessor, John Keats. "One has him so in one's head, one cannot help imitating him sometimes."

If illustrations are to be sought of the importance of Keats's impact on Victorian literature we find perhaps its most convincing mani- festation in the poetry of Arnold. Hood, Tennyson, Morris, Rossetti and others who came under the spell of Keats were all professed admirers of his work, and were content, on the whole, to carry on and exploit the type of poetry which he had developed. Matthew Arnold, by contrast, was a conscientious objector. To find even his verse drawn into the stream is perhaps the most interesting example of the way in which the Victorian poets gave a literal confirmation to Keats's prophecy: "I think that I shall be among the English poets after my death."

PART THREE

ROSSETTI

I loved thee ere I loved a woman, Love.

Rossetti, To Art.

I've fought the good fight. And now it's all over, there's an indescribable peace: I believe in Michael Angelo, Velasquez, and Rembrandt; in the might of design, the mystery of colour, the redemption of all things by Beauty everlasting, and the message of Art that has made these hands blessed. Amen. Amen.

Shaw, The Doctor's Dilemma, Act IV
(creed of the dying painter).

VII

Conflicts in Victorian Taste After 1850

MOST of the information which we possess about the life and tastes of Dante Gabriel Rossetti has been left to us by his brother William Michael Rossetti. In most matters, William Rossetti was a relatively accurate reporter, but there were two things about his brother of which he was somewhat ashamed and which he attempted to minimize as much as possible. The first was Gabriel's chequered relations with women: the second was his passion for the poetry of John Keats. William was never truly fond of Keats,[1] and it horrified him to find that his brother considered him "the greatest modern poet." He was especially horrified when Gabriel asserted the superiority of Keats's work to Shelley's, for William regarded the poetry of Shelley as the supreme of excellence. On Christmas day in 1870, in the studio on Cheyne Walk the two brothers had "a long battle" over whether Keats or Shelley was the greatest modern poet. For a very brief period, Gabriel was persuaded that Shelley was finer than Keats, and William recorded the fact in his diary with considerable triumph.[2] The triumph was, however, very short-lived. Gabriel returned to his early preference in short order, and it is with obvious reluctance that William has to record: "Perhaps, in his last few years, the poetry of Keats was more constantly present to my brother's thoughts than that of anyone else, hardly excepting even Dante."[3]

The fact that by the year 1870 two writers could argue seriously about whether Keats or Shelley was the most important poet since Shakespeare gives some indication of the change in their status since the 1820's and 1830's. By 1870, with a certain group, the reputation of Keats was such that he would rate as the finest poet of the nineteenth century. This group comprised the so-called Aesthetic School. Furthermore, he was being appreciated (with some reservations) by an increasingly large reading public, a public whose standards, although by no means so advanced as those to whom the pursuit of

1. It may be noted that William had to defend his biography of Keats from the charge that he had been unfair to the poet. See W. M. Rossetti, *Some Reminiscences*, New York, 1906, II, 485.

2. See *Rossetti Papers*, New York, 1903, p. 499.

3. *The Works of Dante Gabriel Rossetti*, London, 1911, p. 671. (In subsequent footnotes, this is referred to simply as *Works*.) In his Preface William also states: ". . . Keats whom my brother for the most part, though not without some compunctious visitings now and then, truly preferred to Shelley" (*ibid.*, p. xv).

Beauty had become a cult, had, nevertheless, been considerably modified by a desire for aesthetic pleasure.

In the opening chapter, I suggested that Keats's rise to fame in the latter half of the nineteenth century was occasioned primarily by four factors: a shift in public taste, his great influence on the leading poets of the day, the resurrection of his personality by such biographers as Houghton, and the appreciation of his poetry by leading critics and essayists. In connection with the shift of taste, I suggested that during the interregnum period after the decline of Byron's popularity, new "Victorian" literary standards were hardening, which, in turn, were modified again after 1850. It is this shift after 1850, a shift which paved the way for the revival of Keats, that I wish to examine in the present chapter and to suggest thereby that although the extremism of Rossetti and his group cut them off from their age, the point from which they start is a change of taste shared by the age as a whole. The paradoxical thing about Rossetti is that although he remained aloof from many things Victorian, he represents a recognizable trend, a trend in which he played a considerable role. Arnold was much more of an individual figure. Rossetti brings us to a general consideration of the literary standards of the different periods of the Victorian era.

In spite of the growing reputation of Tennyson in the 1840's, Keats was still an obscure figure. His name was more often mis-spelt in the reviews than not (if and when mentioned).[4] In fact, when Rossetti discovered him in 1845, he supposed that he had found an unknown writer. Holman Hunt had a similar notion. "No other copies of his work than those published in his lifetime had yet appeared," Hunt mistakenly writes referring to his own discovery of Keats. "These were in mill-board covers, and I had found mine in book-bins labelled 'this lot 4d.' "[5] Rossetti went so far as to believe that it was he who had discovered Keats and was responsible for his later fame.[6]

On the surface, Rossetti's claim was absurd. We have seen how Tennyson and his associates were enjoying Keats to the full at a time when Rossetti was still an infant.[7] As for his part in the development of Keats's reputation, it was only one of several factors which, after 1848, combine to make Keats the most influential poet of the latter

4. Coventry Patmore's poems were reviewed in 1844 in these words: "This is the life into which the slime of the Keateses [sic] and Shelleys of former times has fecundated! . . . Nothing is so tenacious of life as the spawn of frogs. . ." (*Blackwood's Magazine*, LVI [1844], 342).

5. W. Holman Hunt, *Pre-Raphaelitism and the Pre-Raphaelite Brotherhood*, London, 1905, I, 106. (Hunt discovered Keats about 1845 but apparently was unaware that in 1841 two editions of the poet had been issued.)

6. See W. M. Rossetti, *Dante Gabriel Rossetti . . . Letters with a Memoir*, London, 1895, I, 100. (In subsequent notes, this work will be referred to simply as *Memoir*.)

7. Reference might also be made to Rossetti's friend W. B. Scott who, as early as 1832 composed an ode: *To the Memory of John Keats*, a praiseworthy undergraduate piece. It is reprinted in his *Poems* (London, 1875).

half of the century. Yet, in another respect, Rossetti's claim had some justification. He could truly say that he was the first Victorian poet who was entirely satisfied with what he understood Keats to represent. It will be apparent that in some respects he narrowed the Keatsian conception of poetry and also that he was careful to conceal his borrowings. But the essential thing is that with the *spirit* of Keats he had no quarrel whatever. He was not looking in Keats for the same values which Matthew Arnold sought (and rarely found), nor was he disturbed, as Tennyson was finally disturbed, by the absence of these values. He never complained, as Tennyson did, that Keats was not a "great sage poet." He was satisfied with what he did find there.

In 1850, the sort of taste which would allow this unqualified satisfaction with the spirit of Keats was exceptional; by 1870 it was distinctly perceptible in Victorian criticism, and by 1890 predominant. With Rossetti, the appreciation of Keats entered a new phase. It was in the moist soil of the Aesthetic Movement (a movement of which Rossetti was certainly the father) that the fame of Keats would best grow.

In the light of historical perspective, the Aesthetic Movement might be regarded as a backwater. As Evans says:

Sometimes one feels that Victorian romanticism is a ghostly masquerade; only when all is quiet in the night do these poets come out and, donning their antique costumes, revive their dreams of long-faded beauty. When day has come they are gone, and the waking world knows them not.[8]

For all this, the movement is nevertheless symptomatic of the direction of the tides of taste in the latter half of the century. In connection with Tennyson, several aspects of aestheticism have already been examined and we have seen in what respects he was affected by its tenets and in what respects he modified them. As T. Earle Welby nicely observes, he gave them a direction of his own:

Tennyson offered to new developments a passive resistance the harder to overcome because he frequently and discreetly adjusted himself to change. He did not present an antithesis to the new poetry: he seemed rather to show how far a consummate artist in poetry who was also an Englishman and a man with a just sense of moral obligations should go along the new paths.[9]

Yet the extent to which he did go along the new paths and, in fact, anticipated them, is one of the most important indications of the

8. B. Ifor Evans, *English Poetry in the Later Nineteenth Century*, London, 1933, p. xxiii. See also the section on Rossetti in *The Victorians and After: 1830–1914*, by Edith C. Batho and Bonamy Dobrée (London, 1935).
9. T. Earle Welby, *The Victorian Romantics*, London, 1929, p. 7.

trend. Like Ruskin, he was a half-way figure in the revolution of taste which culminated in Oscar Wilde.

"To disagree with three-fourths of all England on all points of view" said Wilde when defending the Pre-Raphaelites, "is one of the first elements of sanity."[10] As is the case with most Victorian writings, Rossetti's seem to have been written in opposition to some of the prevailing demands of his age. In 1870, Alfred Austin complained vigorously of this diversity in Victorian literature. "Great poets" he writes, "are the unambiguous representative voice of decisive eras that have arrived at some definite conclusion." Of his own age he continues:

It cannot make up its mind on any one single subject, except that to have plenty of money is a good thing. . . . We have no concord, intellectual, moral, social, or vital; and accordingly, we waste our puny individual or sectional efforts in letting off a series of small fireworks.[11]

Like the tractarian movement, aestheticism was one of these series of fireworks. It constituted a sort of substitute religion in place of the prevailing Victorian faith in progress and its concomitants.[12]

The decline and fall of the phenomenon known as "Victorianism" has sometimes been traced in terms of three periods. The first (1832–50) represents the almost unchallenged rise to power of the middle-class way of life; the second (1850–70) represents its fullest flowering and also the development of forces opposing it; the third (1870–1900) represents its decline. The history of aestheticism and of Keats's reputation and influence can be conveniently followed with reference to these three periods.

The Reform Bill of 1832 is often said to mark a revolution in English history of greater significance than that of 1688. The political influence of the English aristocracy lingered well on into the century, but its days were numbered, and with it went Byron, the aristocrat poet. The new classes, as Matthew Arnold himself admitted, were singularly well equipped for the immediate task in hand: the transformation of England into the manufacturing and trading centre of the world. They were earnest, self-confident, and energetic, and they

10. Address in America on the Pre-Raphaelites. Reprinted by Walter Hamilton, *The Aesthetic Movement*, London, 1882, p. 115.

11. Alfred Austin, *The Poetry of the Period*, London, 1870, pp. 281–8.

12. A character in George Gissing's novel, *The Unclassed* (1883), is a study of the way in which a mind evolving from orthodox "Victorianism" may find a sort of religion in beauty. Gissing describes how Maud reads Rossetti's poems and finds there a new faith. "Their perfect beauty entranced her, and the rapturous purity of ideal passion, the mystic delicacies of emotion, which made every verse gleam like a star, held her . . . high above that gloomy cloudland of her being. . . . That Beauty is the solace of life, and Love the end of being,—this faith she would cling to in spite of all" (New York edition of 1896, p. 217). For a history of the concept of progress, J. B. Bury's *The Idea of Progress* is very useful.

brought with them an ethic which, although apparently designed for the greater glory of God, also served very conveniently for the greater glory of Manchester manufacturing. They imposed their code on the entire nation. "The aristocracy" said Bagehot in 1867, "live in fear of the middle classes—of the grocer and the merchant. They dare not frame a society of enjoyment as the French aristocracy once formed it."[13]

As an historian points out, these new classes, the despised Philistines, were also the book-buyers.[14] One would gather from statistical tables showing the immense numbers of working-hours which the early Victorians laboured, that although they might buy books they would never have time to read them. Victorian taste was seriously affected by the prevailing gospel of work, a peculiar blend of Puritan doctrine and business ideals which is very neatly symbolized by the motto of the Gideons: "Diligent in business; fervent in spirit; serving the Lord." The concept which gave England her pre-eminent position in nineteenth-century commerce and industry was, in its original form, sanctified with the halo of Puritan faith. In the words of Louis Cazamian: "The substance of grace is to discover one's daily task; upon the renunciation of self in effort man is to build day after day toward the painful victory of salvation."[15]

As Halévy, and Weber before him, have shown, even when the theological basis disappears, the concept does not change.[16] The Utilitarians talked a great deal about pleasure, but it is still very hard to imagine John Stuart Mill enjoying himself. "It has been jokingly said of this class" said Arnold, "that all which the best of it cared for was summed up in this alliterative phrase—*Business and Bethels:* and that all which the rest of it cared for was the *Business* without the Bethels."[17]

To the mid-Victorians (at least to those who did not live in the slums) the glowing fruits of the gospel of work would be widely apparent in the increasing prosperity and industrial expansion of the country.[18] England had also been extremely fortunate. With the exception of a mild "Cabinet War" in the Crimea,[19] she was at peace for

13. Quoted by O. F. Christie, *The Transition from Aristocracy: 1832–1867*, London, 1927, p. 77.

14. *Ibid.*, p. 80.

15. Louis Cazamian, *Carlyle*, New York, 1932, p. 6.

16. Max Weber, *Gesammelte aufsätze zur religionssoziologie*, Tübingen, 1922, vol. 1; Elie Halévy, *A History of the English People*, London, 1938, vol. 111.

17. *A French Eton*, in *The Works of Matthew Arnold*, XII, 73.

18. The railroad became a symbol. As Christie says (*op. cit.*, p. 204): "The railroad was a more outstanding phenomenon than the Renaissance, the Reformation, the Revolution, or the Reform Bill."

19. Robert C. Binkley, *Realism and Nationalism: 1852–1871*, New York, 1935, p. 176. He points out, for example, that Anglo-Russian trade continued almost without interruption during the war.

generations. The revolutions which shook Europe in 1848 had only slight repercussions across the channel. Macaulay's smug faith in progress is understandable. The public which bought (and also read) Macaulay had definite conceptions about literature which had their basis in this middle-class way of life. Literature was to be related to the prevailing faith in work and progress, respectability and success, the divine order. They looked first of all for edification, and Macaulay certainly edified them. In poetry, as Amy Cruze shows in her study *The Victorians and Their Books*, Macaulay's *Lays of Ancient Rome* were almost as popular as the infallible Martin Tupper's *Proverbial Philosophy*.[20]

> Not here, O Apollo!
> Are haunts meet for thee.

Another demand of the mid-Victorian book-buyer was that literature must fulfil all the requirements of Mrs. Grundy. Mrs. Grundyism is the feature of Victorian taste on which the most comment has since been lavished by twentieth-century critics. It springs in part from the Puritan and Utilitarian ethic, but more, in this case, from the Victorian conception of the home. Literature was often a family rather than an individual matter.[21] The preliminary hurdle for books was whether or not they were suitable for the parlour table. Just as the standard for the modern motion-picture often appears to be that it will not offend the intelligence of the dullest member of the audience, so the standard of the parlour table appears to have been that nothing must offend the most blushable cheek of the most modest maiden of the land. As Thackeray said of *Punch:* "We will laugh in the company of our wives and children; we will tolerate no indecorum; we like that our matrons and girls should be pure."[22]

Similar restrictions applied also to other arts. The nude, of course, was not favoured. Hawthorne's provincial embarrassment when he visited Europe and witnessed nude statues in the art galleries would have been shared by many middle-class Englishmen.[23] Only twice did Rossetti essay a nude painting, for his patrons objected in strong

---

20. Amy Cruze, *The Victorians and Their Books*, London, 1935, p. 178.

21. A good analysis of the tastes of the Victorian home is to be found in H. V. Routh's *Money, Morals and Manners as Revealed in Modern Literature* (London, 1935).

22. Quoted by O. F. Christie, *op. cit.*, p. 78.

23. Nathaniel Hawthorne, *French and Italian Notebooks*, Cambridge, 1883, p. 171. He speaks of a statue of Eve "with a frightful volume of calves and thighs. I do not altogether see the necessity of ever sculpturing another nakedness." At one point (p. 199) he suggests that sculpture should be abandoned if the figures cannot be decently draped. "Did anybody ever see Washington nude?" he asks. "It is inconceivable" (p. 274). See also *The Marble Faun*, chap. XIV.

terms to such indecencies.[24] One of his patrons would not tolerate so much as an unclothed arm in a picture.

A survey of Victorian periodicals will reinforce the impression of these demands on art. Such a survey has been made by Miss Louise Rosenblatt in her excellent study: *L'idée de l'art pour l'art dans la littérature anglaise pendant la période victorienne*. Decorous rhymed "philosophy" rather than poetry is a recurring injunction in the Victorian periodical. As her survey indicates: "plutôt des leçons morales mises en mauvais vers que de la vraie poésie sans leçon morale apparente."[25]

One wonders, in such a world, where Keats could possibly come in. Was his work suitable for the parlour table? It could hardly be said to fulfil the first requirement of edification. Keats did not expatiate on the virtues of hard work, or offer consoling balm for apparent failure. He did not even discuss the victory of faith over doubt as Tennyson did, nor did he write anything comparable to Shakespeare's *Hamlet*, in which the many profound sayings of Polonius constitute a "store of wisdom." As for the second requirement, *The Eve of St. Agnes* and *Lamia* might certainly be suspected of a certain licentiousness (although that could be left to one's own imagination).

The Victorian parlour would nevertheless play a considerable part in the revival of Keats. The reason for his gaining access to it is that there are features of his work which catered to some aspects of middle-class taste on which Miss Rosenblatt does not touch. Indeed, the twentieth-century literary historian is usually so obsessed with Mrs. Grundyism that he misses everything else in the Victorian scene.

Mr. G. M. Young is one writer who does not miss these other aspects. "On one of its sides" he says, "Victorian history is the story of the English mind employing the energy imparted by Evangelical conviction to rid itself of the restraints which Evangelicalism had laid on the senses and the intellect; on amusement, enjoyment, art; on curiosity, on criticism, on science."[26] Young suggests that the change

---

24. The word "painting" is perhaps not accurate. He did a full-length nude in crayon of Fanny Cornforth called *Spirit of the Rainbow* (see H. C. Marillier, *Dante Gabriel Rossetti*, London, 1899, p. 191), and a three-quarter crayon of a model which is called *Ligeia Siren*. The latter, according to Marillier (p. 172) was afterwards draped. Some other sketches were also done, as for example, that of Lizzie Siddal which Rossetti later used for his *Beata Beatrix* (p. 127). Concerning Rossetti's patrons, see Marillier, p. 135.

25. Louise Rosenblatt, *L'idée de l'art pour l'art dans la littérature anglaise pendant la période victorienne*, Paris, 1931, p. 34. Dickens, she shows, provided amusement. "L'opinion publique victorienne n'offre à la littérature que l'alternative entre l'édification et l'amusement. . . . Il est très utile pour les critiques, quand ils n'aiment pas l'enseignement que leur offre un écrivain, de pouvoir réclamer uniquement une littérature 'amusante'" (*ibid.*, p. 39).

26. G. M. Young, *Early Victorian England: 1830–1865*, London, 1934, II, 417.

can be seen as early as the 1850's. At the beginning of that decade, the Pre-Raphaelite magazine *The Germ* was published, which, although extremely limited in its circulation, was nevertheless something of a tract for the times.[27] The earlier Victorian had been so intensely concerned with the immediate task of salvation, both economic and spiritual, that he had little time or interest in anything not related to such matters. An awareness of other values gradually developed among his successors and the "will to enjoy" reasserted itself. One can find it, for example, in their growing love of ornament and decoration (the manifestations of which, naturally, were not always very happy). In literature, Tennyson would still be cherished first of all for his concern with immediate problems, but an appreciation of his richness of style also contributed to his popularity. It would be a mistake to assume that because of the continued success of Martin Tupper's *Proverbial Philosophy* the mid-Victorians had no interest in anything whatever other than the "lesson." As Wingfield-Stratford points out in *Those Earnest Victorians*, they responded with enthusiasm to any form of workmanship and minutely-laboured details, as for example, Millais' picture of Ophelia. Provided that requirements of edification were first met, a taste for a certain kind of beauty was developing, and Tennyson catered to that taste.[28]

An excellent example of this kind of compromise is provided by Holman Hunt's approach to Keats. Of strong Evangelical tendencies, Hunt recommended *The Eve of St. Agnes* because it illustrated, he

27. An amusing account of how Keats was finding readers in the 1850's is given by Oscar Browning. In 1851, his tutor at Eton introduced Keats to his classes. "We had to compose a copy of Latin verses every week, and one week he set us the speech of Clymene in 'Hyperion' for a subject. I learnt it by heart and could repeat it now [1918]; another time he gave us the 'Pot of Basil,' which I learnt in a similar manner. He often talked to us about Keats & offered a prize to any of his pupils who would learn 'Hyperion' by heart. . . . The consequence was that when I went to Cambridge in 1856 I was *soaked* with Keats, & was always preaching him to the Apostles & other friends, & after I went as a master to Eton in 1860, to my boys. I don't think that he was much known at Cambridge in 1856, nor did Tennyson ever speak to me about him. . . . Do you know the story of 'Keats, what's a Keat?' One day at the Trinity High Table that was said. 'O. B. is going to lecture this evening on Keats.['] A science Fellow said 'Keats? what's a Keat?['] on which there was a great guffaw—Then Langley said, 'It is all very well for you fellows to laugh, but I don't believe that any one of you could quote a single line of Keats.' Of course there is one line which everyone knows, even science men. . . ." Letter to Colvin quoted by E. V. Lucas, *The Colvins and Their Friends*, pp. 326–7.

28. The importance of Tennyson to the Victorians of the 1850's is described by Canon Dixon, who was at Oxford at the time. "It is difficult to the present generation to understand the Tennysonian enthusiasm which then prevailed both in Oxford and the world. All reading men were Tennysonians: all sets of reading men talked poetry. Poetry was the thing: and it was felt with justice that this was due to Tennyson. Tennyson had invented a new poetry . . . his use of words was new, and every piece that he wrote was a conquest of a new region" (J. W. Mackail, *The Life of William Morris*, London, 1899, 1, 44). For many, the sheer intoxication of language was enough in itself. As Dixon says, "We . . . were most absorbed by the language" (*ibid.*, p. 46).

said, "the sacredness of honest responsible love and the weakness of proud intemperance."[29] Yet in the same breath, he revelled in the fact that "it is brimful of beauties that will soon enchant you. . . ."[30]

The periodicals reflect this transition. Reviewers continue to urge the need for what the modern American Protestant calls "uplift," but side by side with this is a call for Keatsian word-painting, the very thing which Matthew Arnold would condemn. For example, when speaking of Arnold I referred to a reviewer of 1867 who rates Tennyson above Arnold not for his superior lesson, but for his "variation of softly brilliant, exquisitely appropriate imagery, picture after picture of breathing, ruddy-tinted life, each picture . . . moving on as in rhythmic starry dance to the music of the whole. . . ."[31]

The transition is understandable. "In the general movement of the English mind" states Young,

few episodes are so instructive as the revolution which in the fifties reduced the Economic Evangelicalism of 1830 from dominant philosophy to middle-class point of view and so prepared the way for the teaching of Pater and Arnold, the practice of Morris and Toynbee, the recognition, after years of derision or neglect, of Ruskin and Browning. "Nothing," Bagehot once wrote, "is more unpleasant than a virtuous person with a mean mind."[32]

In the seventeenth century, the reaction against asceticism which characterized the court and theatre of the Restoration was sudden and violent; in the nineteenth century a similar reaction was very gradual. The development was marked by a series of compromises. The reading public advanced to a certain stage (far enough to admit Keats) and there stopped. The artists and others advanced far beyond to a world of their own. Yet Rossetti could write with some degree of application to himself of his artist in *St. Agnes of Intercession:* ". . . all work, to be truly worthy, should be wrought out of the age itself, as well as out of the soul of the producer, which must needs be a soul of the age."[33] To cite Osbert Burdett:

The artists of any period . . . are often foci of the sub-conscious desires or instincts of their time, and the hunger felt by the Pre-Raphaelites . . . for a departed beauty converted the pursuit of beauty into a religion. . . . A similar, if less conscious, instinct was dimly driving the populations of the new industrial towns. In them it took finally a religious form, and the Tractarian movement owed some of its popularity to its appeal to men's sense of beauty. . . .[34]

29. Holman Hunt, *op. cit.*, p. 85.
30. *Ibid.*, p. 80.
31. See p. 81.
32. G. M. Young, *op. cit.*, p. 488.
33. *Works*, p. 558.
34. Osbert Burdett, *The Beardsley Period*, London, 1925, pp. 45–6.

These subconscious desires provided a sort of back-door entrance
through which the poetry of Keats could enter into the Victorian library.

John Ruskin is the pivotal figure in the transition from one set of
values to another. He was one of the young men who, reflecting a current of the age, attempted to throw off some of the shackles of spiritual and economic asceticism. His aesthetic principles represent an
attempt to unite the mid-Victorian demand for edification with its
nascent demand for beauty. The really significant thing is that Ruskin
had aesthetic principles. His master Carlyle, except for occasional
flashes of appreciation in the early *Miscellanies,* showed little interest
in the beautiful.[35] He joined with Ruskin in attacking utilitarianism
("the philosophy in office"[36] as Chesterton calls it), but his charge
against it was not its lack of awareness to beauty but its absence of
any kind of spirituality and worship. It was characteristic of Carlyle
to despise Keats. He called Allingham a "soft-horn" for admiring the
poet: "Keats wanted a world of treacle!" he said.[37] It was equally
characteristic of Ruskin to love Keats. He bestowed upon Keats's
writings his highest possible praise by comparing the poet's sense of
beauty to Turner's. "Keats . . . put nearly all that may be said of the
pine into one verse. . . . I have come to that pass of admiration for
him now [1859], that I dare not read him, so discontented he makes
me with my own work."[38]

Ruskin's artistic standards may be said to be social and ethical
rather than aesthetic, as a rule. Great art, in his familiar formula of
The Stones of Venice, is produced by a great society, but a great society is not produced by great art, although art may aid it. "You cannot
paint or sing yourselves into being good men;" he told his Oxford
audience, "you must be good men before you can either paint or sing,
and then the colour and sound will complete in you all that is best."[39]
The main line of Ruskin's life-work was directed to the development
of good men. There is a well-known story that, at the age of four, he
chirped a speech to his doting parents: "People, be dood. If you are

35. It is highly ironical that one of the earliest uses of the phrase *art for art's sake*
occurs in connection with Carlyle. Thackeray read the *Miscellanies* and then wrote
to his mother (1839): "Please God we shall begin ere long, to love *art for art's sake.*
It is Carlyle more than any other who has worked to give it its independence." (See
Rose Egan, "The Genesis of the Theory of 'Art For Art's Sake,'" *Smith College
Studies,* II, no. 4 [1921], p. 15.) The phrase here is not used in its ordinary sense.
Carlyle loathed and detested "aestheticism."

36. G. K. Chesterton, *The Victorian Age in Literature,* New York, 1913, p. 38.

37. *Diary of William Allingham,* p. 205.

38. *Modern Painters* (Everyman edition), v, 81. Lady Burne-Jones also testifies to
Ruskin's enthusiasm. In 1862 she and her husband met him at a Swiss inn and he
spent the evening reading Keats to them (*Memorials of Edward Burne-Jones,* New
York, 1904, I, 243).

39. *The Works of John Ruskin,* London, 1905–12, xx, 74.

not dood, Dod will punish you. If you are dood, Dod will reward you. People, be dood." As many have since noted, this text served him for the rest of his life. To the ideal of the good he would, on several occasions, sacrifice the pleasures of beauty.[40]

Yet for him, a life without aesthetic appreciation was narrow, and, finally, immoral. He has a second text to his sermon: "People, love beauty." The delight which the strictly brought-up young man received when he visited Venice and became enthralled by its gorgeous architecture and painting was genuine, and he communicated it to his age. Especially during the period after 1858, after he had lost his faith in Biblical Christianity, did the importance of art seem to him basic. To relate art to goodness was his persistent endeavour, but sometimes it became for him a goal in itself. While in Venice, and under the sway of Titian and Veronese, he was astonished by the power of artists who, like Keats, seem to record only sensuous beauty:

I don't understand it; one would have thought purity gave strength, but it doesn't. . . . Has God made faces beautiful and limbs strong, and created these strange, fiery, fantastic energies, and created . . . gold, and pearls, and crystal, and the sun that makes them gorgeous . . . only that all these things may lead His creatures away from Him? And is this mighty Paul Veronese . . . a servant of the devil; and is the poor little wretch in a tidy black tie, to whom I have been listening this Sunday morning expounding Nothing with a twang—is he a servant of God? It is a great mystery.[41]

Ruskin would eventually desert Veronese for the more chaste genius of Giotto and veer away from the notion of the adequacy of beauty in itself. Yet his influence in insisting upon the vital importance of the aesthetic is beyond question. He applied it to the daily scene, to the drabness of Victorian life, and, by propagating an awareness of these matters, he represents and guides an important trend of the period. Some of the later aesthetes such as Wilde came to distrust his ethical bias, but he had actually paved the way for them, and for Keats too.[42]

I have dealt with Ruskin here because he represents so well the type of transitional figure in the Victorian scene. Emerging from a religious background in many respects similar to that of Carlyle, he goes far beyond the elder prophet in modifying the standards of that background, yet he never goes all the way. If Ruskin had been pressed to justify his love of Keats, he would in the last analysis have had to admit that, on grounds of "message," Keats was not an entirely adequate poet. The later artists such as Rossetti, and critics such as

40. See his attack on "aesthetics" in *Aratra Pentelici*, lecture I. An excellent account of the ethical conflict in Ruskin is given by Henry Ladd, *The Victorian Morality of Art*, New York, 1932, part III.

41. Quoted by E. T. Cook, *The Life of John Ruskin*, London, 1912, I, 520.

42. The strongest claims for Ruskin in this connection are made by R. de la Sizeranne (*Ruskin et la religion de la beauté*, Paris, 1897).

Pater, would not have made a distinction of this kind. Ruskin had struggled to reconcile the good with the beautiful: the aesthetes gave up the struggle. They also abandoned the struggle between faith and science to which Tennyson had devoted so much attention. In Rossetti and Wilde, in Swinburne and Morris (with qualifications), and among a large group of minor writers, controversies and struggles are ruled out of poetry and the enjoyment of beauty becomes the primary requisite. Generally speaking, the poets with whom we have been concerned previously, the poets who loom large between 1830 and 1870 such as Tennyson, Browning, and Arnold, are controversial to a considerable degree. In what I have called the "third period" of the Victorian age, controversy is minimized, and, in terms of new standards of value, Keats's reputation reaches its highest point in the nineteenth century. The absence of edification in his poetry ceases to be a qualifying clause in estimating his worth. As Wilde said to an American audience in 1882:

. . . it is in Keats that one discerns the artistic renaissance of England. Byron was a rebel, and Shelley a dreamer; but in the calmness and clearness of his vision, his self-control, his unerring sense of beauty, and his recognition of a separate realm for the imagination, Keats was the pure and serene artist, the forerunner of the Pre-Raphaelite school, and so of the great romantic movement of which I am to speak.[43]

To sum up then: the Aesthetic Movement carried to its extreme conclusion a tendency which was part of the general direction of taste after 1850. A desire among the reading public to enjoy art and literature as well as to be edified by it enabled Ruskin and Tennyson to introduce the Beautiful into the Victorian parlour. To be sure, in order to make the Beautiful respectable, they dressed her in discreet crinolines, but this was enough in itself to assure Keats of his place.

Among the later artists and critics, Keats's place would be higher, for by them Beauty would be transferred from the parlour to a sort of shrine, and herein Keats would become a major prophet, a "Priest of Beauty" as Wilde called him.[44] In all likelihood, the average Victorian reader would not go so far as the shrine, but the parlour was far enough. In the general dissolution of straightforward Evangelical tastes of the mid-Victorian period, Keats secured his position with the reading public. One might surmise that in view of the lingering conception of his character, he would have had a particular appeal for what the Victorians called the "fairer sex." As we saw in connection with Arnold and other essayists and biographers, the robust

43. Quoted by Walter Hamilton, *op. cit.*, p. 115. This address appears in a modified form in *The Works of Oscar Wilde*, Boston, 1909. I quote from Hamilton because the references there to Keats are more complete.

44. See chapter XII.

males who continued to deride Keats later in the century always fell back on the notion of his lack of the "manly." Among women readers, however, his early fondness for the effeminate and pretty would hardly constitute a bar to an appreciation of his work. *Endymion* seems to have been especially popular with them. According to one woman writer, it was the poem "on which the writer's fame mainly rests."[45] Illustrated editions of it give us an especially vivid notion of the way in which Keats was admired in the Victorian parlour.[46] Another index is a feminist publication entitled *The Victoria Magazine* in which the editor speaks, in an issue of 1870, of the way in which taste has become "effeminized" by the influence of women readers. A gem of Keatsiana is contained in this same issue, an article by a woman which has the promising title: *The Daintiest of Poets—Keats.* The article is almost as promising as the title. She speaks of the "dainty pre-raphaelitism" which Keats employs in his descriptions of the "sweet passion" of love, and while admitting that he is almost dangerously sensuous at times, she justifies it by referring to mythology. "It might seem difficult to deny" she writes, "that a morally enervating influence lurks in the poem [*Endymion*]. But if this were true we must place a ban on the classics, in place of regarding them as an arcana set apart for aesthetic culture." Having established the respectability of *Endymion* she proceeds to enumerate its delights:

'Endymion' will be ever cherished reading for youthful pilgrims on the flowery road of poesy. Wrapt passion, a flood of delicate entrancing images, a most winning versification, a legend redolent of sublimated feelings the most intimately associated with mankind, are powerful reasons this should be so.[47]

The sighs here are distinctly audible.

One can also understand from such appreciations as this why it was that in 1870 Rossetti's poems should go through so many editions. The shift in taste which was bringing about the popularity of Keats developed from the same current of which Rossetti was a part and which cut across the prevailing standards of orthodox "Victorianism." The "Fleshly School" controversy was an indication that Rossetti had gone too far, and that he and his followers had deliberately isolated themselves. In their fondness for beauty itself, however, they were not isolated. More than is generally recognized, the later Victorian reader welcomed both sides of the compromise which Tennyson and Ruskin effected between edification and a sort of decorative beauty.

After this brief bow to the public we can now return to the indi-

---

45. Anon., "The Daintiest of Poets—Keats," *Victoria Magazine,* xv (1870), 58.
46. For example, see the elaborate folio edition printed in London in 1873, with illustrations by F. Joubert from paintings by E. J. Poynter.
47. *Victoria Magazine,* xv (1870), 59.

vidual poets themselves. The remainder of this study will be devoted to the impact of Keats on those writers who, for the most part, accept his work with very few qualifications, and exploit the Keatsian tradition to the fullest possible extent.

VIII

Rossetti's Standards of Poetry and Prophecy

K EATS'S circle of friends had included a fair number of painters and lovers of art who had considerable influence on his
work. Severn and Haydon were painters; Hunt was an art
collector; Hazlitt (whom he admired) was a painter and art-critic.[1]
After his death, the debt to his painter friends was repaid by the influence which his poetry had on Victorian art. As I have indicated,
Holman Hunt was an ardent admirer of Keats, and in May of 1848, he
exhibited his picture of *The Eve of St. Agnes* in the Academy. When
Rossetti saw it and recognized a fellow-admirer of Keats, he sought
out the artist and their important (although short-lived) friendship
developed. "Our common enthusiasm for Keats" says Hunt, "brought
us into intimate relations."

Rossetti came up to me . . . loudly declaring that my picture . . . was the
best in the collection. Probably the fact that the subject was taken from
Keats made him the more unrestrained, for I think no one had ever before
painted any subject from this still little-known poet.[2]

A few months later this Keatsian friendship widened out into the
Pre-Raphaelite Brotherhood, a group in which an admiration for
Keats was almost a badge of membership. Keats seems to have been
a recurring subject for discussion in the meetings, and interest in him
was increased by the publication of Milnes's *Life and Letters of Keats*
in the same year.[3] It has been stated by Mlle. Villard that not only was
Keats responsible for bringing the artists together but the very name
"Pre-Raphaelite" was derived from him.[4] The statement is questionable. Evidence is provided by a letter of Rossetti's written on August
20, 1848, after he had been reading Milnes's biography: "He [Keats]
says in one place (to my great delight) that having just looked over
a folio of the first and second schools of Italian painting, he has come
to the conclusion that the early men surpassed even Raphael himself!"[5] The fact that Keats shared with his successors similar taste

1. See Clarence Dewitt Thorpe, *The Mind of John Keats*, New York, 1926, p. 133 n.,
and Clarke Olney, "Keats and Benjamin Robert Haydon," *PMLA*, XLIX (1934), 258–75.
2. Holman Hunt, *Pre-Raphaelitism and the Pre-Raphaelite Brotherhood*, I, 105–06.
3. See *ibid.*, p. 114, and Frances Winwar, *Poor Splendid Wings*, Boston, 1933, pp.
5–6.
4. Léonie Villard, *The Influence of Keats on Tennyson and Rossetti*, p. 61.
5. *Memoir*, II, 39–40. For the passage which pleased Rossetti, see *The Letters of
Keats*, pp. 259–60.

even in painting is one of the most startling examples of the way in which his work anticipated later developments. Yet he cannot be held responsible for the famous P. R. B. title. Rossetti's "great delight" sprang from the fact that Hunt had already been talking to him about the desirability of going back to the primitives before Raphael. Hunt's surly and self-righteous querulousness when speaking of his own part in the movement makes him a questionable authority, but there is little doubt that he had talked Pre-Raphaelitism to Millais and Rossetti some time before the latter found the statement in Keats.

In any case, Keats's continued influence on the group was striking. A series of designs from *Isabella* was planned, one of which was developed by Millais into his well-known painting, *Lorenzo and Isabella,* a work which Roger Fry considers one of the few "worthy efforts" of the Pre-Raphaelite school.[6] *La Belle Dame sans Merci* served as a subject for Rossetti on more than one occasion, and later painters continued to draw subjects from Keats and to pay tribute to the pictorial qualities of his poetry. In an Appendix to this chapter, there are listed a few of these, and no doubt more could be added.

Since 1848 it has been customary to speak of "Keats and the Pre-Raphaelites" as a sort of closed corporation. Actually the label "P.R.B." is very confusing. Perhaps, as William Rossetti said in one of his few witty moments, it meant nothing more than "Please Ring the Bell." As used by literary historians, Pre-Raphaelitism really means "Rossettiism," which is, as Hunt knew, a somewhat different phenomenon from that recommended in the original manifesto of *The Germ.* Hunt and Rossetti were united in an appreciation of the literal rendering of pictorial detail and fondness for mediaeval themes which they found in Keats, but beyond this, a split was inevitable. Rossetti went his own way and carried with him the "second generation" of Pre-Raphaelites such as Burne-Jones in painting and Morris in both painting and literature.

To bring others round to his point of view was Rossetti's life-long habit. It was said that by sheer bullying he could make anyone a painter. He always had the faculty of attracting young artists and writers and converting them to Rossettiism. This faculty was of considerable service in the matter of fostering the reputation of Keats. Rossetti's influence was not, of course, of such tremendous extent as that of Tennyson. If the laureate had chosen to publish *In Memoriam* in serial form, the final installment expressing the triumph of his faith might have aroused the same response in town and hamlet as the final triumph of Pamela: the church-bells would have been rung. Rossetti had no comparable audience, but within a certain more restricted circle, his word was virtually law, his approbation final. We have evi-

6. Roger Fry, *Reflections on British Paintings,* New York, 1934, p. 110.

By kind permission Macmillan and Co., Ltd.

THE EVE OF ST. AGNES BY HOLMAN HUNT

EXHIBITED 1848

dence of his having introduced Keats to many, and he must have made several "converts."[7] The Christmas argument of 1870 in which he had tried to force Keats on his brother William would have been repeated several times, and hence his belief that he was responsible for Keats's growing fame.

Together with Dante, Keats was his favourite poet although, as we shall see shortly, there were others whom he ranked almost as highly. He appears to have appreciated the character of Keats as well as his poetry. "He seems to have been a glorious fellow"[8] he remarked on one occasion, and there is a rather touching entry in his Notebooks where he says:

> Could Keats but have a day or two on earth
> Once every year![9]

In later years, Rossetti's feeling for Keats was fortified by his own sense of isolation. "The weltering London ways where children weep" had ignored Keats, and now London seemed unfriendly to his successor:

> A city of sweet speech scorned,—on whose chill stone
> Keats withered, Coleridge pined, and Chatterton,
> Breadless, with poison froze the God-fired breath.[10]

The extravagant praise which Rossetti lavished on Chatterton in later years springs in part, no doubt, from his own strange persecution complex. Keats's belated recognition could make him vitriolic, as the following recently published note will show:

Nowadays, when the Poems of John Keats are in every library, and the Quarterly Review at every butterman's and fishmonger's (by the way, it is surprising that these worthy people are not afraid of dirtying their goods by the contact) my reader is almost sure to remember that the young poet, lying worldsick on his deathbed, requested that his epitaph might be:
Here lies one whose name was writ in water.[11]

The note was to have been appended to his *Epitaph for Keats*, a few lines in the same strain which he never published. In 1880 he composed a sonnet in which the development of the poet's fame is referred to in a manner less biting:

7. See *Preraphaelite Diaries and Letters* (ed. W. M. Rossetti), London, 1900, p. 95.
8. *Memoir*, II, 39.
9. *Works*, p. 246.
10. *Tiber, Nile, and Thames,* written in January, 1881. Cf. W. M. Rossetti, *Dante Gabriel Rossetti as Designer and Writer*, London, 1889, p. 171.
11. *Dante Gabriel Rossetti: An Analytical List of Manuscripts in the Duke University Library* (ed. Paull Franklin Baum), Duke University Press, 1931, p. 11

Thou whom the daisies glory in growing o'er,—
   Their fragrance clings around thy name, not writ
   But rumour'd in water, while the fame of it
Along Time's flood goes echoing evermore.

In the history of Keats's reputation among the Victorians, these lines represent something of a landmark.

On Keats's poetry Rossetti has left a number of comments which may be considered in connection with the individual poems. His general estimate was that Keats represents "the one true heir to Shakespeare."[12] In an earlier chapter, some pains were taken to show what was signified when the average Victorian critic compared Keats to Shakespeare. Arnold, it was found, likened Keats to Shakespeare on grounds of expression, but ranked him nevertheless as a poet of the second order. When Rossetti referred to Keats as the heir to Shakespeare, did he mean anything different from what Arnold and others meant?

It will be found that Rossetti's method of reading Keats is not strikingly different from that of his contemporaries. He enjoyed what his fellow-Victorians enjoyed in Keats: the sheer richness of expression in some of the early pieces, the weird "Celtic twilight" in the atmosphere of *La Belle Dame sans Merci,* the mediaeval colouring of *The Eve of St. Agnes.* He knew the letters, and he knew and appreciated *Hyperion.* But for him, as for the others, Keats was not what T. S. Eliot calls (with reference to Middleton Murry) a "messianic" poet. He was not much concerned about the earlier poet's potentialities as a sort of philosopher. The difference between Rossetti and his contemporaries lies in the fact that he was content that this should be so. Such an evaluation, although also hinted at by Fitzgerald and by David Masson, is exceptional enough to be considered unique. He does not deplore Keats's apparent remoteness from nineteenth-century problems because he does not seek such things in poetry. And inasmuch as he valued Shakespeare for something different from what Arnold meant by "high seriousness," his yoking of Keats with Shakespeare was much more complete than Arnold's was intended to be. Furthermore, in his own poetry, Rossetti breaks away from Tennyson's and Arnold's practice of blending Keatsianisms with Victorian themes; he disengages this foreign element from the Keatsian strain and presents it without any admixture from the world of controversy.

Rossetti shared with many other young men of the Fifties the desire to become emancipated from various aspects of middle-class asceticism. Perhaps owing to his different religious background, he underwent no apparent struggle comparable to that of Ruskin. He seems almost to have been born emancipated. Evelyn Waugh describes him as "a man of the South, sensual, indolent, and richly versatile, exiled in the narrow, scrambling, specialized life of a Northern city . . . an artist born into an age devoid of artistic standards."[13] Of his own search for Beauty, Rossetti wrote:

> This is that Lady Beauty, in whose praise
> Thy voice and hand shake still,—long known to thee
> By flying hair and fluttering hem,—the beat
> Following her daily of thy heart and feet,
> How passionately and irretrievably,
> In what fond flight, how many ways and days!
> (*House of Life*, LXXVII)

Beerbohm has painted an amusing and revealing scene showing the poet's childhood. In a roomful of long-bearded fiery Italian exiles arguing excitedly about politics, Rossetti is to be seen lying on the floor writing, completely aloof from the issues under discussion. He remained aloof for the rest of his life. The "condition of England question" did not interest him in the least. On reading the opening article of Ruskin's *Unto This Last*, he wrote to Allingham: "Who *could* read it or anything about such bosh!"[14]

An indifference to politics is also characteristic of most of Rossetti's successors. The principles of 1789 would stir the attention of Swinburne for a period, and Morris would embody a later political faith, but among most of the later poets, political idealism is dead. W. B. Scott writes with horror of conversations which he had early in the Seventies with Gosse, O'Shaughnessy and John Payne:

Another jaunty tenet they all held was *art for art's sake;* what matters the sense, motive or morals of a poem, if it is beautiful? . . . One of them called the year of the Franco-German war (that war that changed the face of Europe . . .) "the year when Regnault died."[15]

In the Nineties, indifference hardened into a pose. As someone said of Beardsley: "Social questions bored him undisguisedly. Indeed by Social he would only have understood . . . an extravagantly dressed society of polished people . . . who despised the middle-class virtues as rather vulgar."[16]

This lack of interest in politics and political poetry was one of the many things which attracted Rossetti to Keats. One of the reasons he preferred Keats to Shelley was, according to William, his resentment

---

13. Evelyn Waugh, *Rossetti*, London, 1928, p. 13.
14. *Letters of Dante Gabriel Rossetti to William Allingham*, London, 1897, p. 228. See also *Memoir*, II, 355.
15. William Bell Scott, *Autobiographical Notes*, II, 198.
16. Haldane Macfall, *Aubrey Beardsley*, New York, 1927, pp. 54-5.

against "those elements in Shelley's poetry where the abstract tends to lose sight of the concrete, *or where revolutionary philanthropy, rather than the world of men and women, is the dominant note.*"[17] In the last book of *Endymion*, when the youth returns to the "world of men and women" after a series of Shelley-like flights, he cries out in words which seem a reply to Shelley's *Alastor*:

> O I have been
> Presumptuous against love, against the sky,
> Against all elements, against the tie
> Of mortals each to each. . . .
>   My sweetest Indian, here,
> Here will I kneel, for thou redeemed hast
> My life from too thin breathing: gone and past
> Are cloudy phantasms.
>   (*Endymion*, IV, 638 ff.)

It was natural for Rossetti to choose, among the earlier writers, the only one besides Lamb who seems to have escaped the political contagion of the age.[18] Interestingly enough, Rossetti's sum total of political poems is about the same as Keats's, although *Wellington's Funeral* gives him, perhaps, a slight edge. He wrote a few scattered sonnets, one of which (rather ironically) has subsequently become oft-quoted in the popular press: *On the Refusal of Aid Between Nations*. On social questions there is, of course, that curious *tour de force, Jenny*. But like his single excursion into social issues in painting (the picture, *Found*), it is the exception which proves the rule.

During a visit to Brussels, Rossetti wrote home characteristically: "I believe we saw all the town today, except a lot of scientific and industrial silliness. . . ."[19] Towards science Rossetti was not so much indifferent as actually hostile. Tennyson and Ruskin had both been extensively interested in science and attempted to come to terms with it, and Browning under the cloak of Karshish the Arab Physician, had dealt with the clash of science and faith in which his contemporaries were vastly interested.[20] Rossetti, as William said, was "superstitious in grain, and anti-scientific to the marrow,"[21] and in his poetry he broke completely with the world of Herbert Spencer, which to him was anathema. The kind of Keatsian romanticism which his poetry represents is a conscious revolt from the standards of science, one of the several revolts in the later nineteenth century.[22] In 1883, in his

17. *Works*, p. 671. (Italics mine.)
18. Cf. Crane Brinton, *The Political Ideas of the English Romantics*, London, 1926, p. 4.
19. *Memoir*, II, 80.
20. See William O. Raymond, "Browning and the Higher Criticism," *PMLA*, XLIV (1929), 590 ff.
21. *Works*, p. xi.
22. See Robert C. Binkley, *Realism and Nationalism: 1852–1871*, p. 56.

penetrating analysis of what he calls the "Religion of Beauty,"
F. W. H. Myers drew attention to this side of Rossetti:

We may observe in Rossetti the reaction of Art against Materialism, which
becomes more marked as the dominant tone of science grows more soulless
and severe. The instincts which make other men Catholics, Ritualists,
Hegelians have compelled him, too, to seek "the meaning of all things that
are" elsewhere than in the behaviour of ether and atoms, though he can
track his revelation to no source more explicit than the look in a woman's
eyes.[23]

The Victorian "philosophy in office" had its basis, as we have seen,
not only in Evangelical asceticism but in scientific utilitarianism.
Scientists and middle classes had been allies for a considerable period.[24] The alliance was seriously threatened by the mid-century
geologists' and biologists' attacks on the Biblical fundamentalism to
which the Victorian perilously clung, and it was even more seriously
threatened after 1870 when science seemed to be challenging the
very faith in progress which Macaulay and Spencer had preached.
The alliance was patched up, however, principally to the benefit of
the scientists. In literature, the direct expression of this viewpoint is
the phenomenon known as Naturalism, with its prophet Zola. Irving
Babbitt quotes a definition of naturalism as "romanticism going on
all fours,"[25] which is actually nonsense. Naturalism is utilitarianism,
shorn of its Biblical faith, going (if one likes) on all fours.

Rossetti's successors in the latter part of the century were not slow
to recognize an old enemy in new disguise. As a recent article shows,
while they appreciated the attack which Naturalism effected against
Victorian prudery, they were violently opposed to its materialistic
and anti-romantic basis.[26] In whatever guise scientific standards appeared, the Aesthetic School was united in opposing them. Even
Morris, who preached a sort of communism, is a persistent opponent
of the scientific.

In Rossetti's own revolt against science he had Keats as a model
and reference point. Keats was for the banishing of Newton:

> Philosophy will clip an Angel's wings,
> Conquer all mysteries by rule and line,

23. F. W. H. Myers, "Rossetti and the Religion of Beauty," *Cornhill Magazine*,
XLVII (1883), 223.

24. For an account of the early union of science and middle classes in the sphere of
education, see H. McLachlan, *English Education Under the Test Acts*, Manchester,
1931.

25. Irving Babbitt, *Rousseau and Romanticism*, Cambridge (U. S. A.), 1935, p. 104.
It is true, of course, that Zola himself in *Germinal* and other novels shows a remarkably
"romantic" imagination, but his own efforts and those of his "school" are basically
anti-romantic.

26. Clarence R. Decker, "The Aesthetic Revolt Against Naturalism in Victorian
Criticism," *PMLA*, LIII (1938), 844–56.

Empty the haunted air, and gnomed mine—
Unweave a rainbow, as it erewhile made
The tender-person'd Lamia melt into a shade.

Haydon relates how Keats at a banquet had proposed a toast damning
Newton, and when Rossetti was reading the painter's *Correspondence and Table Talk*, he wrote enthusiastically to his mother about
the incident:

There is also a splendid anecdote of Keats' proposing as a toast at a gathering—"Confusion to the memory of Newton!" and, on Wordsworth's wish-
ing to know *why* before he drank it, the reply was "Because he destroyed
the poetry of the rainbow by reducing it to a prism." That is magnificent.[27]

Here was further cause for preferring Keats to Shelley, a poet who
has been labelled "A Newton Among the Poets." Keats provided a
realm for poetry in which science and the discussion of the conflict
between science and faith do not exist.

The latter was the most significant aspect of Rossetti's appreciation
of Keats and his own writing of poetry. Not only was he indifferent to
politics and hostile to science, he was also not interested in anything
in the nature of exhortation and argument. "In all poetic literature"
William Rossetti observed, "anything of a didactic, hortatory, or ex-
pressly ethical quality was alien from my brother's liking."[28] The dividing line between what Oliver Elton calls "pure and applied literature" is distinctly drawn by Rossetti. In most Victorian poetry, the
two are blended, and its readers sought, as we have seen, for a sugar-
coated tonic-pill. When a reviewer remarked of the volume of 1870
that it was "a publication in certain aspects fitted to startle and per-
plex that British Philistine with whose features Mr. Matthew Arnold
has made us familiar,"[29] he meant that the Philistine would cavil not
only because Rossetti might be charged with having done those
things which he ought not to have done, but also for having left un-
done those things which he ought to have done. Emersonian "metre-
making argument" was not to Rossetti's liking.

Rossetti was not a formal critic and, unlike Gautier and other
French writers who were effecting a similar revolutionary conception of poetry during the same period, he issued no formal treatise

27. *Memoir*, II, 328. I have been unable to locate this anecdote in the *Correspondence
and Table Talk*, which was published in 1876. It is possible that he was thinking back
to Haydon's *Autobiography* of 1853 in which the story is told. If my interpretation is
correct, Rossetti is making a good story better by bringing Wordsworth's query into it,
for Haydon does not mention it in this connection.

28. *Works*, p. 671.

29. "The Poems of Dante Gabriel Rossetti," *Fraser's Magazine, New Series*, I (1870),
613.

setting forth his views.[30] The direction of his poetics is nevertheless quite clear. His position would be formally stated by the aesthetic group, by Pater for example in 1868, and most unconditionally by Wilde, as in an address of 1882:

In choosing his subject, the artist is the spectator of all time. Past and present are alike real to him. For him no form is obsolete, no subject out of date. But all things are not fit subjects for poetry. Into the sacred house of Beauty the true artist will admit nothing which is harsh or disturbing, *nothing about which men argue*. If he writes on these subjects, he does so, as Milton expresses it, with his left hand.[31]

Rossetti's fundamental vigour would have led him to avoid, in public address, the rather affected phrasing which Wilde employs,[32] but the ideas are his own.

Nothing about which men argue, such a conception was vital to the complete acceptance of Keats's poetry. To employ the labels of a recent reviewer, Keats was whole-heartedly accepted by Rossetti insofar as he wished a poet to be neither a "Cassandra" nor a "Comrade."[33] Rossetti cherished Keats for the very things he had not done. His most significant comment on the early poet was written in this vein. "I value more the privilege of seeing great things in loneliness than the fame of a prophet," wrote Keats. The sentence delighted Rossetti when he first read it in 1876,[34] and a few years later, on reading Caine's essay on Keats, he recalled it:

Keats did not die so much too early if there was any danger of his taking to the modern habit eventually of treating material as product, and shooting it all out as it comes. Of course, however, he wouldn't; he was always getting choicer and simpler; my favourite piece in his works is "La Belle Dame sans Merci"—I suppose about his last. . . . You quote some of Keats's sayings. *One of the most characteristic,* I think, is in a letter to Haydon. *"I value more the privilege of seeing great things in loneliness than the fame of a prophet,"* . . . Keats wrote to Shelley: "You, I am sure, will forgive me

30. Miss Louise Rosenblatt (*op. cit.,* pp. 101–02) finds a substitute for a formal treatise in the prose tale which Rossetti composed in 1849: *Hand and Soul.* See *Works,* p. 549.

31. Quoted by Walter Hamilton, *op. cit.,* p. 116. (Italics mine.)

32. The style of Rossetti's *Hand and Soul* anticipates Wilde, but Rossetti considered it a "prose poem," and the style of his scattered critical notices is markedly different. Caine speaks of Rossetti's reception of Wilde's poetry, his "quick recognition of the gifts that underlay a good deal of amusing affectation" (Hall Caine, *My Story,* New York, 1909, p. 159).

33. Andrews Wanning, "Neither Cassandra Nor Comrade," *Furioso,* I (1941), 53. It may be noted that the twentieth-century "Comrade" usually prefers Shelley to Keats. For example, see Stephen Spender's essay on Keats and Shelley in *From Anne to Victoria* (ed. Bonamy Dobrée), London, 1937, pp. 574–88.

34. Benjamin Robert Haydon, *Correspondence and Table Talk,* London, 1876, II, 12. Rossetti quoted it from this source when writing to his mother. (See *Memoir,* II, 328.)

for sincerely remarking that you might curb your magnanimity and be more of an artist, and load every rift of your subject with ore." Cheeky! But not so much amiss. *Poetry and no prophecy, however, must have come of that mood; and no pulpit would have held Keats's wings.*[35]

In the light of Rossetti's conception of what poetry did *not* have to deal with in order to be great, his reason for ranking Keats higher than did his fellow mid-Victorians is best expressed in this statement. The bar between Keats and the more orthodox Victorian tastes is thereby dropped, and as a later chapter will show, such a reading would apply to most of Rossetti's successors.

In the sphere of what he actually had accomplished, Keats's work was almost exactly calculated to suit Rossetti's tastes. "All poetry" he said, "affects me deeply, and often to tears. It doesn't need to be pathetic or yet tender to produce this result."[36] Such poems as *La Belle Dame sans Merci* and *The Eve of St. Agnes* were of a kind to affect him particularly deeply, for they fulfilled the two things which Rossetti especially sought: intensity and highly-finished pictorial power (whether rich or simple).

A desire for intensity and a desire for the pictorial, these give us a clue to Rossetti's criteria in reading. Like Matthew Arnold, his main interests in English literature were centred in his own century (although he was infinitely more favourably disposed towards its literature than Arnold would allow himself to be). Aside from Shakespeare and Donne, poetry before Blake does not seem to have attracted his attention. It is significant that he never refers to Spenser, whose ethical bias, in all probability, must have offset whatever attraction he might have had for Rossetti. Chaucer and Milton he mentions but seldom, and as for the eighteenth century, he would have shared the opinion of his friend Burne-Jones:

Walpole lived in a horrid set of years and people; all the century through is like a wet Saturday afternoon to me, and the word eighteenth century sinks me down into despair. When Blake comes I begin to revive, and when Coleridge comes I am wide awake, and have been happily staring and seeing ever since.[37]

Eighteenth-century polish was not enough for Rossetti.[38] Without some form of intensity, literature would indeed resemble a wet Satur-

35. Hall Caine, *Recollections of Rossetti*, London, 1928, pp. 119–20. (Italics mine.) Caine's essay on Keats was later published in his *Cobwebs of Criticism*, London, 1883.

36. Hall Caine, *Recollections*, p. 84.

37. *Memorials of Edward Burne-Jones*, II, 319. It might be added that Rossetti had high praise for two other eighteenth-century romantics besides Blake: Chatterton and Christopher Smart.

38. For a detailed account of Rossetti's reading see Albert Morton Turner, "Rossetti's Readings and His Critical Opinions," *PMLA*, XII (1927), 465–91. This study is thorough, but little attempt is made by the author to explain the basis of Rossetti's likes and dislikes.

day afternoon. Byron, who failed to satisfy Rossetti on other counts, was valued for his sheer force. In early life Maturin and others of the Tale of Terror school were favourites with Rossetti, and later *Wuthering Heights* attracted him. "A fiend of a book" he called it, "an incredible monster. . . . The action is laid in hell,—only it seems places and people have English names."[39] One may recall Pater's comment on Prosper Mérimée: "Exaggerated art! you think. But it was precisely such exaggerated art, intense, unrelieved, an art of fierce colours, that is needed by those who are seeking in art . . . a kind of artificial stimulus."[40] The writings of Poe fascinated Rossetti for a similar reason.

One can understand why he disliked Wordsworth and was wildly enthusiastic about Browning. In the first place, Wordsworth's themes stood in his way in a manner in which Browning's more objectified philosophizing did not. There is an amusing story that when he saw two camels strutting in the zoo he exclaimed: "There go Ruskin and Wordsworth virtuously taking a walk."[41] Not only Wordsworth's often unvarnished moralizing but his fondness for narrative unheightened by intense excitement (at its best, for example, in *Michael*) would seem dull to the author of *Sister Helen*.

To the Society founded in his name, the poetry of Robert Browning represented a sort of Bible: to Rossetti, it represented something different. For twenty-five years he regarded Browning's volumes as the most exciting publications issued by any contemporary.[42] The early enthusiasm which Rossetti had for *Sordello* may perhaps have a touch of the perverse, but his general appreciation is understandable and it is not, as sometimes thought, an inexplicable aberration from his canons of taste. As DeVane shows, it disintegrated largely for personal rather than for literary reasons.[43]

Browning's influence on Rossetti's poetry is sometimes quite marked. *A Last Confession* is most close to *Men and Women*, and *Jenny* also owes something to the older poet's technique. Beyond this, Rossetti's appreciation of Browning's dramatic power in particular, and his general taste for the intense and exciting in other writers, has had a more marked influence on his work than has generally been recognized. One of the soundest observations he ever made upon poetry is this:

39. *Letters to Allingham*, p. 58. See also W. M. Rossetti's comment: "Any writing about devils, spectres, or the supernatural generally . . . had always a fascination for him" (*Works*, p. xvi).

40. Walter Pater, *Miscellaneous Studies*, London, 1920, p. 27.

41. Albert Morton Turner, *op. cit.*, p. 480.

42. See *Memoir*, I, 102.

43. For a detailed account of the friendship of Browning and Rossetti and the reasons for its breakdown, see William Clyde DeVane, "The Harlot and the Thoughtful Young Man," *Studies in Philology*, XXIX (1932), 463–84.

It seems to me that all poetry, to be really enduring, is bound to be as *amusing* . . . as any other class of literature; and I do not think that enough amusement to keep it alive can ever be got out of incidents not amounting to events. . . .[44]

Much of Rossetti's writing (especially *The House of Life*) suffers from a lack of the "amusing," but he had an awareness of its value. At his best, as *Sister Helen* will show, he could tell a story supremely well, much better than Keats or Tennyson. "Incidents not amounting to events" are especially a weakness of Tennyson; and Rossetti, like the Spasmodics, was conscious of the danger although he by no means avoided it, especially in such pieces as *Rose Mary*. His attempt to avoid it depended not only upon a more dramatic arrangement of his narratives (in the manner of Browning), but upon endowing them with the sort of intensity and heightened colouring which he admired so much in nineteenth-century literature. Morris in the violent *Defence of Guenevere* volume surpasses him in this respect.[45]

In Rossetti, combined with a taste for the intense there is a taste for the pictorial which has an even more marked effect on his verse. It constitutes a current (for which Keats must be held largely responsible) which crosses and often obscures the "amusing" part of his own work. In the succeeding section I shall deal with it in detail. I refer to it here to round out this account of the bases of Rossetti's preferences in literature. "Picture and poem" he wrote, "bear the same relation to each other as beauty does in man and woman: the point of meeting where the two are most identical is the supreme perfection." One can readily understand Rossetti's response to Tennyson (at least the early Tennyson) whose picture-poem *The Palace of Art* he illustrated with drawings. According to William, "Tennyson reigned along with Keats, and Edgar Poe and Coleridge along with Tennyson."[46]

Rossetti's preference for Keats and Coleridge above all other English poets except Shakespeare is in entire accord with his standards of excellence. Both poets, in different degrees, catered to both sides of his taste. The weird spell of *Christabel* always fascinated him, and he found there also such pictorial vignettes as:

44. *Memoir*, I, 419.
45. Among the later aesthetes, the adjective "intense" became a *cliché*. In his amusing *Ballade of Aesthetic Adjectives*, Andrew Lang drew attention to it:

> Prince, it is surely as good as a play
> To mark how the poets and painters agree;
> But of plumage aesthetic that feathers the jay,
> "Intense" is the adjective dearest to me!
>
> *Ballades in Blue China* (London, 1885)

46. *Works*, p. xv.

> Her stately neck and arms were bare;
> Her blue-veined feet unsandal'd were,
> And wildly glittering here and there
> The gems entangled in her hair.

Of all Coleridge's poems *Christabel* was his favourite. For other aspects of Coleridge he had little concern. The "six years" during which Coleridge turned aside from philosophy and theology and concentrated on such pieces as *The Ancient Mariner* were all that counted to Rossetti. As he says in his sonnet:

> Six years, from sixty saved! Yet kindling skies
> Own them, a beacon to our centuries.

In the instance of Keats the balance was probably in favour of the pictorial, but Rossetti found there as well a weird intensity at times. Hence *La Belle Dame sans Merci* was his favourite and he linked it with the work of the Spasmodics. Speaking of *Keith of Ravelston* he says: ". . . I have always regarded that poem as being one of the finest, of its length, in any modern poet—ranking with Keats's *La Belle Dame sans Merci*, and the other masterpieces of the condensed and hinted order so dear to imaginative minds."[47] There are innumerable passages in Keats (aside from the weirder poems) where intensity is stressed:

> What men or gods are these? What maidens loth?
> What mad pursuit? What struggle to escape?
> What pipes and timbrels? What wild ecstasy?

Intensity was, for Keats, a fundamental quality in art. There is a fine passage in one of the letters where he refers to a painting by West:

It is a wonderful picture, when West's age is considered; But there is nothing to be intense upon; no women one feels mad to kiss, no face swelling into reality— The excellence of every art is its intensity, capable of making all disagreeables evaporate, from their being in close relationship with Beauty and Truth. Examine "King Lear," and you will find this exemplified throughout.[48]

Other qualities of Keats, which we shall consider in the next section, would have had equal fascination for Rossetti. If he was not influenced by the example of Keats's richness of description it was certainly not owing to a failure to respond to it. Rossetti was not, like Arnold, an exacting reader, and he was prepared to admit to his "House Beautiful" a considerable variety of nineteenth-century liter-

47. *Memoir*, I, 420.
48. *Letters of Keats*, p. 71.

ature. His standards were such, however, that his preference was for those poets who avoid, as a rule, either the abstract or the controversial; whose work has a sort of fire and excitement about it; whose phrasing is highly wrought. Finding one or another of these ingredients absent in a poet, he might (as in the case of Byron) still retain admiration. But Keats was the poet *par excellence,* the poet whose work was "more constantly present" to his thoughts "than that of anyone else, hardly excepting even Dante," because Keats gave him exactly what he expected from great poetry. "With a great poet" said Keats, "the sense of Beauty overcomes every other consideration. . . ."[49] Rossetti's assumption that he was the first to appreciate Keats may have been inexact chronologically, but it was quite true that he was the first whose standards were such that Keats did seem entirely adequate, the "true heir to Shakespeare." The shift of values which is discernible in Victorian taste after 1850 is carried along by Rossetti to a point which anticipates the time when Keats would attain his final apotheosis.

49. *Letters of Keats,* p. 72.

IX

Keats's Influence on Rossetti

I T is not precisely known when Rossetti discovered the poetry of
John Keats. The *Memoir* states that it was in 1845 or 1846, but
in William Rossetti's notes to the *Works* the date mentioned is
1844.[1] At all events, he had discovered Keats some time before beginning work on his own precocious pieces such as *The Blessed Damozel*, one version of which was completed when he was nineteen.[2]

Rossetti's study of Keats was extensive. On the individual poems
he made various remarks which are to be found in three sources:
in some scattered references in his letters, in the marginal comments
which he made in his volume of Keats (these were published in the
Manchester Quarterly in 1882), and in a series of letters to H. B. Forman (privately printed in 1919). The dominant impression which
these comments give is that Rossetti knew his Keats thoroughly. He
had some opinion to offer on almost all of the poems, not merely the
better-known ones. In writing to Forman he noted a detail in *The
Cap and Bells* and referred to it as "the only unworthy stuff Keats
ever wrote except an early trifle or two,"[3] and his *Marginalia* show
that he knew the trifles of which he was speaking. Rossetti might
describe himself, in the words of Oscar Browning, as "soaked with
Keats."[4]

A surprising feature of the *Marginalia* which no one seems to have
noticed is that no comments on *Lamia, The Eve of St. Agnes* and
Isabella are printed. He referred to *Isabella* once in his letters, but not
to the others. We can assume, however, that the first two at least were
among his favourites. In the rest of Keats's work he singled out especially *La Belle Dame sans Merci* and *The Eve of St. Mark*. Of the
latter fragment his opinion was that "with *La Belle Dame sans Merci*"
it is "the chastest and choicest example of his maturing manner, and

1. See *Works*, p. 671, and R. L. Mégroz, *Dante Gabriel Rossetti*, London, 1928, p.
41. There is a reference to his youthful reading of Keats in an early version of *The
Portrait*; see *An Analytical List of Manuscripts in the Duke University Library*, p. 68.

2. For an account of the revision of the poem, see R. L. Knickerbocker, "Rossetti's
'The Blessed Damozel,'" *Studies in Philology*, XXIX (1932), 485–504.

3. Dante Gabriel Rossetti, *John Keats: Criticism and Comment* (Rossetti's Letters
to H. B. Forman, privately printed), London, 1919, p. 21. He once told Swinburne
that if *The Cap and Bells* had been Keats's only poem, "it would justify all Maga's
insolence to Keats" (Edmund Gosse, *The Life of Algernon Charles Swinburne*, New
York, 1917, p. 295).

4. See p. 100, n. 27.

shews astonishingly real mediaevalism for one not bred as an artist."[5]
We have seen some of the reasons why *La Belle Dame* would attract
Rossetti; *The Eve of St. Mark* is another matter. Those aspects of
Keats which had appealed so strongly to the youthful Tennyson and
which led to what Babbitt calls the "confusion" of painting and poetry had an even stronger appeal for Rossetti, himself a painter.
"Colour and metre" said Rossetti, "these are the true patents of nobility in painting and poetry, taking precedence of all intellectual
claims."[6] In his own work we are usually conscious that the experience which he is describing has been first seen with the painter's eye
for arrangement and significant detail, and then worked into poetry.
To take an example at random, here is the lonely Dante at the licen-
tious court:

> And pages hushed their laughter down,
> And gay squires stilled the merry stir,
> When he passed up the dais-chamber
> With set brows lordlier than a frown;
> And tire-maids hidden among these
> Drew close their loosened bodices.
>   (*Dante at Verona*, 78–84)

The scene has the pattern and grouping of a design. So too he employs details of colour:

> Through the small room, with subtle sound
> Of flame, by vents the fireshine drove
> And reddened. In its dim alcove
> The mirror shed a clearness round.
>   (*My Sister's Sleep*, 16–19)

When Rossetti congratulated George Meredith on one of his
poems, the latter replied: "It is quite destitute of the lumen purpu-
reum which I like to give. How a work without colour can please you
at all, astonishes me."[7] Keats's lavish provision of this "lumen pur-
pureum" ran no danger of displeasing Rossetti. "The next Keats must
be a painter" he told Morris, and implied that Keats's genius in translating the pictorial into words had actually exhausted the possibilities
of poetry, and hence future artists would have to turn more and more
to painting.[8] Time and time again Keats would seem to have anticipated the very effects which Rossetti sought:

> Bertha arose, and read awhile,
> With forehead 'gainst the window-pane.
>
> From plaited lawn-frill, fine and thin,

5. *John Keats: Criticism and Comment*, p. 9.
6. Quoted by T. Earle Welby, *The Victorian Romantics*, p. 132.
7. Janet Camp Troxell, *Three Rossettis*, Cambridge (U. S. A.), 1937, p. 6.
8. *Memorials of Edward Burne-Jones*, I, 145.

> *She lifted up her soft warm chin,*
> *With aching neck and swimming eyes,*
> *And daz'd with saintly imageries.*
> (*The Eve of St. Mark*, 48 ff.)

The lines which I have italicized seem to me a remarkable rendering of the scene which Rossetti painted in his most famous picture, the *Beata Beatrix*. He wrote no poem on that particular picture, although many times the details of the lifted chin and straining neck appear,[9] and above all the strangely mystical "breathless" effect which he uses, for example, in *The Blessed Damozel*:

> The wonder was not yet quite gone
> From that still look of hers.

If Keats was the first Pre-Raphaelite poet, Bertha was the first Pre-Raphaelite "model."

The Eve of St. Mark also served Rossetti in other ways. One of the most memorable of his early poems is *My Sister's Sleep*, a poem all the more remarkable when we realize that it was not founded on actual experience. The theme was perhaps suggested to him by Thomas Hood's short poem *The Death Bed*, but for handling the theme he seems to have gone to Keats. The vivid details of the fireside scene in *My Sister's Sleep* owe much to a similar scene in *The Eve of St. Mark*. As Landor said in one of his *Imaginary Conversations*: "Young poets imagine feelings to which in reality they are strangers." But this, as he goes on to say, is not mere copying. "The copybook acts on the imagination. Unless they felt the truth of the verisimilitude, it could not take possession of them."[10] *My Sister's Sleep* shows how completely Rossetti was possessed with the scene in Keats's poem.

Such statements bring us to the thorny question of Rossetti's debt to Keats, both in the matter of general influence and of actual parallels. Since Rossetti's death a fair quantity of ink has been employed in showing either that Rossetti owes a good deal to Keats or that he was entirely independent. It seems to me that both sides in the dispute leave out of account a very important factor in the situation, that is, Rossetti's *attitude* to borrowing from Keats and other poets.

The early biographers of Rossetti such as A. C. Benson took for granted that he had drawn from Keats. Benson emphasized especially that the influence of Keats was responsible for Rossetti's "deliberate

---

9. The "Rossetti neck" appears many times in the poems. See, for example, *The House of Life*, x, xxxi, and *Rose Mary*, i, 73–4:
> Then over her mother's lap leaned she,
> And stretched her thrilled throat passionately. . . .

10. *Works of Walter Savage Landor*, v, 307.

intention of wringing beauty out of the moment and the scene."[11] Most readers of Rossetti have felt similarly, although, like Benson, they do not cite passages to prove their case. In 1909, a more systematic study appeared by Kurt Horn: *Zur Entstehungsgeschichte von Dante Gabriel Rossettis Dichtungen*, in which the influence of Keats and other poets is discussed in some detail. This might have settled the problem, but a year later, James Routh published an article in which the debt to Keats is flatly denied and dismissed as a "fallacy." "I have been unable to find" he says, "a single specific parallel, in rhythm, in subject-matter, or in sentiment. Moreover there are marked dissimilarities just where one would expect the reverse."[12] In 1914, Mlle. Léonie Villard's study was issued, and, although she does not refer to Routh (or to Horn for that matter), her examination would serve as a reply to his contention.[13] A direct reply to Routh, and one which seems to have been written independently of Mlle. Villard was brought out in 1926 by Hill Shine.[14] Shine cites a number of interesting parallels, and once again we might suppose that the matter could be considered settled. Unfortunately, the leading Rossetti editor of the present day, P. F. Baum, refuses to be convinced. Without referring to any passages in particular, Baum nevertheless waives the possibility of Keatsian influence sometimes almost as peremptorily as Routh did in 1910. "Though his range was limited" asserts Baum, "he [Rossetti] never sought to enlarge his experience from the poetry of others."[15] We appear to be back where we started.

My own contention is that the reader who senses the influence of Keats in certain passages and the scholar who examines the passages minutely and often finds *exact* parallels absent, are both right. For example, Oliver Elton refers to Rossetti's poem *Spring* which, he says, "may or may not be meant to remind us, but which does remind us, of Keats, and which well bears the comparison; it is an English watercolour of the best school:

> The young rooks cheep 'mid the thick caw o' the old:
> And near unpeopled stream-sides, on the ground,
> By her Spring cry the moorhen's nest is found,
> Where the drained flood-lands flaunt their marigold."[16]

11. A. C. Benson, *Rossetti*, London, 1926, p. 141. On p. 99 he speaks of Keats as a "Pre-Raphaelite" poet and refers to *The Eve of St. Mark* and *The Eve of St. Agnes*. He does not, however, refer to any parallel passages or echoes of any kind.

12. James Routh, "Parallels in Coleridge, Keats, and Rossetti," *MLN*, xxv (1910), 36.

13. Léonie Villard, *The Influence of Keats on Tennyson and Rossetti*, pp. 68–89.

14. Hill Shine, "The Influence of Keats upon Rossetti," *Englische Studien*, 61 (1926), pp. 183–219.

15. *The Blessed Damozel* (ed. Paull Franklin Baum), Chapel Hill, 1937, Introduction, p. xxxv. Elsewhere Mr. Baum is not so definite on the point as he is here and in his notes to the poems refers to occasional echoes.

16. Oliver Elton, *A Survey of English Literature: 1830–1880*, London, 1932, ii, 11.

Elton's intuitive sense is surely correct here, but exact parallels would be hard to find. Of one thing, however, there is no doubt. It is not *"meant* to remind us" of Keats, and in this we have a clue to our problem.

In Rossetti's Notebooks we find the sentence: "I was one of those whose little is their own."[17] As R. L. Knickerbocker shows in connection with *The Blessed Damozel,* Rossetti was almost fanatical on the subject of borrowing.[18] When Leigh Hunt suggested to him that Dante had influenced his writing of *The Blessed Damozel,* he was displeased and wrote to his aunt:

Where Hunt, in his kind letter, speaks of my "Dantesque heavens," he refers to one or two of the poems the scene of which is laid in the celestial regions, and which are written in a kind of Gothic manner which I suppose he is pleased to think belongs to the school of Dante.[19]

With regard to Keats, Rossetti was especially on the alert. Letters to his family show how conscientious he could be. Christina, who was not a reader of Keats, was rather offended when Gabriel pointed out that one of her poems echoed *Isabella.* "Is it so very like Keats?" she asked. "I doubt if I ever read the lines in question, never having read the *Isabella* through."[20] William was similarly censured. When he submitted his *Mrs. Holmes Grey* to Gabriel for inspection in 1849, he received this reply:

I do not know if you remember that at the beginning of the *Eve of St. Mark* there are the lines—
> "The city streets were cool and fair,
> From wholesome drench of April rains."

This is like the beginning of your poem; and, though of course the statement of a fact from observation cannot even be a reminiscence of what has been done before, *still I think it is perhaps as well not to have at the very outset a line which some people might manage to draw conclusions from.*[21]

William seems to have carried out instructions rather violently. I have never seen the original draft about which Gabriel is speaking, but the opening of *Mrs. Holmes Grey,* as published in 1868, is certainly a long way from Keats:

> The English "Rainy weather" went from mouth
> To mouth, with "Very" answered, or a shrug

---

17. *Works,* p. 607.
18. See R. L. Knickerbocker, *op. cit.,* pp. 492–3.
19. *Memoir,* ii, 38.
20. *Rossetti Papers,* p. 99.
21. *Memoir,* ii, 64. (Italics mine.) It may be noted that Gabriel is quoting Keats's lines from memory. In the poem, the streets were *"clean* and fair."

Of shoulders, and a growl, and "Sure to be!
Began the very day that we arrived."[22]

We have then two factors with which to contend in the problem of Rossetti's possible debt to Keats. One is that he was determined, if possible, to avoid the charge of having imitated Keats. By the time Rossetti was publishing poetry it was no longer possible to do as Hood had done, that is, to borrow directly from Keats and blissfully assume that no one would notice. Secondly, we have seen that Rossetti was fairly "soaked" with Keats's work and that with the earlier writer's whole approach to poetry he was in complete accord. A third fact to note is Rossetti's method of composition, laborious and painstaking, every line wrought and rewrought before taking its final form. He was not the kind of poet who would let some borrowing slip by to the press unnoticed, and thence eventually, alas, into the hands of the aspirant for a Ph.D. or the source-hunter of the scholarly journals.

Bearing these facts in mind, we can hypothesize that Rossetti, no matter how deeply attracted to Keats, would avoid directly borrowing anything so obvious as a plot from Keats. He was not likely to attempt to retell the story of *Isabella*. Further, if and when he sensed the influence of Keats (which would crop up in spite of himself) he would try to eliminate it or to disguise it in such a way that the similarity could not be directly traced (much as William did in the case of *Mrs. Holmes Grey*). This, I believe, accounts for the comparative scarcity of exact parallels. The influence is nevertheless still there, and as Elton did in the instance of *Spring*, we sense it even though the poet has striven to obscure it.

For an example of how Rossetti contrives to be both derivative and original at the same time, we might consider *The Bride's Prelude*, in which traces of Tennyson as well as of Keats are to be found. This long, unfinished narrative is probably the most picturesque poem which Rossetti ever wrote. "For profusion and passion of pictorial detail I do not think that Rossetti ever wrote anything more noticeable than 'The Bride's Prelude.' "[23] Such was the opinion of William, and Gabriel himself said: "Its picturesqueness is sufficient to make it pass muster, though it has no other quality to recommend it."[24] The story itself, as Rossetti knew, is not very substantial and so like Keats in *Endymion*, who laboured to make "4000 lines of one bare circumstance,"[25] he developed an elaborate setting to make up for the deficiency in narrative. As is the case with nearly all works of Rossetti,

22. Published in *The Broadway*, February, 1868. See R. D. Waller, *The Rossetti Family*, Manchester, 1932, p. 292.

23. *Works*, p. 648.

24. *Poems, Ballads, and Sonnets* (ed. Paull Franklin Baum), New York, 1937, Introduction, p. 124 n.

25. *Letters of Keats*, p. 52.

The Bride's Prelude fulfils the requirement which Poe made of a poem, that it produce a single, vivid *effect*. Here the effect sought seems to be a kind of stifling dreariness. This is produced in part by the slow-moving narrative itself, but more by other devices.

For one thing, there is a highly appropriate stanza-form which drags its slow length along page after page. It was certainly not developed from Keats, whose metrical experiments, except in the odes, were not extensive, but it may owe something to Tennyson.[26] Also there is the weird atmosphere of the poem and here the influence of Tennyson is quite marked. Especially in the first half of the poem are we constantly conscious of a brooding heat in the air which, perhaps more than anything else, contributes the effect of dreariness and stagnation which Rossetti sought. Tennyson had secured the same effect in his early Keats-like Mariana poems:

> Nor bird would sing, nor lamb would bleat,
>   Nor any cloud would cross the vault,
> But day increased from heat to heat,
>   On stony drought and steaming salt. . . .
>   (*Mariana in the South*, 37–40)

Compare this with Rossetti's opening stanza:

> "Sister," said busy Amelotte
>   To listless Aloÿse;
> "Along your wedding-road the wheat
> Bends as to hear your horse's feet,
> And the noonday stands still for heat."[27]

And later:

> She would have pushed the lattice wide
>   To gain what breeze might be;
> But marking that no leaf once beat
> The outside casement, it seemed meet
> Not to bring in more scent and heat.
>   (*The Bride's Prelude*, 101–05)

The above passage echoes Tennyson's:

> The house thro' all the level shines,
> Close-latticed to the brooding heat,
> And silent in its dusty vines. . . .

26. Baum points out one of the few cases where Keats may have influenced Rossetti's stanza-forms. In *The Staff and Scrip* the short fifth line was perhaps suggested by *La Belle Dame sans Merci* (*Poems, Ballads, and Sonnets*, p. 23 n.). Baum states that *The Bride's Prelude* stanza-form was derived from the ballads (*ibid.*, p. 124 n.) but there is also a resemblance to Tennyson's *Lady of Shalott* (itself modelled on ballads) in which an identical triple rhyme is employed, although here modified by omitting the refrain.

27. Kurt Horn has also drawn attention to this passage. The others are my own. See *Zur Entstehungsgeschichte von Dante Gabriel Rossettis Dichtungen*, Bernau, 1909, p. 56.

These examples, together with several others, illustrate the way in which Rossetti was derivative. When he was drawing from earlier poets, it was his practice to exploit devices and techniques which they had used rather than precisely parallel details.[28]

The influence of Keats on the poem is more direct and Rossetti is not so successful in concealing it. A passage in *The Eve of St. Agnes* which Rossetti probably knew by heart (for he echoes it several times) describes the moonlight scene in Madeline's chamber:

> A casement high and triple-arch'd there was . . .
> And *diamonded* with panes of quaint device,
> Innumerable of stains and splendid dyes,
> As are the tiger-moth's deep-damask'd wings;
> And in the midst, 'mong thousand heraldries,
> And twilight saints, and dim emblazonings,
> A shielded scutcheon blush'd with blood of queens and kings.[29]

Keats is describing a castle chamber at midnight; Rossetti is describing one at noon; and yet Keats's account still serves Rossetti's purposes. The detail stressed by Keats is the play of colours from the moonlight passing through stained glass. Aloÿse's chamber is pictured with the sunlight passing through coloured objects:

> Within the window's *heaped* recess
> The light was counterchanged
> In blent reflexes manifold
> From *perfume-caskets of wrought gold*
> And gems the bride's hair could not hold
> All thrust together: and with these
> A slim-*curved lute.* . . .

One may note in passing how some of the phrases here seem transposed from stanzas xxxi and xxxiii of *The Eve of St. Agnes*, where Porphyro "heap'd" with delicacies the "golden" dishes and "baskets" which stood in the moonlight, and filled the room thereby with "perfume," and also that Keats speaks of the "hollow lute" which Porphyro plays. But the important thing is that Rossetti, in succeeding stanzas, seems to describe not only the same items which Keats mentions, but also follows the same sequence. Keats tells how the casement light "threw *warm gules* on Madeline's *fair breast*" and:

> Rose bloom fell on her hands, together prest,
> And on her *silver cross* soft amethyst,
> And on her hair, a glory like a saint.
> (Stanza xxv)

28. For example, compare the use of sound effects: *The Bride's Prelude*, 146–50, and 277–80, with *Mariana*, 61–71; also the picture of the stagnant pool: *The Bride's Prelude*, 266–70, and *Mariana*, 37–40.

29. Italics mine here and in subsequent passages from *The Eve of St. Agnes* and *The Bride's Prelude*.

Rossetti follows in similar order. Instead of a silver cross, however, he pictures a silver belt. It is especially interesting that the reflections from the scarlet stained glass of Keats reappear in Rossetti as reflections through another scarlet coat of arms but here, instead of by means of a window, the belt-clasp which Amelotte is wearing is the reflecting object:

> The *belt was silver,* and the clasp
>   Of *lozenged arm-bearings;*
> A world of mirrored tints minute
> The rippling sunshine wrought into't,
> That *flushed* her hand and *warmed* her foot.
>   (*The Bride's Prelude,* 31–5)

Furthermore, the next items which Keats describes are the pearls and jewelry, the former in Madeline's hair:

> Of all its *wreathed pearls her hair* she frees;
> Unclasps her *warmed jewels* one by one.

Rossetti's account follows:

> At least an hour had Aloÿse,—
>   *Her jewels in her hair. . . .*

And Keats (as Rossetti does) also goes on to describe the "rich attire" of Madeline. We may wonder what happened to the "pearls" which Keats mentioned? Rossetti changes the order slightly, but they appear at once:

> Over her bosom, that lay still,
>   The vest was rich in grain,
> With *close pearls* wholly overset. . . .

This section is an exceptionally good piece of evidence.[30] Here, where Rossetti follows out, step by step, and in almost the same order, a scene in Keats which he must have loved, it is especially revealing to see what he does with it. Analysis shows, I think, why it is so hard to find the direct echo. He throws us off the track by employing sunlight rather than moonlight. But more than this, he seems consciously to be avoiding the exact terms which Keats had used. Not only does the stained-glass window become transformed into a clasp, but he has cast about for other ways of remaining independent. Keats's window had been "*diamonded* with panes of quaint device." Rossetti carefully avoids the word which Keats had coined and substitutes "lozenged." Again, he does not wish to say that "a

30. Previous commentators have referred in general terms to the passage, but no one appears to have worked over it in detail to show exactly what Rossetti drew from Keats and in what ways he changed things. (Cf. Hill Shine, *op. cit.,* pp. 203–04; Léonie Villard, *op. cit.,* pp. 77–8; and Kurt Horn, *op. cit.,* p. 58.)

shielded scutcheon blush'd with blood of queens and kings," but says in place of this: "lozenged *arm-bearings*," the light from which "flushes" the figure of Amelotte. Both poets are certainly wringing beauty out of the moment and of the scene.

I have dealt with these passages of *The Bride's Prelude* in some detail because I think they show to a certain extent in the poetry of Tennyson, and to a marked extent in the poetry of Keats, how Rossetti contrives to secure effects similar to those achieved by poets from whom he derives and yet how scrupulously careful he is to avoid, if possible, the direct parallel. It is this, I think, which accounts for Routh's impression: "There are marked dissimilarities just where one would expect the reverse."[31] Exactly! for Rossetti usually tried to see to that, but the patching is not always a successful blind.

The debt to Keats in this particular instance appears, then, to have been conscious. In many of the others which follow it is likely that Rossetti was unaware of his source. As Matthew Arnold complained of Tennyson, so might Rossetti complain of Keats: "One has him so in one's head, one cannot help imitating him sometimes."

The "astonishingly real mediaevalism" which Rossetti found in some of Keats's poems becomes even more important in his own work than it had been in Keats. When reviewing the poems of his friend Hake in 1873, Rossetti remarked: "Though much has been said concerning the matter-of-fact tendencies of the reading public which poets desire to enlist, it must we think be admitted that the simpler and more domestic order of themes has not been generally, of late years, the most widely popular."[32] He might have been thinking of the anti-Wordsworthian cast of his own poetry in which the "simpler and more domestic themes" of Victorian England were, as a rule, conspicuously absent. The incidents of *A Last Confession* (although occurring in 1848) are too highly coloured by the "Lombardy Coast" to be simple, and *Jenny*, although contemporaneous, is scarcely domestic. Many of the poems, such as *The House of Life* and *The Stream's Secret*, seem to be set in a realm where historical time is forgotten. The main body of narratives such as *Rose Mary*, *Sister Helen*, and *The Bride's Prelude*, are set in the Middle Ages. Rossetti was drawn to the past by its colour and, as he saw it, its romantic mystery.[33] In *The Bride's Prelude* we have seen how the picturesque mediaevalism of *The Eve of St. Agnes* left its mark on Rossetti's poem. These same scenes influenced his writing in other instances as well. What is perhaps an unconscious echo occurs in a recently published sonnet (written in 1848) called *Happy and Thankful*. In it, he de-

31. James Routh, *op. cit.*, p. 36.
32. *Works*, p. 634.
33. Léonie Villard notes that both poets ignored the battlefield (*op. cit.*, p. 74). In Keats's case, *Otho the Great* may be regarded as an exception.

scribes his beloved, surrounding her with an air of awe-inspiring saintliness much as Keats has done with Madeline:

> She should be with me now, shedding on all
> A something holy, *like the crown a Saint*
> *Has round her temples,* or a sun glow on
> Iced rocks in the blue North when their peaks fall
> And become water; *for my soul is faint*
> At seeing all *this glory* thus alone.[34]

Bearing in mind Rossetti's familiarity with the following passage, we can see how the details influenced him:

> Rose-bloom fell on her hands, together prest . . .
> And *on her hair a glory, like a saint:*
> She seem'd a splendid angel, newly drest,
> Save wings, for heaven:—*Porphyro grew faint.* . . .
> (*The Eve of St. Agnes,* xxv)

In *The Bride's Prelude* and in the poem quoted above the emphasis falls on the description of the woman. In *The King's Tragedy,* Rossetti returns to the scene again, now however, for details of setting rather than for the description of a person. In *The Bride's Prelude* he employed the effects of light transmitted through coloured glass; there, however, he was referring to sunlight. Almost as if the moonlight-scene in Keats was too good to lose, Rossetti uses it directly in *The King's Tragedy:*

> And the rain had ceased, and the moonbeams lit
> The window high in the wall,—
> Bright beams that on the plank that I knew
> Through the painted pane did fall,
> And gleamed with the splendour of Scotland's crown
> And shield armorial.
> (*The King's Tragedy,* 629–34)

Here Rossetti is especially careful to avoid identical phrases, but that he has taken over from Keats the notion of moonlight passing through a stained-glass "shielded scutcheon" and casting light on the floor seems to be beyond question.[35]

34. *An Analytical List of Manuscripts in the Duke University Library,* pp. 64–5. (Italics mine.)

35. As Shine remarks: "It is striking that in both passages the light is moonlight, that the object it shines through is a coat of arms, and that the same mistake is made: namely, the power to transmit the colours of the stained glass through the glass and upon an object within the room, is attributed to moonlight; whereas moonlight possesses no such power" (Hill Shine, *op. cit.,* p. 200). Baum objects that it is not clear whether Rossetti really has repeated Keats's error. Surely one could not ask for anything more explicit than Rossetti's lines describing what happens when the moonlight disappears:

A passage which had some influence on both Tennyson and Arnold also attracted Rossetti:

> The arras, rich with horseman, hawk, and hound,
> Flutter'd in the besieging wind's uproar;
> And the long carpets rose along the gusty floor.
> (*The Eve of St. Agnes*, XL)

Rossetti, like Coleridge in *Christabel*, is more accurate and speaks of the floor-covering as rushes:[36]

> The night-wind wailed round the empty room
> And the rushes shook on the floor.
> (*The King's Tragedy*, 623–4)

The change is indicative not only of a greater desire for accuracy on Rossetti's part but also of his basic method of obscuring his sources.

The King's Tragedy shows as well an instance in which Rossetti draws on his favourite *The Eve of St. Mark*. The title page of William Rossetti's popular edition of Keats had been illustrated by a picture of Bertha bending over the firelight with her shadow on the wall looming up mysteriously.[37] Gabriel would have approved of the illustrator's choice of this scene in Keats. When writing *The King's Tragedy*, in order to give atmosphere to the chamber in which James is to die, he emphasizes the ghostly, spectre-like quality of the shadows:

> But the fire was bright in the ingle-nook,
>   And through empty space around
> The shadows cast on *the arras'd wall*
> 'Mid the *pictured* kings stood sudden and *tall*
>   *Like spectres* sprung from the ground.[38]

These were the principal elements in Keats's mediaeval poems which Rossetti took over to adapt to his own purposes. Although he left no formal comments on *The Eve of St. Agnes*, his use of the poem indicates the extent of his appreciation. Occasional isolated phrases

---

>   And the climbing moon fell back;
>   And the royal blazon fled *from the floor*,
>   And nought remained on its track. . . .
> Cf. *Poems, Ballads, and Sonnets* (ed. P. F. Baum), p. 250 n.
> 36. Cf. *Christabel*, 174–5:
>   And now doth Geraldine press down
>   The rushes of the chamber floor.
> 37. Thomas Seccombe is the illustrator of this edition published in the series of *Moxon's Popular Poets*, London, n. d. The title page is of interest not only because of the scene from *The Eve of St. Mark* but because Keats's name is mis-spelt: "*Keat's Poetical Works.*"
> 38. Cf. *The Eve of St. Mark*, 74–9 and 83–7.

which echo elsewhere in his poems also suggest how it had affected him. For example, Shine notes a parallel with *The Blessed Damozel*:[39]

> Until her bosom must have made
> The bar she leaned on *warm*.
> (*The Blessed Damozel*, 45–6)

> Unclasps her *warmed jewels* one by one.
> (*The Eve of St. Agnes*, xxvi)

Another which might be added occurs in *Rose Mary*:

> And the *lights throbbed* faint in unison.
> (*Rose Mary*, 1, 239)

Keats had likened Porphyro to a "throbbing star" (stanza xxxvi). The point is worth noting that Tennyson took over the exact phrase itself ("throbbing star"), as we have seen, whereas Rossetti echoed only the device.

Keats's other strictly mediaeval poem is *La Belle Dame sans Merci* but here there is no particular sign of influence on Rossetti in spite of his admiration for its concentrated "Celtic" qualities. Its theme of the bewitching siren was one which seems always to have interested him, and in *Eden Bower* he develops it intensively.[40] In this poem, of course, he is much closer to another work of Keats in which the siren theme is employed at greater length, that is, *Lamia*.

It was inevitable that the snake-woman in *Eden Bower* would have much in common with the snake-woman in *Lamia*, but the two poems are otherwise markedly different.[41] *Lamia* is a puzzling mixture of a kind of Drydenesque humour with highly intense passages having that "sort of fire" in them which Keats himself noted.[42] *Eden Bower* contains nothing intentionally humorous, for its author, although having a great sense of humour himself, never introduced it into his

---

39. Hill Shine, *op. cit.*, p. 202.

40. Concerning the origins of the Lilith legend see Oliver Elton, *op. cit.*, ii, 13, and Mario Praz, *The Romantic Agony*, London, 1933, p. 218.

41. Compare the opening lines of *Eden Bower* with *Lamia*, 1, 59–60. See also Hill Shine, *op. cit.*, p. 202. Shine likewise draws attention to a "gruesome detail" in *Lamia* which may have influenced Rossetti:

> Mark how, possess'd, his *lashless eyelids* stretch
> Around his demon eyes!
> (*Lamia*, ii, 288–9)
> . . . a memory all in vain,
> Upon the sight of *lidless* eyes in Hell.
> (*The House of Life*, lxiii)

(See Shine, p. 196.) It might be added that the same term is used most effectively by T. S. Eliot in *The Waste Land*, 137–8:

> And we shall play a game of chess,
> Pressing lidless eyes and waiting for a knock upon the door.

42. *Letters of Keats*, p. 402.

poetry.[43] Rossetti wanted, rather, a single, powerful effect. Consequently, his account of the snake-woman is vastly different in tone from that of Keats. Another interesting difference is that Rossetti makes no reference to the colouring of the snake in *Eden Bower*. Keats's flashing description of Lamia must have been hard for Rossetti to pass by and he returns to it in other poems.[44] This absence of colour in *Eden Bower* may perhaps be owing to the shortness of line in Rossetti's stanzas, but there seems here again a deliberate attempt to avoid echoes.

It appears that *Lamia* left some impression on Rossetti's poetry but that its influence is not comparable to that of Keats's mediaeval poems. What then of *Isabella?* Mlle. Villard suggests that its morbidity might have had a certain fascination for Rossetti,[45] but to my knowledge, no one has indicated a parallel or even any sign of influence on Rossetti's work. My own suggestion (which is offered for what it is worth) does not provide a parallel of phrasing but of general conception.

This suggestion relates to *The Blessed Damozel*, the sources of which have been considerably disputed. Dante's influence on the poem appears to be relatively certain both in the matter of devices and in aspects of the general conception.[46] As we have seen, however, Rossetti himself denied that the poem was influenced by "Dantesque heavens," and, in addition, suggested that its atmosphere was "Gothic." Indeed, there is a marked difference in *spirit* between Dante's almost purely mystical concept of the lovers' relations and Rossetti's strange blending of the mystical and physical, producing what a French critic calls "cette sorte d'extase prolongée où la spiritualité et la sensualité se mêlent."[47] It is this fusion which constitutes Rossetti's originality, and according to Watts-Dunton, his main object as an artist:

To *eliminate asceticism from romantic art, and yet to remain romantic, to retain that mysticism which alone can give life to romantic art, and yet be as sensuous as the Titians who revived sensuousness at the expense of mysticism, was the quest, more or less conscious, of Rossetti's genius.*[48]

43. I refer later to *The Burden of Nineveh* as an exception. Rossetti called Keats's *Lines on the Mermaid Tavern* "sadly futile" (*Marginalia*, p. 6), but his own experiment with humorous poetry, *The Ballad of Jan Van Hunks* (first published in 1929) is one to which the words "sadly futile" more properly apply.

44. Compare *Lamia*, I, 48–54, *The Card Dealer*, 21–4, and *Rose Mary*, I, 36–40.

45. Léonie Villard, *op. cit.*, p. 71.

46. On the influence of Dante, see R. D. Waller, "The Blessed Damozel," *Modern Language Review*, xxvi (1931), 129–41. Baum, in his edition of *The Blessed Damozel* (Chapel Hill, 1937) is more sceptical of the influence of Dante. (See Introduction, pp. xxxi–xxxv.)

47. Albert J. Farmer, *Le mouvement esthétique et "décadent" en Angleterre*, p. 18.

48. *The House of Life* (ed. P. F. Baum), Cambridge, 1928, Introduction, p. 27.

Nowhere is the compromise better handled than in *The Blessed Damozel*. The physical, non-Dantesque elements are to be found not only in the richness of details such as the yellow hair and the warmth of the damozel's bosom, but in the central idea of union and separation:

> There will I ask of Christ the Lord
> Thus much for him and me:—
> Only to live as once on earth
> With Love,—only to be,
> As then awhile, for ever now
> Together, I and he.

The "heaven" sought is a renewal of the earthly bliss, without which the damozel, in spite of the presence of Cecily, Gertrude, Magdalen, Margaret, and Rosalys, is lonely. The 1850 version of the poem contains lines which make this especially clear:

> Alas for lonely Heaven! Alas
> For life wrung out alone!

The words are spoken by the lover on earth. They indicate not only that he may be unworthy to join her, but from her point of view, they reinforce the notion that in this paradise of lovers, heavenly bliss is incomplete in itself without the company of the beloved, in fact wretchedly lonely. Rossetti later removed the lines, perhaps because they make the situation *too* explicit, but his general intention is clear enough. The poem is built around two themes: first, the almost helpless yearning of the lover on earth for reunion with his beloved, and second, the lonely yearning of the damozel in heaven. Rossetti considered the second of these to be the more important. He told Caine: "I saw that Poe [in *The Raven*] had done the utmost it was possible to do with the grief of the lover on earth, and so I determined to reverse the conditions, and give utterance to the yearning of the loved one in heaven."[49] Where in his reading might he have found something which would contribute to this conception? Let us turn to *Isabella*, a poem which Rossetti certainly knew before writing *The Blessed Damozel*. Keats describes the murder of Lorenzo and the way in which, after death, he strives to return to his beloved on earth. The conception of the after-life in *Isabella* is deliberately vague and Keats in no way anticipates Rossetti's stellar spaces or Catholic elysium. On one point he is, however, perfectly clear: the loneliness of the dead lover without his loved one:

> Ah! when a soul doth thus its freedom win,
> *It aches in loneliness*—is ill at peace. . . .
>
> (*Isabella*, xxviii)[50]

49. T. Hall Caine, *Recollections* (1882), p. 248.
50. The italics here, and in the three following quotations, are mine.

In a vision, the lover returns and strives to speak:

> Strange sound it was, when the pale shadow spake;
>   For there was *striving*, in its piteous tongue,
> To speak *as when on earth it was awake*,
>   And Isabella on its music hung. . . .
> (*Isabella*, xxxvi)

In Rossetti, the damozel's striving to reach the lover is much more effectively represented by means of the falling leaves, the rain, and the bird's song:

> Ah sweet! Even now, in that bird's song,
>   *Strove* not her accents there,
> Fain to be hearkened?
> (*The Blessed Damozel*, 61–3)

The significant passage is the one in which Keats's lonely lover addresses Isabella from beyond:

> I am *a shadow now, alas! alas!*
>   Upon the skirts of human-nature dwelling
> *Alone: I chant alone the holy mass*,
>   *While little sounds of life are round me knelling* . . .
> Paining me through: those sounds grow strange to me,
>   *And thou art distant in Humanity.*
>
> Though I forget *the taste of earthly bliss*,
>   That paleness warms my grave, as though I had
> *A Seraph chosen from the bright abyss*
>   *To be my spouse:* thy paleness makes me glad;
> Thy beauty grows upon me, and I feel
> A greater love through all my essence steal.
>
> The Spirit mourn'd "Adieu!"—*dissolv'd, and left*
>   *The atom darkness in a slow turmoil.* . . .
> (*Isabella*, xxxix, xl, xli)

The passage constitutes one of the few fine things in a work which Keats knew himself was a "weak-sided Poem."[51] That Rossetti would have admired it is beyond doubt; that it would have some bearing on the central conception of *The Blessed Damozel* seems to me probable. The loneliness of the lover and his striving to be in touch once more with "earthly bliss," his reference to the sounds about him, his anticipation of union with her as his "spouse" after her death, and finally her fading away as the vision of the damozel faded—these things might appear to have given Rossetti some hints for his poem.

51. *Letters of Keats*, p. 391. The passage in the poem was one which Browning loved. He used to cite it as an example of Keats's "supreme mastery of language" (*The Poems of John Keats*, ed. E. de Sélincourt, p. 463).

These elements are seemingly blended with the more mystical Dantesque features of the poem to make that highly original fusion which is Rossetti's own.

In 1848, according to Holman Hunt, a London phrenologist had on display in his studio pictures of two heads by means of which he illustrated the "bumps" of genius.[52] They were the heads of Keats and Dante, a curious combination perhaps, but one which Rossetti would have understood and approved. Rossetti had the faculty of moulding the "bumps" into a new head of genius of his own.[53]

One further point in this connection: in making this suggestion about *Isabella* I am not calling into question the influence of Dante which has been so often marked. But the difference between Rossetti's conception of the after-life and the "Dantesque heavens" was stated by the poet himself when he wrote to his aunt that *The Blessed Damozel* was "written in a kind of Gothic manner."[54] Baum remarks that "it does not help us much to know that Rossetti thought of the poem as written 'in a kind of Gothic manner.' "[55] Perhaps it does, however, if Keats is the Gothic artist Rossetti had in mind.

Evidence of further influence of Keats may be considered more briefly. These examples will show again how a consciousness of Keats's work affects his handling of a situation and also aspects of his style. With regard to the Odes, a revealing contrast is to be found between Arnold and Rossetti. Arnold's favourite appears to have been *To Autumn*. Rossetti, in his *Marginalia*, ranks it in the second class, giving his first choice to the *Ode to a Nightingale* and *Ode on a Grecian Urn* along with the mediaeval narratives.[56] Some of his landscape poems seem, nevertheless, to derive from the Autumn ode. Elton, as we have seen, referred to *Spring*, and Shine cites several parallels between the sonnet *Autumn Idleness* and *To Autumn*.[57] As in the case of Tennyson and Arnold, it is not so much a matter of phrasing here as an attitude towards the landscape which the two

---

52. W. Holman Hunt, *Pre-Raphaelitism and the Pre-Raphaelite Brotherhood*, I, 261.

53. I have referred only to the Keatsian and the Dantesque in connection with *The Blessed Damozel*. Baum mentions the possibility of another contributing influence: Bailey's *Festus*. Coleridge's poetry does not seem to have been a factor in this poem. James Routh (*op. cit.*, p. 222) who was searching for signs of Coleridge's influence, indicates only one point:

> And every soul, it pass'd me by,
> Like the whiz of my cross-bow!
> (*The Ancient Mariner*)

> And the souls mounting up to God
> Went by her like thin flames.
> (*The Blessed Damozel*)

54. See Rossetti's comment on Dante, p. 125 of this chapter.

55. *The Blessed Damozel* (ed. P. F. Baum), Introduction, p. xxxvi.

56. *Marginalia*, p. 9.

57. Hill Shine, *op. cit.*, pp. 192–3.

poets hold in common. Descriptions of nature are not frequent in Rossetti, but when his taste was for out-of-doors scenery, he could appreciate, as Arnold and Tennyson appreciated, the objectified rendering of landscape which the mature Keats gave in *To Autumn* and elsewhere. *Autumn Idleness* is in the same spirit:

> The sunlight shames November where he grieves
> In dead red leaves, and will not let him shun
> The day, though bough with bough be over-run.
> But with a blessing every glade receives
> High salutation; while from hillock-eaves
> The deer gaze calling, dappled white and dun. . . .

Without quite the freshness of the original, this is good nevertheless, and it is still another example of the way in which Keats's rendering of landscape anticipated the Victorians.

In describing an experience which he had in the British Museum when witnessing the arrival of "a winged beast from Nineveh," Rossetti was no doubt conscious that he would have to avoid imitating Keats's *Ode on a Grecian Urn*. The stone figure is hardly a thing of beauty and a joy for ever, but like the urn, it is a foster-child of silence and slow time and suggests similar associations with an age-old civilization. Perhaps with the object in mind of reinforcing his originality, Rossetti, in his first version of *The Burden of Nineveh*, broke away from the tone of Keats's ode by combining a sort of slap-stick humour with his reflections on antiquity.

> Here, while the Antique-students lunch,
> Shall Art be slang'd o'er cheese and hunch,
> Whether the great R. A.'s a bunch
> Of gods or dogs, or whether *Punch*
> Is right about the P. R. B.

This, as I noted in connection with *Eden Bower*, was not natural for Rossetti and he later tried to unify the poem by removing its humorous sections. Keats shows in *The Mermaid Tavern* and elsewhere that he can, when he wishes, write successful poetry with a note of fanciful humour. Throughout the *Ode on a Grecian Urn*, in keeping with the subject, is a much rarer element than humour, an element of what is meant today by "metaphysical wit."[58] Rossetti has none of it, and *The Burden of Nineveh* consequently never equals such things as:

> Thou, silent form, dost tease us out of thought
> As doth eternity: Cold Pastoral!

Keats's great lines have a juxtaposition of opposites which is delightful; it is not humour, but wit in the best sense of the word. Wit is

58. See Cleanth Brooks, *Modern Poetry and the Tradition*, Chapel Hill, 1938, pp. 237–8.

fundamentally serious and Keats's ode has real unity.[59] Humour is not serious of course, and because Rossetti can manage only a bouncing sort of humour he has to abandon it in the interests of unity. One thing he does manage extremely well, however, is that in his reflections on this ancient piece of sculpture he usually avoids echoing Keats's lines. What influences him most is devices. Keats addresses the urn with a series of questions:

> What men or gods are these? What maidens loth?

Rossetti likewise (italics mine):

> What song did the brown maidens sing,
> From *purple mouths* alternating,
>   When that was woven languidly?
> What vows, what rites, what prayers preferr'd,
> What songs has the strange image heard?
>   (*The Burden of Nineveh*, 23–7)

The first line may remind us of Sir Thomas Browne's *Urn Burial*,[60] the second of Keats, not however of the *Ode on a Grecian Urn* but rather the *Ode to a Nightingale*. The phrase "purple mouths" echoes Keats's choice lines:

> With beaded bubbles winking at the brim,
> And purple-stained mouth. . . .
>   (*Ode to a Nightingale*, ii)[61]

The parallel here is not far-fetched inasmuch as on another occasion Rossetti echoed the passage more directly (italics mine):

> And as I stooped, her own lips rising there
> *Bubbled* with *brimming* kisses at my *mouth*.

Significantly enough, he had to defend this particular Keatsian line when Buchanan attacked him in *The Fleshly School of Poetry*.[62]

Rossetti's poetry is not nearly so rich in figures of speech (especially metaphors) as that of Keats. One type of figure which he often employs, however, is personification, especially in his sonnets. As Baum observes, his method of making the figure appear natural, rather than "elevated" reminds us of Keats's *Ode on Melancholy* with its personifications of Joy, Pleasure and Melancholy.[63]

59. *Lamia* does not seem to be nearly so successful in this respect.
60. In chap. v of the *Urn Burial*, Browne begins his list of questions with the sentence: "What song the Syrens sang . . ." etc.
61. Hill Shine (*op. cit.*, p. 206) does not mention the two passages to which I refer, but cites a third in *Rose Mary* (italics mine):
    The drops run in from the *beaded brink*. . . .
62. *Works*, pp. 618–9 (*The Stealthy School of Criticism*).
63. *The House of Life* (ed. P. F. Baum), Introduction, p. 18. Cf. also Kurt Horn, *op. cit.*, p. 114. Sonnets I, XXIII, and LXXVII are good examples.

Of Keats's sonnets Rossetti had mixed opinions. He liked best the sonnet on Chapman's Homer and also *To Homer*. The first line of the latter he pronounced to be "the greatest line in Keats"[64] and in his poem *Found* he quotes it:

"There is a budding morrow in midnight:"—
So sang our Keats, our English nightingale.

Of actual influence there appears to be no trace. In the general resemblance between the two poets, their mutual concern with the sonnet is of interest. Garrod points out that Keats's odes develop from his experiments with expanded sonnets, and Baum has shown that *The Stream's Secret* is a "highly elaborated sonnet."[65] For the poet who likes to pack his "moment's monument" into the most concentrated forms, the sonnet (or its derivatives) is ideal.

There remains finally *Endymion,* which Rossetti happily described as "a magic toy, fit for the childhood of a divine poet."[66] Here, where discursiveness rather than concentration was the rule, Rossetti might not be expected to find much to his taste. In reality, knowing the poem well, he echoes some of its better passages on several occasions. Shine draws attention to a plausible parallel in the case of *Rose Mary,*[67] and there is another in the difficult lyric *Love's Nocturne* in which the lover calls upon Echo to whisper his words of love to the ear of his beloved one.[68]

Isolated words and expressions in *Endymion* which may have influenced Rossetti have been pointed out by others.[69] On this point in general, in view of Rossetti's habits of word-searching, one is not so apt to go astray in attributing parts of his poetic vocabulary to earlier writers as one is in the case of other poets who appear to borrow. Especially in *The House of Life* do we see signs of his expeditions to the British Museum. His habit was to search through old romances in order to "pitch upon stunning words for poetry."[70] Keatsian phrases appear there also:

Unto my lady still this harp *makes moan.*
(*The House of Life,* ix)

64. *Marginalia,* p. 8. For his comments on the sonnets in general, see *John Keats: Criticism and Comment,* p. 6 and p. 11.

65. On Garrod's point, see Arnold chapter, p. 83. On *The Stream's Secret,* cf. *Poems, Ballads, and Sonnets* (ed. P. F. Baum), Introduction, p. xxxv.

66. *Marginalia,* p. 2. His close reading of *Endymion* is apparent in his letters to Forman where he notes instances of deficient syllables, shifts in the rhyme-scheme and the like. (See *John Keats: Criticism and Comment,* pp. 5–7.)

67. Hill Shine (*op. cit.,* p. 208) compares *Endymion,* iv, 182–7 with *Rose Mary,* iii, 16–20. The plausibility of the parallel is increased by the fact that Rossetti regarded this part of *Endymion* as the "finest passage of poetry in the work" (*Marginalia,* p. 2).

68. Cf. *Endymion,* i, 947 ff. and *Love's Nocturne,* 1–5, 71–7, and 85–91.

69. For example, see Hill Shine, *op. cit.,* p. 207.

70. Joseph Knight, *Life of Dante Gabriel Rossetti,* London, 1887, p. 28.

The expression to "make moan" is all too common in Keats. It appears in *La Belle Dame,* in the *Ode to Psyche* and in *Isabella.* Rossetti, too, is overly-fond of having his lovers "moan."[71] With many of Keats's more effeminate phrases however he fortunately makes a complete break. In reading *Endymion* he remarked: " 'Orby,' 'Sphery,' and all such forms are execrable, and disfigure the poem throughout."[72]

For the most part, Rossetti's use of words resembles Keats's not so much in the matter of particular parallel expressions as in their general approach to vocabulary, in the fact that both found the romance of the dictionary.[73] To Keats, a dictionary was almost as exciting reading as Chapman's translation of Homer. With Rossetti a flair for fine phrases becomes more precious, more mannered. His highly decorative polysyllabic words and daring alliterative effects (especially with the consonant "w") make us conscious of the virtuoso, and virtuosity, as one writer notes, is the sign of an artist to whom form itself has become more important than the experience which he is trying to portray.[74] In his quest for ornamental perfection, Rossetti goes beyond Keats, developing the earlier poet's style along his own lines. Here, as in other respects, he acquires the device itself, taking his lead from Keats. As Elton notes:

In another of his favourite usages Rossetti follows Keats, who followed the Jacobeans. This is in the invention of pictorial or musical double compounds. . . . Such are *wind-warm, field-silence, osier-odoured, soul-winnowing . . . soft-littered.*[75]

Such a sonnet as *Through Death to Love* is fairly packed with compounds:

> —what angel-greeted door
> Or threshold of wing-winnowed threshing-floor
> Hath guest fire-fledged as thine, whose lord is Love?

The second line here recalls Keats's *To Autumn* which also abounds in such expressions as *stubble-plains* and *thatch-eves,* and includes the lines picturing Autumn:

71. See *Rose Mary,* II, 35: "the heart has since made heavy moan." Also *The Bride's Prelude,* 320: "To sit at gaze while I made moan," and 739: "till something made me moan."

72. *Marginalia,* p. 4.

73. According to William Rossetti: "His practice with poetry is first to write the thing in the rough, and then to turn over dictionaries of rhyme and synonyms so as to bring the poem into the most perfect form" (*Rossetti Papers,* p. 393).

74. Albert Guérard, *Art for Art's Sake,* New York, 1936, p. 59. Concerning Keats's importance in the revival of alliteration in nineteenth-century poetry, see George Saintsbury, *History of English Prosody,* London, 1910, III, 542.

75. Oliver Elton, *op. cit.,* II, 18. On Keats, see David Watson Rannie, "Keats's Epithets" in *Essays and Studies by Members of the English Association,* vol. III. See also *A Concordance to the Poems of John Keats,* p. xv. Keats used 258 different double compounds in his poetry.

Sometimes whoever seeks abroad may find
Thee sitting careless on a granary floor,
Thy hair soft-lifted by the winnowing wind. . . .

These double compounds are a sign not only of the virtuoso but of the artist who loves concentration. "One benefit I do derive . . . as a result of my method of composition" Rossetti remarked. "My work becomes condensed. Probably the man does not live who could write what I have written more briefly than I have done."[76] What he called a "flawless gift" in Keats,[77] was the gift of concentration. This does not mean simply that a narrative might not sprawl beyond one hundred lines; it meant that every line should be loaded with ore. He wrote to Caine in this connection: "You say an excellent thing when you ask, 'Where can we look for more poetry per page than Keats gives us?' "[78]

To conclude this account: I suggested that as Tennyson grew older and developed away from many aspects of his early likeness to Keats, he left the exploitation of the Keatsian "tradition" to other more receptive hands, which were not lacking in the later Victorian age. Of these, Rossetti's were the most important in the matter of torch-bearing. His poetry has often been said to mark a romantic renaissance. To be more specific, it marked a sort of Keatsian revival or renaissance, for with the other major romantic poets (except parts of Coleridge) Rossetti has little in common. We have seen how he reacted against Wordsworth and Shelley, and even Byron was not in his line. Generally speaking, much of Rossetti's style and his whole approach to poetic experience seems a natural development of some of the lines laid out by Keats in the second decade of the century.

In the matter of Keats's more specific influence, I have tried to show how Rossetti's determination to be original conflicted with his thorough knowledge of Keats and deep appreciation of both Keats's aesthetic sense and features of his technique. In spite of Rossetti's desire to be original, some influence was inevitable, but because of that desire, the influence is often very effectively concealed or appears under conditions strikingly different from those in Keats. It is for this reason that so much of Rossetti's poetry has the paradoxical quality of being both original and yet derivative. He borrows methods from Keats but often fuses them into something new and original of his own. Sometimes, as in *The Bride's Prelude*, the influence is obvious enough: at other times, we sense it in spite of its transformation under Rossetti's careful handling.

Of the more general impact of Keats on Rossetti's poetry, we

76. *Memoir*, I, 416.
77. Hall Caine, *Recollections* (1928), p. 180.
78. *Ibid.*, p. 119.

might refer to Baum's remark on Dante's influence: "Without Dante and his fellow poets 'The Blessed Damozel' would not have been what it is, could hardly have been written at all: yet the influence of Dante is vague and general, prevasive [sic] rather than precise."[79] The interesting question whether Rossetti would have been a poet at all if he had not read Keats can be waived here, but one thing is relatively certain. He would have been a very different poet.

Finally, as we have seen, Rossetti's taste as a reader was such that he could appreciate Keats with less reservation than his fellow-Victorians, and his role as a proselytizer is important. But, as a poet, although equipped to develop fully some of the motifs which Keats's work suggested, he was not equipped to expand and improve upon others. Instead, as was the habit of Tennyson, he narrowed the values for which Keats's poetry stood. "What is wrong with Rossetti?" asks Evelyn Waugh.[80] Like jesting Pilate we would not stay for an answer, but we may wonder why the question does not apply to Keats as well.

I suspect that it is more than a matter of the difference in the amount of time which has elapsed since the death of both poets, a time during which Keats's place has become fixed and Rossetti's remains much disputed. Pater's finely-phrased comment is useful here:

For Rossetti the great affections of persons to each other—swayed and determined, in the case of his highly pictorial genius, mainly by that so called "material" loveliness—formed the great undeniable reality in things, the solid resisting substance in a world where all beside might be but shadow.[81]

The implications of the statement apply in part to Keats as well, but with Rossetti that "shadow" has become perceptibly darker, and much more of the complexity of experience is obscured by it than in the case of Keats.

For one thing, while Rossetti followed up to the full Keats's "astonishingly real mediaevalism," he did not share the earlier poet's reverence for the "beautiful mythology of Greece" (as he called it in his Preface to Endymion). Fausset complains that the Pre-Raphaelites had no appreciation of Hyperion,[82] which is not entirely true. Rossetti called Hyperion the "crown of Keats's genius," and his comment on the poem is excellent in itself. Yet it is true that Hyperion left no mark on his poetry and further, that he scarcely ever touched upon mythological themes.[83]

79. The Blessed Damozel (ed. P. F. Baum), Introduction, p. xxxvi.
80. Evelyn Waugh, Rossetti. Heading for final chapter.
81. Walter Pater, Appreciations, London, 1920, p. 213.
82. Hugh I'Anson Fausset, Keats, p. 9.
83. See Douglas Bush, Mythology and the Romantic Tradition, p. 410. Rossetti's comment on Hyperion is on p. 5 of his Marginalia.

To admire but disregard *Hyperion* meant something more than abandoning the possibilities of mythological themes. Even in the version of the poem published in 1820 (the version which Rossetti knew)[84] there were signs that Keats was moving forward to what I called in an earlier chapter a "third stage" of beauty in which the poet, without becoming either a "Cassandra" or "Comrade," yet struggles to make his world include "the agony, the strife of human hearts." In arriving at such a conception, Keats demonstrated his great capacity to develop. One of the most astonishing features of Rossetti's artistic career, as Baum has noted, is that his work never developed.[85] He experimented with different styles from time to time, but he did not develop.

What seems to mark the dividing line between the qualities of the two poets is something hard to define but easy enough to sense. Both Rossetti and Keats might say with Walter de la Mare:

> Look thy last on all things lovely,
> Every hour. Let no night
> Seal thy sense in deathly slumber
> Till to delight
> Thou have paid thy utmost blessing. . . .

Yet the twist would be different in either poet. With Keats (as with many artists so strongly conscious of both beauty and death) the morbid often becomes dominant. The term "morbid" is an adjective misused by righteous readers, but it will serve to express a quality common to such poems as *Isabella* and the *Ode on Melancholy*. At his best, however, Keats is conscious of "*all* things lovely," and experience for him is fresh. With Rossetti, the freshness is rarer. It is as if everything has been said, and we are conscious in his poetry of what Waugh calls "a sonorous re-echoing of dark perceptions,"[86] in place of the fresh exploration of vivid perceptions which Keats gives in his best odes, or in the sonnet *On First Looking Into Chapman's Homer*.

This difference is reflected in the differences of style (aside from the more "mystical" element in Rossetti) between the two poets. We have seen how Rossetti developed some features of Keats's highly-wrought style. But he develops them to a point where often they simply obstruct communication between poem and reader. The following is exceptional:

> O love, my love! if I no more should see
> Thyself, nor on the earth the shadow of thee,

84. *The Fall of Hyperion: A Dream* was first issued in 1856 by Milnes. It was privately printed and the circulation seems to have been very limited. Fitzgerald, for example, who saw it first in manuscript form, never knew that it had been printed and was unable to get any information on the subject.

85. *Poems, Ballads, and Sonnets* (ed. P. F. Baum), Introduction, pp. xxi–xxii.

86. Evelyn Waugh, *op. cit.*, p. 156.

Nor image of thine eyes in any spring,—
How then should sound upon Life's darkening slope
The ground-whirl of the perished leaves of Hope,
The wind of Death's imperishable wing?
(*The House of Life*, IV)

That is in Rossetti's grand manner, and grand it is in the best sense of the word. But it is extremely rare. Usually the phrasing is obtrusive, and even the more chastened style of such pieces as *The Blessed Damozel*, although not obtrusive to the same extent, is almost equally conscious of itself.

If by comparison with Keats's work, Rossetti's seems more restricted in scope, it is nevertheless almost expansive by comparison with some of the poetry at the end of the century. He is the link between Keats and later writers, and through his example and influence, the Keatsian strain becomes predominant in later nineteenth-century poetry.

PART FOUR

MORRIS, SWINBURNE AND SOME OTHERS

Of Keats read everything. To like Keats is a test of fitness for understanding poetry, just as to like Shakespeare is a test of general mental capacity.

George Gissing, letter to his sister, 1885.

X

William Morris and His Masters

THE argument which had been waged between Gabriel Rossetti and his brother William over the relative merits of Keats and Shelley might easily have been duplicated in some conversation between Algernon Charles Swinburne and William Morris. Speaking of his Oxford days, Morris remarked: "Our clique was much influenced by Keats, who was a poet who represented semblances, as opposed to Shelley who had no eyes, and whose admiration was not critical but conventional."[1] When Swinburne was at Oxford in 1857, he fell under the spell of Morris, but in this matter of Keats and Shelley, he belonged to a different "clique." The two poets, who share with Rossetti the centre of the stage in Victorian poetry after 1870, present a revealing contrast in their attitude to Keats. I shall deal first with Morris.

If Morris did not know the poetry of Keats when he went up to Oxford in 1853 he would not long have been allowed to remain in this state of ignorance. His friends Fulford and Burne-Jones were both Keats enthusiasts, and like the Pre-Raphaelites a few years earlier, their group regarded an admiration of Keats as a sort of badge of membership.[2] R. W. Dixon, also of the group, used to "praise Keats by the hour."[3] According to Burne-Jones, when they visited the continent in 1855, "we took a volume of Keats with us, and no other book."[4]

Swinburne also entertained some youthful admiration for Keats, but it diminished as he grew older. Morris' boyish worship never changed. In 1894, after a furious dispute about which version of *La Belle Dame sans Merci* should be used, he brought out the Kelmscott edition of Keats's collected poetry, a tribute which he denied to Coleridge.[5] His vigorously-worded distinction between Keats and Coleridge is highly entertaining:

As to the Coleridge-Keats question, you don't quite understand the position. . . . Keats was a great poet who sometimes nodded: we don't want

1. *The Collected Works of William Morris*, London, 1910–15, XXII, Introduction, p. xxvi.
2. J. W. Mackail, *The Life of William Morris*, London, 1899, I, 39, 43.
3. *The Letters of Gerard Manley Hopkins to Richard Watson Dixon*, London, 1935, p. 6.
4. J. W. Mackail, *op. cit.*, p. 72. See also *Memorials of Edward Burne-Jones*, I, 112.
5. Concerning the *La Belle Dame* dispute, see *Coll. Works*, I, Introduction, p. xxv.

to make a *selection* of his works. Coleridge was a muddle-brained meta-physician, who by some strange freak of fortune turned out a few real poems amongst the dreary flood of inanity which was his wont. It is these real poems only that must be selected. . . . Christabel only just comes in because the detail is fine; but nothing a hair's breadth worse must be admitted. There is absolutely no difficulty in choosing, because the difference between his poetry and his drivel is so striking.[6]

He then names four poems of his choosing and a fifth possibility, about which he is somewhat doubtful because it is "rather tainted with Wordsworthianism."

Wordsworth and Coleridge were only two of the many idols of English literature toppled off their pedestals by Morris' blunt independence. According to Mackail, he was an omnivorous reader,[7] but few readers have been so difficult to satisfy. He was even more particular than Matthew Arnold. Keats and Chaucer were perhaps the only English poets who satisfied him permanently and whole-heartedly. Like Rossetti, he was not much attracted to Spenser and other Elizabethans, and he despised Milton. Of Milton he wrote: "The union in his works of cold classicalism with Puritanism (the two things which I hate most in the world) repels me so that I *cannot* read him."[8] Even Shakespeare, whose *Troilus and Cressida* may have influenced Morris' *Scenes from the Fall of Troy*, did not attract much of his attention.[9]

Although he was more at home in the poetry of the nineteenth century, Morris was still highly critical. At an early age he had read Scott extensively, but Byron did not interest him in the least.[10] Scawen Blunt tells an amusing story in this connection: "Morris was very dogmatic, with violent likes and dislikes . . . and of the work of those he was averse to, he would pretend never to have read a word." On one occasion, someone quoted to him the lines:

> There was a sound of revelry by night
> And Belgium's Capital had gathered then
> Her Beauty and her Chivalry. . . .

"This he [Morris] declared to be rubbish, and that he had not a notion whom they were by."[11]

Shelley also was not to his liking, not only because he had "no eyes" but because he lacked the human touch. Like Rossetti and

6. J. W. Mackail, *op. cit.*, II, 310.
7. *Ibid.*, I, 38.
8. *Coll. Works*, XXII, Introduction, p. xv.
9. *Ibid.*, p. xxxi. "Shakespeare did not much attract me, as I have not much sympathy with the dramatic form."
10. *Ibid.*, "I never read Byron; even now I have only read Don Juan, the Vision of Judgment, and Cain, which I consider a fine piece."
11. Wilfred Scawen Blunt, *My Diaries*, New York, 1931, I, 25.

Tennyson, Morris' tastes were too earth-bound to enable him to participate to the full, as Swinburne could, in the flight of the skylark. He complained that *To a Skylark* "doesn't bring up any thoughts of humanity."[12]

Browning, by contrast, provided these "thoughts of humanity" which were lacking in Shelley, and Morris ranked him among his few favourites.[13] In his early writings he was profoundly influenced by Browning.[14] Yet after *The Defence of Guenevere* volume, Morris' interest in Browning diminished, and for that poet's later work he had little regard.[15] So too with Tennyson. After *Maud*, he lost interest in a poet who had for some time aroused his "defiant admiration."[16] At Oxford he had perceived limitations even in the early poems. "Tennyson's Sir Galahad is rather a mild youth" he said.[17] Such limitations were all too obvious in the *Idylls of the King*, and when Morris expressed his scorn of this bowdlerizing of Malory, Tennyson never forgave him.[18]

Rossetti's poetry also appealed to him strongly for a period, and according to Morris himself, the influence did him "a great deal of good."[19] Yet by 1870, when he reviewed Rossetti's poems in *The Academy*, it was obvious enough that Morris was not satisfied with much of what his "master" had written. A recurring charge in the review is that the author of *The House of Life* is wilfully obscure.[20] Of other Victorian poets Morris has left little record. Swinburne (except in a few early poems) was not to his taste,[21] and Arnold he never mentions.

So far as is known, at no time did Morris see fit to take exception to anything in Keats, and he always held him to be "the first of modern English poets."[22] Such an estimate would have little significance coming from the type of reader who exclaims every time he reads a

12. J. W. Mackail, *op. cit.*, I, 57.
13. In reviewing Browning's *Men and Women* Morris stated: ". . . I place Robert Browning . . . high among the poets of all time, and I scarce know whether first, or second, in our own" (*Coll. Works*, I, 347). Browning's influence on Morris has been traced by R. G. Watkin in a rather disappointing essay, *Robert Browning and the English Pre-Raphaelites*, Breslau, 1905, pp. 52–7.
14. "As artists, Keats and Tennyson—the early miraculous Tennyson—meant more to him; but in Browning he found an influence even more stimulating, a keenness of delight in life, a directness and vividness in realizing and grasping life such as he was now [1855] finding in himself" (J. W. Mackail, *William Morris and His Circle*, Oxford, 1907, p. 9).
15. J. W. Mackail, *Life*, I, 219.
16. *Ibid.*, p. 45.
17. *Ibid.*, p. 45.
18. Wilfred Scawen Blunt, *op. cit.*, I, 229.
19. *Coll. Works*, XXII, Introduction, p. xxxi.
20. Cf. May Morris, *William Morris: Artist, Writer, Socialist*, Oxford, 1936, I, 102–03.
21. ". . . I never could really sympathize with Swinburne's work; it always seemed to me to be founded on literature, not on nature" (J. W. Mackail, *Life*, II, 74).
22. J. W. Mackail, *Life*, I, 219.

new book: "This is the finest work I've ever read!" Coming from one as particular as Morris, it represents perhaps the highest compliment paid to Keats by any Victorian reader.

Of more interest, however, is a statement which Morris made in a letter to Keats's early friend, Charles Cowden Clarke. In 1870 Clarke had written to him: ". . . I am sure that you would not have had a more devoted admirer, and Brother in the faith of Love and Beauty, than in . . . John Keats. . . ." In reply, Morris spoke of "Keats, for whom I have such boundless admiration, and whom I venture to call one of my masters."[23]

As Mackail notes, the word "master" is one which Morris did not use freely.[24] He reserved it for Chaucer and Ruskin, and, at one time, for Rossetti. According to Mackail, Keats's influence on Morris is such that he is an even more important master to him than Chaucer was. "It will be easily recognized that while the world which he elected to make his own was largely that of Chaucer, his poetical affinities were with Keats more than with any other poet."[25]

These are the words of a very distinguished and level-headed reader of Morris, yet no one seems to have followed up the suggestion nor does Mackail himself bring forward any evidence to support it. That Keats was Morris' favourite poet since Chaucer is clear enough; but whether Keats actually influenced his poetry is not an easy matter to discover. He once told S. C. Cockerell that *La Belle Dame sans Merci* "was the germ from which all the poetry of his group had sprung."[26] This is a useful hint but it is not the whole story. Next to Browning, Morris is, in many respects, the most original of Victorian poets. His originality was apparent even in his earliest volume. Several poems in *The Defence of Guenevere* owe something to thirteenth and fourteenth century romances,[27] but Swinburne (who knew of this) was not far wrong when he said that its author "held of none, stole from none, clung to none, as tenant, or as beggar, or as thief."[28] According to Tinker, "an investigation of its 'sources' hardly repays the effort that must be expended upon it."[29] Certainly in few other poets are we less conscious of lines or phrases which seem to echo earlier writers.

The reason for this lack of echoes gives us a clue to Morris' method of reading Keats. In reading and writing alike, Morris did not "look upon fine phrases like a lover." Keats's faculty of packing a world of

23. J. W. Mackail, *Life*, I, 200.
24. J. W. Mackail, *William Morris and His Circle*, p. 9.
25. J. W. Mackail, *Life*, I, 200.
26. Sidney Colvin, *John Keats*, New York, 1917, p. 470.
27. See Georges Lafourcade, *La jeunesse de Swinburne*, Paris, 1928, II, 41.
28. J. W. Mackail, *Life*, I, 131.
29. Chauncey B. Tinker and Carl P. Rollins, *Addresses Commemorating the One Hundredth Anniversary of the Birth of William Morris*, Overbrook Press, 1935, p. 12.

suggestiveness into a single line constituted one of the principal attractions of his poetry for most Victorian readers. To Morris, such a faculty was of no great importance. He valued Keats for other reasons, and his appreciation of the earlier poet is therefore as unique as was Rossetti's along a different line.

More perhaps than any other poet, Keats is responsible for the "touchstone" method of reading poetry. In one of his letters, he remarks how "any one grand and spiritual passage of poetry" can serve a mature reader "as a starting-post towards all 'the two-and-thirty Palaces.' "[30] His letters abound in allusions to such passages, in casual references to Shakespeare, for example, to which his initiated friends would be expected to respond. These have been the stock-in-trade of the literary letter-writer, but Keats, of course, did more. He created touchstones of his own which have stamped themselves on later generations. Perhaps the choicest sample for most Victorians is to be found in the *Ode to a Nightingale*. "What I most love" said Burne-Jones, "are little things . . . that make me tingle every time I say them—whereof the crown and ensample are those piercing ones,

> Magic casements, opening on the foam
> Of perilous seas, in faery lands forlorn."[31]

Tennyson, as we have seen, referred to these same "wild and wonderful" lines as "the last perfection" and cited them to show the superiority of Keats to Coleridge.[32] Watts-Dunton mentions that he himself could never read them without his voice quavering with emotion. "The finest in English poetry" he called them.[33] How would Morris react to such a passage? In all probability he would be unlikely to retain it in his memory as an isolated touchstone, a key to the poem itself. For him the whole poem was the important thing. The rich phrasing of a particular passage merged into a total impression, which he retained, but the touchstone itself, except in rare instances, was not likely to remain with him. His personal letters give evidence of this. Never do we find allusions of the kind common to a literary man writing to his friends. He refers seldom enough to poets, but never to particular lines. On the occasion which Scawen Blunt describes when Morris failed to recognize the two best-known lines of Byron, he may, perhaps, have been posing.[34] But the pose was very close to his real character.

30. *Letters of Keats*, p. 103.
31. *Memorials of Edward Burne-Jones*, ii, 264.
32. *The Diary of William Allingham*, p. 327.
33. T. Watts-Dunton, *Old Familiar Faces*, London, 1916, p. 7.
34. See p. 150 of this chapter. According to May Morris, her father's unpublished correspondence is also lacking in literary allusions. Cf. B. Ifor Evans, *English Poetry in the Later Nineteenth Century*, p. 101.

Morris' indifference to fine phrases had several important effects on his own poetry. It made his work the least "quotable" of any ranking poet of the century. One cannot call up the mood of *Jason* by citing a few touchstone passages. In the first place, one is quite likely not to remember any. There is a genuine democracy about Morris' verse. It is on a good average level, but its parts almost never stand out. One can occasionally recall the peculiar music of some of his lyrics:

> Christ keep the Hollow Land
> All the summer-tide;
> Still we cannot understand
> Where the waters glide. . . .

The Defence of Guenevere also has some memorable passages, but the rest of his writing has the same lack of distinctive small units as has the tapestry-work to which it has been so often compared. The length and even tempo of *The Earthly Paradise* make the reader feel, as G. K. Chesterton says, like a fly crawling across a wall-paper.[35] Burne-Jones, who preferred the Keatsian purple passages, drew attention to their absence in the work of his friend:

As to Morris's poetry . . . you cannot find short quotations in him, he must be taken in great gulps. Chaucer is very much the same sort of person as Morris. . . . They are neither of them typical artists—typical poets but not typical artists.[36]

Unless a radical shift of taste occurs, Morris' poetry will always suffer more neglect than it deserves, owing to its lack of Keatsian fine passages. Of *The Earthly Paradise* tales he himself remarked in a letter to Swinburne: "Yet they are all too long and flabby, damn it!"[37] On this score, he was unable to profit, as Rossetti and Tennyson had profited, from the example of Keats. On the other hand, one great benefit Morris did derive from his want of interest in touchstones was his remarkable originality. Rossetti and Arnold had to struggle against a tendency to echo Keats's phrasing directly. Morris underwent no such struggle.

Inevitably, of course, there would be in his work occasional echoes of Keats's expressions. Miss Maud Bodkin draws attention to one example in the well-known lyric *A Garden by the Sea:*

> And though within it no birds sing
> And though no pillar'd house is there
> And though the apple boughs are bare
> Of fruit and blossom. . . .

35. G. K. Chesterton, *Chaucer*, London, 1940, pp. 156–7.
36. *Memorials of Edward Burne-Jones*, ii, 265.
37. Letter to Swinburne, Dec. 21, 1869 (May Morris, *William Morris*, i, 642).

The phrase "no birds sing" recalls Keats's *La Belle Dame sans Merci,* and this association gives an added effect to the blending of luxuriance and mortality which characterizes the poem.[38] Again, a stanza in *Rapunzel* shows an echo of Keatsian phrasing:

> If it would please God make you sing again,
>   I think that I might very sweetly die,
> My soul somehow reach heaven in joyous pain,
>   My heavy body on the beech-nuts lie.
>   (*Coll. Works,* I, 67)

In the *Ode to a Nightingale,* Keats writes of the effect of the bird's song on him:

> Now more than ever seems it rich to die,
>   To cease upon the midnight with no pain,
>   While thou art pouring forth thy soul abroad
>   In such an ecstasy!
> Still wouldst thou sing, and I have ears in vain—
>   To thy high requiem become a sod.

But these are rare instances. Morris' method of reading saved him from fears of appearing derivative. If he did sometimes find that he was echoing an earlier poet too closely, his method seems to have been either to cancel the passage or write it over again completely. Rossetti's habit of carefully working over his lines was not to Morris' liking.[39] In writing *The Earthly Paradise* for example, he described a character in terms obviously too closely reminiscent of Chaucer's *Prologue:*

> I trow a right fat man was he,
> He had a brown face and eyen white;
> His red hair in the sun shone bright;
> He was as fierce as any knight.
> I trow that in the town council
> Always for hanging spoke he well,
> If men debated on some thief.[40]

Instead of trying to iron out the Chaucerisms here, Morris simply cancelled the passage altogether.

May Morris mentions a theory of her father's about the best way of using source material for such stories as those in *The Earthly Paradise.* "When you are using an old story" he said, "read it through, then shut the book and write in your own way."[41] In the case of his

---

38. Maud Bodkin, *Archetypal Patterns in Poetry,* London, 1934, pp. 117–8.
39. "When he was dissatisfied with a poem, he wrote it afresh, or wrote another instead of it" (J. W. Mackail, *Life,* I, 52).
40. Reprinted in *Coll. Works,* III, Introduction, p. xvii.
41. *Ibid.,* p. xxii.

"masters" in poetry, as well as with these old stories, Morris shut up the books and wrote in his own way. What he retained, then, from such a poet as Keats was not key phrases but such other things as types of versification, tone, methods of handling a narrative. And in these spheres Keats does serve as Morris' master.

Keats represented for Morris one of the few great English poets who wrote narrative verse, and it was in this role that he had a special appeal for the author of *The Earthly Paradise*. "I abominate introspective poetry"[42] he wrote, and by "introspection" he meant not only the intrusion of the subjective into poetry but the intrusion of any form of allegory. Morris believed in the story for the story's sake. When someone asked him what one of his poems "meant" he became indignant. "I told him I meant what I said in writing;" he said, "and you know, my dear, Wordsworth's primrose by the river's brim is quite good enough for me in itself; what on earth more did the man want it to be?"[43] In spite of later excursions into socialism, Morris' fundamental conception of the role of poetry is well represented in the familiar *Apology:*

> Dreamer of dreams, born out of my due time,
> Why should I strive to set the crooked straight?
> Let it suffice me that my murmuring rhyme
> Beats with light wing against the ivory gate,
> Telling a tale not too importunate
> To those who in the sleepy region stay,
> Lulled by the singer of an empty day.

Keats is never so completely detached as Morris is, but more than any other major poet, he avoids using verse as a vehicle to set the crooked straight. One can search for "meanings" in *Endymion, Lamia* and *Hyperion,* but they are never so obtrusive as in *Prometheus Unbound* or even in the *Idylls of the King.* Morris was able to read Keats's stories as stories and to appreciate them as such. Ruskin was not entirely justified when he coupled Keats's handling of mythological tales with that of Morris,[44] yet of all nineteenth-century mythological poets Keats comes closer to Morris than does any other. Morris learned many lessons from his predecessor's pictorial treatment of myth.

Although Morris went far beyond Keats in making his stories detached, he followed very closely Keats's method of making his stories pictorial. In his rather startling study of Morris, Dixon Scott makes the statement that although Morris is a great poet, he is not a great

42. Quoted by B. Ifor Evans, *op. cit.,* p. 100.
43. May Morris, *op. cit.,* I, 430.
44. *Coll. Works,* II, Introduction, pp. xvii–xviii.

narrative poet.[45] I myself share this heresy and believe the same charge applies to Keats. Morris said that his own poems were "of the nature of a series of pictures"[46] and like the "first Pre-Raphaelite poet," he fills in every item of his pictures so that the narrative becomes obscured. Even in the more terse stories of the *Defence of Guenevere* volume, we are conscious of the author's greater interest in scene than in action:

> Along the dripping leafless woods,
> The stirrup touching either shoe,
> She rode astride as troopers do;
> With kirtle kilted to her knee,
> To which the mud splash'd wretchedly. . . .[47]

That is as original as anything in the book, but it is also evidence of how Morris is committed to the Keatsian method of story-telling.

Much better examples occur in *The Life and Death of Jason* and other later poems. *The Defence of Guenevere* collection is in many respects much less close to Keats. Take, for example, this passage from *Sir Peter Harpdon's End*:

> . . . once a-going home,
> Without my servants, and a little drunk,
> At midnight through the lone dim lamp-lit streets,
> A whore came up and spat into my eyes. . . .

Morris' mediaevalism in *The Defence of Guenevere* is in a class by itself. His early interest in the Middle Ages as the ideal setting for poetry[48] was reinforced by the practice of Keats, and sometimes, as in *Golden Wings*, we may be reminded of Keats or Tennyson. This early volume has, however, a note of its own. Most of the poems are, if anything, closer to Browning and occasionally to Poe. Keats, in *The Eve of St. Agnes*, had pictured the colour of the Middle Ages and in *La Belle Dame* opened up a world of mystery. Morris was indebted to Keats's example, but he went beyond this to explore the passion and brutality of mediaeval life.[49] We are, of course, conscious of Keatsian colour effects in *The Defence of Guenevere*, but there is little sign of actual derivation:

45. Dixon Scott, *Men of Letters*, London, 1917, p. 281.
46. *Coll. Works*, xxii, Introduction, p. xxxii.
47. *The Haystack in the Floods*. This particular example was drawn to my attention by E. K. Brown. See also A. Clutton-Brock, *William Morris*, London, 1931, p. 84.
48. In spite of his socialism, Morris retained this view to the last. When lecturing on the Pre-Raphaelites in 1891 he said: "When an artist has really a very keen sense of beauty, I venture to think that he can not literally represent an event that takes place in modern life. He must add something to qualify or soften the ugliness and sordidness of life in our generation" (May Morris, *William Morris*, 1, 304).
49. Concerning the originality of Morris, see Elisabet C. Kuster, *Mittelalter und Antike bei William Morris*, Berlin, 1928, p. 50.

> And every morn I scarce could pray at all,
>   For Launcelot's red-golden hair would play,
> Instead of sunlight, on the painted wall,
>   Mingled with dreams of what the priest did say. . . .
>   (*King Arthur's Tomb*, I, 20)

Dixon Scott is of a different opinion. *The Eve of St. Agnes* he says, served Morris as "raw material" in several of his poems. Scott takes, for an example, the stanza describing the casement in Madeline's chamber:

The coloured light that splashes these pages of *Guenevere* drew much of its splendour from those dyes: yet in all that stanza of Keats there is not one cardinal word that Morris himself ever used. He thrust through the writing to the solid substance itself, to the gules and traceried stone—stacked these in the Aladdin's cave of his memory . . . and then, when the time came to use it . . . he had mapped the carven casement out afresh:—

> Because it seemed a dwelling for a queen,
>   No belfry for the swinging of great bells,
> No bolt or stone that ever crush'd the green
>   Shafts, amber and rose walls, no soot that tells
> Of the Norse torches burning up the roofs
>   On the flower-carven marble could I see. . . .[50]

I cite this passage because it represents the only account of which I know where Keats's influence is considered and explained. Yet the example itself is hardly convincing. That Morris thought in terms of pictures rather than phrases is true, but it is in his later, weaker volumes, that Keats-like pictures seem more prevalent. Generally speaking, *The Defence of Guenevere* has a fire in it which suggests that its author could have developed where Keats left off in 1820. Morris never fulfilled that early promise. Instead his next volume seems to return to the style of the earlier Keats. The leisurely-moving *Jason* reminds us of *Endymion* rather than of the most mature work of the poet Morris called his master.

The versification of *The Earthly Paradise* and of *The Life and Death of Jason* owes much to Keats. Morris was never attracted to the Spenserian stanza as a narrative-medium, and blank verse he despised. He remarked to Watts-Dunton that "the use of blank verse as a poetic medium ought to be stopped by Act of Parliament for at least two generations."[51] Instead, he turned to two measures both of which had been developed by Keats. In *Jason*, in most of *The Earthly Paradise* and *Love is Enough* he employs a loose heroic couplet. He uses it as Keats used it in *Endymion* and *Lamia*, that is, with consid-

50. Dixon Scott, *op. cit.*, p. 289. (The passage is from *Rapunzel.*)
51. T. Watts-Dunton, *op. cit.*, p. 248.

erable enjambment to secure variety. According to Saintsbury, Morris was able to profit by some of Keats's errors in handling heroics,[52] and indeed the standard of craftsmanship is higher than in *Endymion*. There are still many "pouncing rhymes," however, which illustrate the dangers of the medium.[53]

In several tales of *The Earthly Paradise* Morris uses a shorter couplet, the octosyllabic, in place of the prevailing heroics. Saintsbury has pointed out that here again Morris was profiting from the example of Keats.[54] In *The Ring Given to Venus* there is an analogy not only of versification but of the atmosphere of *The Eve of St. Mark*. Morris describes a minster-close where a wedding procession is in progress. The first line of the passage reminds us directly of Keats's *Eve of St. Agnes* (italics mine):

> Innumerable of *stains and splendid dyes*,
> As are the *tiger-moth's deep-damask'd wings*,

but the atmosphere calls up *The Eve of St. Mark*. Morris writes:

> Such dyes as stain the parrot's wing,
> The May-flowers or the evening sky,
> Made bright the silken tapestry . . .
> . . . silken webs from some far shore,
> Whereon were pictured *images*
> Of *other beasts* and other trees
> *And other birds than these men knew.* . . .
> (*Coll. Works*, vi, 139–40)

Morris recalls from Keats not phrases but pictures. In *The Eve of St. Mark*, the beasts and birds were described by name:

> . . . doves of Siam, Lima mice,
> And legless birds of Paradise,
> Macaw, and tender Av'davat. . . .
> (*The Eve of St. Mark*, 79–81)

Morris' memory would not have stored up such phrases: he would have remembered the scene itself.

So too in other instances. A good example occurs in Book vi of *The Life and Death of Jason*. Morris had the same delight as his predecessor in describing luxurious banquet-scenes. The hall in the palace of King Æetes is as wonder-provoking to the mariners as is the hall in Lamia's palace to the citizens of Corinth:

52. George Saintsbury, *A History of English Prosody*, iii, 323.
53. For example: And streets of well-built towns, with trembling seas
      About their marble wharves and palaces. . . .
      (*Coll. Works*, ii, 96–7)
54. G. Saintsbury, *op. cit.*, p. 325.

The pillars, made the mighty roof to hold,
The one was silver and the next was gold
All down the hall; the roof, of some strange wood
Brought over sea, was dyed as red as blood,
Set thick with silver flowers, and delight
Of interwining figures wrought aright.

(*Coll. Works*, II, 98)

In Book II of *Lamia*, Keats had also pictured a "roof of awful richness" and walls hung with "splendid draperies," but most interestingly, he conveyed an impression of spaciousness by describing alternating pillars down the hall:

The glowing banquet-room shone with wide-arched grace.
A haunting music, sole perhaps and lone
Supportress of the faery-roof, made moan
Throughout, as fearful the whole charm might fade.
Fresh carved cedar, mimicking a glade
Of palm and plantain, met from either side,
High in the midst, in honour of the bride:
Two palms and then two plantains, and so on. . . .

(*Lamia*, II, 121–8)

It is as if Morris had seen the banquet-room as Keats saw it, then, as he said, "shut up the book" and recreated it anew:

. . . and strange dainty things they ate,
Of unused savour, and drank godlike wine;
While from the golden galleries, most divine
Heart-softening music breathed about the place;
And 'twixt the pillars, at a gentle pace,
Passed lovely damsels, raising voices sweet
And shrill unto the music, while their feet
From thin dusk raiment now and then would gleam
Upon the polished edges of the stream.

(*Coll. Works*, II, 98)

Lamia's feast was also an "earthly paradise," a palace of polished marble in which "beautiful slaves" passed in and out amid strains of music mingling with human voices while the wondering guests feasted on strange foods and wines.[55]

Morris' capacity to write poetry with his proverbial facility and speed may be attributed, in part, to a memory stored with pictures from reading, pictures which had flashed upon that inward eye which is the bliss of the artist's solitude.

The influence of Keats on *The Earthly Paradise* is not always beneficial. Both Morris and Keats, in introducing their longest poems,

55. See *Lamia*, II, 172–90; 204–10; 215–20; and I, 380–4.

hailed Chaucer as their master. Morris' two invocations may remind us of Keats's wish:

> . . . that I may dare, in wayfaring,
> To stammer where old Chaucer used to sing.
> (*Endymion*, i, 133–4)

From Chaucer, Morris may have taken over his device of a story-telling framework and also something of the pace of a Chaucerian narrative. But it is Keats rather than Chaucer who is the more responsible for the style of both *Jason* and *The Earthly Paradise*. The resemblance is especially noticeable in the many passages where the effects of love are described, as for example, when Jason meets Medea:

> Her fair face reddened, and there went and came
> *Delicious* tremors through her. . . .
> As with the cup he touched *her dainty hand,*
> Nor was *she loth awhile* with him to stand,
> Forgetting all else in *that honied pain.*
> (*Coll. Works*, ii, 101–2. Italics mine)

In *Troilus and Criseyde* and elsewhere, Chaucer had dwelt on the conventional love gestures, but the tone is very different:

> And therewithal he bleynte and cride, "A!"
> As though he stongen were unto the herte.
> (*Knight's Tale*, 1078–9)

Morris' adjectives "dainty," and "honied," and "delicious" call up the atmosphere of *Endymion*. One of the things which we miss most, in passing from Guenevere to Medea, is that Morris somehow lost the art of delineating stark passions. Instead, everything is softened down to the level of the sighing lovers of *Endymion*. A better example occurs in *The Land East of the Sun and West of the Moon*:

> But round
> His *fluttering heart* her arms she wound,
> And kissed his *pale cheeks* red again,
> And hung above *his lovesome pain.* . . .
> His *parched mouth* felt her *odorous breath,*
> His weary burning head did rest
> Upon the heaven of her sweet breast,
> His *mazed* ears heard her *tender speech.* . . .
> (*Coll. Works*, v, 118. Italics mine)

The theme of the dream and metamorphosis of the lover in *The Land East of the Sun and West of the Moon* has an interesting analogy with that of Keats's poem, but it is in the descriptions of love-making that the resemblance is most noticeable. A typical example from Keats's poem will illustrate:

Stretching his indolent arms, he took, O bliss!
A naked waist. . . .
At which soft ravishment, with doating cry
They trembled to each other. . . .
"O known Unknown! from whom my being sips
Such darling essence, wherefore may I not
Be ever in these arms?"
(*Endymion*, II, 712–41)

Morris himself remarked that although Chaucer's poetry had considerable effect on his own, he was not affected by Chaucer's style. "In fact I cannot think that I ever consciously aimed at any particular style."[56] Unconsciously perhaps, when writing some of the poems which he published in the Sixties, he was attracted to a Keatsian style as well as to Keatsian versification. Here, for once, not only the descriptions remained with him but a tone of description as well.

By 1876 however, when *Sigurd the Volsung* appeared, it was apparent that Morris had broken away from Keats and from many aspects of mediaevalism itself. *Sigurd* is of interest here only insofar as it shows a certain parallelism between Morris' development and that of his predecessor. This point has been noted by Miss Bodkin:

We may perhaps compare Morris's visit to Iceland with that of Keats to the Scottish mountains. Although Keats's journey appears as a less momentous incident in the history of his soul than was that of Morris, yet when Keats visited the mountains, desiring thereby to "strengthen" his "reach in Poetry," he seems to have found there images that called forth and helped to actualize sterner elements of his character than had yet found expression in his verse.[57]

Both poets, after their respective trips, turned from romance to epic. In the Icelandic sagas, Morris found a mythology in keeping with his own Northern vigour, and Keats found in his Titans a symbol of mighty struggle which his earlier love-stories could not give. Finally, both poets later abandon the epic and return at the last to something approximating romance.

From many points of view, Morris was the Victorian poet best equipped to carry on where Keats left off. Unlike Rossetti and Tennyson, he did not share to the full Keats's sense of fine phrasing, but more than either of them, he was aware of the freshness of Keats. Chesterton said of him that he was "the first of the Aesthetes to smell mediaevalism as a smell of the morning; and not as a mere scent of decay."[58] The fascinating vigour of Morris' personality leads us to

56. J. W. Mackail, *Life*, I, 197.
57. Maud Bodkin, *op. cit.*, p. 119. See also C. H. Herford, "Mountain Scenery in Keats," in *Keats Memorial Volume*, London, 1921, pp. 96–104.
58. G. K. Chesterton, *The Victorian Age in Literature*, p. 200.

imagine that he would have sensed Keats's poetry in the same way. Yet as a poet, as heir to Keats, Morris is disappointing just as Rossetti, if considered in the same light, is disappointing. In a sense, Rossetti took poetry *too* seriously: Morris did not take it seriously enough. I do not subscribe to the legend (perpetrated by those who never read Morris closely) that he was an amateur dabbler in poetry. He was, on the contrary, a highly-skilled craftsman. The difference may be indicated by comparing Morris' celebrated remark about how easy poetry is to write with Keats's oft-repeated complaints that poetic composition left him in a state of exhaustion and fever.[59] After *The Defence of Guenevere* volume, Morris writes as if he were afraid of such exhaustion and fever. According to Middleton Murry, it was the very greatness of Keats's accomplishment that was directly responsible for Morris' attitude. Keats's success, says Murry, discouraged Morris by convincing him that there was little more that could be done in great poetry, and he therefore "had the splendid sanity not to take himself very seriously as a poet."[60] There is some truth in Murry's point that Keats discouraged his successor, but few would regard Morris' attitude as an example of "splendid sanity."

On the other hand, Morris contributed mightily to the Victorian revival of Keats. In spite of his distinct originality, his two most popular works are stamped with the mark of his master in versification, in tone, in handling of pictorial narrative, and sometimes even in phrasing. Like Rossetti, but unlike Swinburne, he is part of the "Keats tradition." As Cowden Clarke asserted when he wrote to Morris in 1870: "I am sure that you would not have had a more devoted admirer, and Brother in the faith of Love and Beauty, than in my beloved friend and schoolfellow, John Keats. . . ."

59. After writing what is sometimes thought to have been his first poem, Morris exclaimed: "Well, if this is poetry, it is very easy to write" (J. W. Mackail, *Life*, I, 52). It is likely, however, that Morris had to struggle at first to reach perfection. Smoothness came only later.
60. *The Great Victorians* (ed. H. J. and Hugh Massingham), London, 1938, II, 330.

XI

Swinburne

WHEN Swinburne's *Atalanta in Calydon* appeared in 1865, a reviewer writing for the *Athenaeum* pronounced that it might be linked with the poetry of Keats.[1] This sort of linking seems to have become almost commonplace in Victorian criticism. It had been applied to Tennyson, Coventry Patmore, Sidney Dobell, Alexander Smith, Morris and Dante Gabriel Rossetti, in each case with some considerable justification. In the case of Swinburne it was much less appropriate. Somewhat in the manner of Arnold, Swinburne took exception to the place which Keats held in the affections of his contemporaries and he attempted to avoid Keats's influence. Like war, literary taste sometimes makes strange bedfellows. We do not often speak of Swinburne and Matthew Arnold in the same breath, yet with respect to Keats the two poets have much in common. I suggested earlier that amidst the swelling chorus of praise which the later Victorians accord to Keats, the voice of Matthew Arnold sounds like a discordant croak. Almost equally discordant is the shrill shriek of Swinburne.

Keats's effect on Swinburne has been examined in a very able and scholarly essay by Georges Lafourcade,[2] and I therefore do not propose to treat their relationship in much detail beyond aligning it with the present study as a whole.

Swinburne's principal comment on Keats is contained in an article which he wrote for the *Encyclopaedia Britannica* in 1881.[3] Had it been written at an earlier date, it would have been considerably more favourable. During the ten-year period from 1857 to 1867,[4] Swinburne was strongly under the influence of the Pre-Raphaelite poets to whom Keats was a master and model, and, at that time, his own estimate of Keats would have been coloured by theirs. In 1867 for example, he took strong exception to Matthew Arnold's coupling of Keats with such an unimportant writer as Maurice de Guérin. Guérin, he shows, is in the minor rank of writers together with such poets as Gray and Cowper. Keats is a giant by comparison, one who was "able

1. *The Athenaeum*, no. 1953 (1865), p. 281.
2. Georges Lafourcade, *Swinburne's Hyperion and Other Poems: With an Essay on Swinburne and Keats*, London, 1927. (In subsequent notes, this work is referred to as *Essay*.)
3. It was published in 1882 and is reprinted in Swinburne's collected works.
4. Georges Lafourcade, *La jeunesse de Swinburne*, Paris, 1928, I, 144, and II, 38–9.

to do for nature what in his own day Shelley could not achieve nor Wordsworth attempt; above all Greece and all Italy and all England in his own line and field of work." In this field, he says, "all the giants and all the gods of art would fail to stand against him for an hour. . . ."[5]

During this same period Keats's poetry had some influence on Swinburne's own, both indirectly through the examples of Morris and Rossetti, and directly through his study of Keats's work. Lafourcade has shown how Swinburne in 1857 deliberately engaged in a series of "prosodic exercises" modelled on other poets in order to acquire facility and high literary finish.[6] One of the most interesting of these exercises was his *Hyperion*, in which, like a veritable mocking-bird, he copies Keats's story and style. As a result of this early apprenticeship, Swinburne acquired some things from Keats which remained with him always. Unlike Morris, he did not relish Keats's versification, but he was strongly attracted by many features of Keats's diction, and these left their stamp on his later work.[7] A rich and exotic vocabulary is one of the principal reasons for the epoch-making sonority of *Poems and Ballads* and other volumes of Swinburne. Since their author drew much of this richness from Keats, Grierson's statement that Swinburne's poetry stems from Keats has some justification.[8]

Yet except for this enrichment of vocabulary, Swinburne probably owes less to Keats than does any other Victorian poet of note except Browning. It is strange that Arnold, who would appear to have much less in common with Keats than a poet usually associated with the Pre-Raphaelites, actually drew more from him than did Swinburne. Arnold's *Tristram and Iseult* is much closer to Keats than is Swinburne's early *Queen Yseult*. In Swinburne's later poems, the difference is even more marked.

There are three good reasons why Swinburne's appreciation of Keats was limited and his debt to Keats restricted. Most important of these is one which Lafourcade does not choose to develop in his essay. It is Swinburne's emphasis upon music. Swinburne reserves his highest praise for the great singers of poetry rather than for the pictorial poets, the Shelleys rather than the Keatses. Although the Pre-Raphaelites and Parnassians fascinated him, and although under their guidance he tried, for a time, to give colour to his own verse, his genius was not along their line. For his own purposes, when he spoke of art for art's sake he usually meant music for music's sake.

5. *The Complete Works of Algernon Charles Swinburne* (Bonchurch edition), London, 1925–27, xv, 109.

6. G. Lafourcade, *Swinburne: A Literary Biography*, London, 1932, p. 70.

7. G. Lafourcade, *Essay*, pp. 70–6.

8. See Arnold chapter, p. 74.

As in Shelley, the only colour which strikes us in Swinburne's poetry is white. His world, as Lafourcade notes, is monochromatic.[9] To have painted in words, as Keats did, was not enough for Swinburne, and what music he did find in Keats was not to his taste. Of Morris' *Earthly Paradise* Swinburne complained of the absence of "swift and spontaneous style." "Top's is spontaneous and slow" he said, "and especially my ear hungers for more force of variety and sound in the verse."[10] The same objection would apply to Keats. Compare, for example, Swinburne's description of the song of the nightingale with Keats's ode:

> The torrent-tide of song, then free burst out
>   And in a tempest whirl of melody rush'd
> Through the stirred boughs. . . .
>   Dash'd down a precipice of music, rent
> By the mad stream of song; whirl'd, shook, rang out, spoke. . . .[11]

The rush of the verse here is far removed from the "plaintive anthem" of Keats and reminds us rather of Shelley's outbursts in *The Skylark* or in *Prometheus Unbound:*

> The joy, the triumph, the delight, the madness!
> The boundless, overflowing, bursting gladness,
> The vaporous exultation not to be confined!

Lafourcade and others have often compared Swinburne to Leconte de Lisle, Gautier, and the poets of the French Parnassian school. Actually he has not so much in common with these Keats-like *ciseleurs* as he has with the later symbolists such as Mallarmé, who believed that three-quarters of the pleasure of a poem was lost when the poet named an object directly, or such as Verlaine, whose credo was, "De la musique avant toute chose."

> Car nous voulons la Nuance encore,
> Pas le Couleur, rien que la nuance!
> Oh! la nuance seule fiance
> Le rêve au rêve et la flûte au cor!

Like Shelley,[12] Swinburne anticipates the symbolist's evaluation of words for their sound effects rather than for their denotation of actual objects. This tendency is superbly imitated in his parody of his own style:

Only this oracle opens Olympian, in mystical moods and triangular tenses—
Life is the lust of a lamp for the light that is dark till the dawn of the day when we die.

9. G. Lafourcade, *La jeunesse de Swinburne*, II, 538.
10. Quoted by Holbrook Jackson, *William Morris*, London, 1926, p. 134.
11. G. Lafourcade, *Essay*, p. 149, and *La jeunesse de Swinburne*, II, 539.
12. See Henri Peyre, *Shelley et la France*, Le Caire, 1935.

Although Swinburne acquires vocabulary from Keats, he puts it to vastly different uses. When Keats is obscure it is usually simply a matter of an over-packed line, as for example in *The Eve of St. Agnes:*

> Clasp'd like a missal where swart Paynims pray. . . .

Swinburne's obscurity results rather from a deliberate manipulation of words for a certain musical effect:

> Time with a gift of tears
> Grief with a glass that ran.[13]

As E. K. Brown notes:

. . . Swinburne dwells, not in a world of objects, but in a world of words. If one looks in his poetry for the clear shapes of particular things, which stand forth in soft outline in the poems of Rossetti [or Keats], one will be not only disappointed but exasperated.[14]

In an earlier chapter, I referred to a remark by D. W. Rannie that if poets are divided into three classes, "those who paint (or carve), those who sing, and those who prophesy, we must unhesitatingly place Keats in the first class." Swinburne, on the other hand, is to be found not only among the singers but among the prophets. The second reason for his breaking away from the Keats tradition is the absence of prophecy in Keats. Swinburne refers to him as "the most exclusively aesthetic and the most absolutely non-moral of all serious writers on record."[15] Even Gautier, he says, has more political interests than Keats.[16] This conception, which was all to Keats's credit in the estimations of Rossetti or Morris or Wilde, finally told against Keats in Swinburne's estimation. After 1867, under the influence of Mazzini, Swinburne tried to grow away from aestheticism and set out to preach politics in verse. Instead of an *Eve of St. Agnes* we find him writing *The Eve of Revolution*. As he expresses it in the *Prelude* to *Songs before Sunrise:*

> For Pleasure slumberless and pale
> And passion with rejected veil
> Pass and the tempest-footed throng
> Of hours that follow them with song
> Till their feet flag and voices fail.

The transition is perhaps never complete in Swinburne and the clash of aestheticism and politics confuses his theories.[17] Yet as Lafourcade

13. T. S. Eliot, *Selected Essays*, London, 1932, pp. 326–7.
14. E. K. Brown, "Swinburne: A Centenary Estimate," *University of Toronto Quarterly*, VI (1937), 220.
15. *Complete Works of Swinburne*, XIV, 158.
16. *Ibid.*, p. 159.
17. For an account of the way in which Swinburne's criticism can be unified, see Lafourcade's attempt to find a centre (*La jeunesse de Swinburne*, II, 320–81).

shows, in his later years Swinburne often finds himself in agreement with Arnold:

All sane men must be willing to concede the truth of an assertion which [Arnold] seems to fling down as a challenge . . . that a school of poetry divorced from any moral idea is a school of poetry divorced from life.[18]

There is something supremely funny in thinking of Swinburne condemning Keats for his aestheticism, but such is the case. Here again Swinburne finds that Shelley is the poet *par excellence* rather than Keats.

Most strange of all however is Swinburne's attitude towards the character of Keats. Herein is to be found the third reason for the strict qualifications of his liking for the earlier poet. In connection with Arnold, I have traced the history of the Victorian conception of Keats's character and showed how Arnold and others were deeply offended by what they conceived to be the absence of the manly and the gentlemanly in the Cockney poet. One might not expect to find the author of *Dolores* in such company, but there indeed he is, and in the front rank. "I would rather read Arnold on Keats than write on Keats myself" said Swinburne in 1879.[19] As it turned out, he did both. He read Arnold's essay on Keats, remarked that it was extremely just to Keats's "manhood,"[20] and then wrote his own study, in which Arnold's strictures are echoed closely enough. Throughout, as Lafourcade notes, Swinburne is continually judging Keats's poetry through Keats's character. A good sample of "two-edged homage" is his comment on the *Ode to a Nightingale:*

The *Ode to a Nightingale,* one of the final masterpieces of human work in all time and for all ages, is immediately preceded in all editions now current by some of the most vulgar and fulsome doggerel ever whimpered by a vapid and effeminate rhymester in the sickly stage of whelphood.[21]

In spite of his flashes of insight, Swinburne is one of the least satisfactory of critics. As Dryden said of Buckingham, "Railing and praising were his usual themes." What made Swinburne rail so clamorously in the case of Keats was his dislike of effeminacy. In 1876 he sensed it in *The Cap and Bells* and remarked to Gosse how alarming it was that Keats should have "gone back to his gallipots" at the last. "It gives one a horrid thought" he said.[22] Two years later, when the Fanny Brawne letters were published, the "horrid thought" was confirmed and he wrote in his essay:

18. *Complete Works of Swinburne,* xiv, 160. See also Lafourcade, *Essay,* p. 55.
19. *Complete Works of Swinburne,* xviii, 313.
20. *Ibid.,* xiv, 301.
21. *Ibid.,* pp. 295–6. See also Lafourcade, *Essay,* p. 52 n.
22. Edmund Gosse, *The Life of Algernon Charles Swinburne,* p. 295.

. . . while admitting that neither his love-letters, nor the last piteous out-cries of his wailing and shrieking agony, would ever have been made pub-lic by merciful or respectful editors, we must also admit that, if they ought never to have been published, it is no less certain that they ought never to have been written; that a manful kind of man or even a manly sort of boy, in his love-making or in his suffering, will not howl and snivel after such a lamentable fashion.[23]

This "high moral tone" seems strange from one whose verses fell on the Victorian age, as Hardy said, like "a garland of red roses" about "the hood of some smug nun." It is tempting to lay all the blame on Watts-Dunton, but the roots of it are in Swinburne himself. One reason is his own aristocratic background, but another, equally im-portant it seems to me, is psychological. Many incidents in Swin-burne's biography might be cited to show that he has the small man's passionate desire to assert his masculinity. The recurrence of the ad-jective "manly" in so much of his criticism is not merely the voice of Victorian England and Watts-Dunton. It has its roots in Swinburne's own personality. As for his sneer about Keats and the "gallipots," Mario Praz's comment is worth noting:

. . . the retort might have been made to Swinburne that if by "loving like a gentleman" he meant loving in the way approved by such exquisite gentlemen as the Maréchal Gilles de Rais and the Marquis de Sade, then Keats was certainly not a gentlemanly lover.[24]

Swinburne's critical opinions are of such a hectic nature that by judicious selection, one could present a vastly different picture of his estimate of Keats than the one which I have presented. I believe however, that in spite of ecstatic outbursts of praise on some occa-sions, and in spite of early imitations, Swinburne's respect for Keats's art is not very deep. His own poetry is on the periphery of the Keats tradition.

23. *Complete Works of Swinburne,* xiv, 297.
24. Mario Praz, *The Romantic Agony,* p. 239.

XII

The Last Decades

SWINBURNE'S essay of 1882, with its deprecatory attitude towards the apotheosis of Keats was, as he personally admitted, hotly challenged by his friends.[1] The tide in favour of Keats was by that date so strong that the usually self-reliant Swinburne turned to Arnold for support. He might have turned to others as well, such as W. J. Courthope and R. H. Hutton (to whom I have referred earlier), and also to Coventry Patmore. Although some traces of Keatsian influence are apparent in his earlier work, Patmore became strongly opposed, as he grew older, to Keats's growing fame. Replying to Colvin, who had spoken of Keats as a "Shakespearean spirit," Patmore affirmed that "he was the most un-Shakespearean poet that ever lived." Poets, he adds, are of two types, the masculine such as Shakespeare, and the feminine such as Keats. "In the first class, which contains all the greatest poets, with Shakespeare at their head, intellect predominates."[2] Patmore's point of view would have been shared by many righteous readers who were offended by the Fanny Brawne letters published in 1878. Yet in most literary circles of the closing decades of the century, Patmore, Swinburne, and Arnold represented a minority opinion. By 1895, to deplore Keats was literary heresy.

I intend to conclude this account with some evidence of Keats's fame at the time of the centennial of his birth, but first there are some further points in connection with his influence. One of the most extraordinary features of Keats's impact on the Victorians is that his influence extended over such a long period. From the time of Hood in the 1820's to the end of the century, he is the poet's poet. In widely varying degrees, all the major Victorian poets draw from his work. Attention has been concentrated on these more important figures, but of course the lesser and more derivative ones would provide innumerable instances as well. The work of R. W. Dixon (1833–1900), for example, was so indebted to Keats that his friends feared that it would never be properly appreciated as original writing. Mention might also be made of R. H. Horne (1803–84), a schoolfellow of Keats, who later attained considerable fame as a Victorian poet. Horne is

1. G. Lafourcade, *Essay on Swinburne and Keats*, p. 58 n.
2. Coventry Patmore, "Keats," *St. James's Budget*, July 2, 1887, p. 21. Patmore's study may be contrasted with a book on Keats (published in 1880) by Frances Owen. Owen treats Keats's themes seriously and regards him as a poet of the first order.

still a very readable poet today, yet his fame was very short-lived. When his one-time popular epic *Orion* was published in 1843, *The Westminster Review* affirmed that the poem was as "classic in its way as Keats's *Endymion*."[3] Actually, although the love-allegory suggests *Endymion*, the main account of the giants seems to draw from *Hyperion*. As we find also with Robert Bridges at a later date, Horne read Keats for his themes rather than for his phrasing,[4] and in this sphere his debt is considerable. As Douglas Bush remarks, no reader of *Orion* can help exclaiming, "This is a combination of *Endymion* and *Hyperion!*"[5]

When dealing with Arnold, I referred also to the interesting case of the Spasmodic poets who, while professing a reaction against Tennyson, were deeply influenced by Keats. Alexander Smith was especially drawn to Keats. The list might be extended indefinitely, but we may take leave of most of them by citing a comment which "Michael Field" passed on Sir Lewis Morris (1833–1907), a popular imitator of Keats. "He loves Keats" writes Field, and adds, "Ah, poor Keats, nauseous in his disciples!"[6]

I have not as yet mentioned a better-known figure, George Meredith. His early volume of poems (1851), which includes *Love in the Valley*, shows a very distinct Keatsian strain. "Endymionisms" are common in such pieces as *The Wild Rose and the Snowdrop*, *The Rape of Aurora*, and *Angelic Love*, but they are especially noticeable in the long poem *Daphne*. Meredith unfortunately chose to imitate the most cloying effects of Keats. He describes the "delicious panting vows" of Apollo, and of the nymph he writes:

> There the young green glistening leaflets
> Hush'd with love their breezy peal;
> There the little opening flowerets
> Blush'd beneath her vermeil heel.

Again:

> Palms that like a bird's throbb'd bosom
> Palpitate with eagerness,
> Lips, the bridals of the roses
> Dewy sweet from the caress!

These recall *Endymion*, but sometimes there are echoes of *The Eve of St. Agnes*, as for example:

> All her dreamy warmth revolving,
> While the chilly waters woo'd.[7]

3. *Orion* (ed. Eric Partridge), London, 1928, Introduction, p. xxix.
4. There are echoes of Keats in some of the other poems as well, e.g., *The Urn* (1848).
5. Douglas Bush, *Mythology and the Romantic Tradition*, p. 281.
6. Quoted *ibid.*, p. 428.
7. George Meredith, *Poems*, London, 1851, pp. 54, 59, 53.

If Meredith had not later abandoned the style of *Daphne,* he might have shared the honour with Keats of being known to Victorian ladies as "The Daintiest of Poets."

Had Matthew Arnold seen the volume, he would have felt additional cause to exclaim about Keats: "What harm he has done to English poetry!" Much as Arnold might deplore it however, the influence persisted. We might expect to find that in the last decades of the century it would have worn itself out, but in spite of a certain reaction to which I shall refer, it is even more pervasive from 1870 on than it had been in the 1850's. In these last decades, it becomes inextricably blended with strains of Tennyson, Rossetti and many others, so blended in fact, that there is seldom much point in attempting to sift it out as an isolated element.

The fostering of Keats's fame by the Pre-Raphaelites passes from their hands during this period to the "Aesthetic School" and to others. Tennyson blamed aestheticism on French influences and thundered against "the poisonous honey brought from France." The young aesthetes themselves were naturally only amused by his outburst,[8] and although French models were indeed their ideal, they might have retorted that they were simply developing tendencies latent in the work of Keats, to whom Tennyson himself owed so much. As a French critic notes, the ultimate sources of English aestheticism are not French but national.[9] Oscar Wilde considered Keats more responsible than any other for the aesthetic Renaissance of which he himself was a curious sort of symbol.[10]

The Garden of Eros and *Charmides* will show how Wilde was inevitably led to copy Keats. Again in *The New Helen,* which follows the *Ode to a Nightingale* in stanza form, he bursts into such lines as:

> Thou wast not born as common women are!

and also in *Camma:*

> As one who poring on a Grecian urn
> Scans the fair shapes some Attic hand hath made. . . .

Examples could be multiplied *ad infinitum,* but there would be little point in the case of Wilde, a poet whose borrowings from his predecessors are so glaring that oftentimes his poems seem to us to be simply parodies (especially when he borrows from Arnold).[11] The more significant fact is his method of reading Keats. In one of his last poems (*Glykypikros Eros*), he muses on the fact that if he had taken his art seriously he might have shared Keats's glory,

8. W. B. Scott, *Autobiographical Notes,* II, 196.
9. A. J. Farmer, *Le mouvement esthétique et "décadent" en Angleterre,* pp. 4–10.
10. See p. 104.
11. On Wilde's sources in general, see B. Fehr, *Studien zu Oscar Wilde's Gedichten,* Berlin, 1918.

Keats had lifted up his hymeneal curls from out the poppy-seeded wine,
With ambrosial mouth had kissed my forehead, clasped the hand of noble
    love in mine.

Clearly enough, Wilde associated the early poet with his own particular conception of beauty. Tennyson had sensed in Keats certain po-
tential tendencies in the direction of decadence, and thus had turned
away from his influence in later years. Wilde, on the contrary, cherished this side of his poetry. The overtones of the following para-
graph (written after Wilde's visit to the grave of Keats in Rome)
require no comment:

As I stood beside the mean grave of this divine boy, I thought of him as
a Priest of Beauty slain before his time; and the vision of Guido's St. Se-
bastian came before my eyes as I saw him at Genoa, a lovely brown boy,
with crisp, clustering hair and red lips, bound by his evil enemies to a tree,
and though pierced by arrows, raising his eyes with divine, impassioned
gaze towards the Eternal Beauty of the opening heavens.[12]

Wilde's literary master, Walter Pater, might be mentioned in
this connection. When contrasting the different stages of Victorian
thought, it is often convenient to compare the attitudes of Carlyle,
Ruskin and Pater towards some particular subject. Unfortunately, in
the matter of their attitude to Keats, we possess surprisingly little
direct evidence of Pater's view. It is a strange gap in Pater's studies
of romanticism that he has left us no essay on a poet whose work
would seem a model of the very beauties he sought in art. Perhaps
he felt that in his essay on *Aesthetic Poetry* especially, and also in his
six or seven other studies of romantic writers,[13] he had said all that
he wished to say about the value of poetry such as that of Keats.
There are scattered references throughout his writings which give
clues to his estimate, as for example when he praises the "fulness of
imagery" in *The Eve of St. Agnes*.[14] In his essay on Lamb, he ranks
Keats above Coleridge, Wordsworth, and Shelley as one of "the disinterested servants of literature." The poets contemporary with Keats
he says, "were greatly preoccupied with ideas of practice—religious,
moral, political," and in the long run, their poetry suffers by comparison with those "who may have seemed to exercise themselves
hardly at all in great matters, to have been little serious, or a little

12. Oscar Wilde, "The Tomb of Keats," *Irish Monthly*, v (1887), 476–7.
13. These include his "Postscript" to *Appreciations* and his studies of Wordsworth,
Coleridge, Lamb, Mérimée, Amiel, and in the same connection, Rossetti and Morris
(*Aesthetic Poetry*). In occasional references, he seldom speaks of Byron or Shelley, but
Victor Hugo is a recurring name, especially in *The Renaissance*. A useful study of Pater's
tastes is that by A. J. Farmer, *Walter Pater as a Critic of English Literature*, Grenoble,
1931.
14. Walter Pater, *Appreciations*, p. 44.

indifferent, regarding them." Keats and Lamb had the virtue, for Pater, of having remained aloof.

Of this number of the disinterested servants of literature, smaller in England than in France, Charles Lamb is one. In the making of prose he realizes the principle of art for its own sake, as completely as Keats in the making of verse.[15]

From Pater's comments on Rossetti and Morris and other writers, it would not be difficult to show how Keats must have attracted him. One thing is clear. Like Rossetti, he does not deplore the absence of "ideas of practice" in Keats. He values him as the complete exponent of art for art's sake. Thus although Pater may have done little to foster Keats's fame in the way of writing a detailed study, the general approach to art which he preached was of great importance in that connection.

It might seem that Keats's appeal would be especially noticeable among Pater's many followers in the closing years of the century, among those who could appreciate his poetry from the point of view of art for art's sake. Yet the extraordinary thing is that Keats's popularity was by no means limited to this group. A good example is provided by George Gissing, who although interested in aestheticism, gropingly made his own way in another direction. Yet no "pure" aesthete could have praised Keats more warmly than did Gissing in the letter which I have quoted on the title page of this section: "Of Keats read everything. To like Keats is a test of fitness for understanding poetry, just as to like Shakespeare is a test of general mental capacity."[16]

A writer much more independent of the Aesthetic Movement than Gissing is James Thomson ("B. V."). Although more interested in Shelley, Thomson had many good things to say in Keats's favour throughout his essays, and in at least one of his poems, admiration led to imitation:

> O happy bud, for ever young,
>   For ever just about to blow!
> O happy love, upon whose tongue
>   The Yes doth ever trembling grow!
> O happiest twain, whose deathless bower
> Embalms you in life's crowning hour![17]
>   (*The Fadeless Bower*)

15. *Ibid.*, p. 109. In his two studies of Flaubert Pater makes further comments on the value of objectivity. (Reprinted in *Sketches and Reviews*, New York, 1919.)

16. *Letters of George Gissing to Members of His Family*, London, 1927, p. 160.

17. For this information concerning Thomson, I am indebted to an unpublished dissertation in the Yale University Library, *The Prose Writings of James Thomson* ("B. V.") by Lyman A. Cotten.

So too with certain writers of the "Catholic School" of the closing years of the century did Keats find exponents and defenders. According to Jacques Maritain, the artist who believes in art for art's sake is essentially an idolator, and in order to find happiness, the artist must seek for something better-beloved than his own creations. "God" he adds, "is infinitely more loveable than art."[18] Many of the later Victorians found Him so, yet in the process of conversion, they did not abandon their favourites in art. Of these, the most renowned today is Gerard Manley Hopkins, whose grandfather, incidentally, had been a fellow-student of surgery with John Keats at Guy's Hospital in London.[19] Like many Victorian poets, Hopkins launched into poetry with direct imitations of Keats. Some of the rather delightful poems written in his 'teens, which Father Lahey has reprinted, illustrate the most obvious borrowing from *The Eve of St. Agnes*.[20] As George Meredith had done, Hopkins went his own way in poetry in later years, but as a commentator on Keats he is of particular interest. His correspondence contains many references to the earlier poet, and he followed articles on him with interest. "Keats' genius was so astonishing" he wrote, "unequalled at his age and scarcely surpassed at any, that one may surmise whether if he had lived he would not have rivalled Shakespeare."[21] While admitting Keats's faults, Hopkins had some very sensible things to say in reply to those such as Patmore who deplored the young poet's sensuousness. Especially of interest is a remark which anticipates the twentieth-century approach to Keats: "He was, in my opinion, made to be a thinker, a critic, as much as a singer or artist in words."[22]

Hopkins' attitude may have influenced his friend Robert Bridges, whose method of evaluating Keats was somewhat different from that of his fellow-Victorians. Bridges professed to dislike the Pre-Raphaelites, and many of the things which they cherished most in Keats did not seem to him to be of such great importance. His privately printed study of Keats (1895) is not much concerned with the poet's word-painting. It concentrates rather on analysing the thought of such pieces as the revised *Hyperion* and also *Endymion*. He does not shirk their allegories, and he regards the second *Hyperion* as embodying some of Keats's deepest convictions, an example of its author's "earnestness."[23]

If Bridges drew from Keats in his own poetry, it was primarily on

18. Jacques Maritain, *Art and Scholasticism*, London, 1930, p. 74.
19. *The Letters of Gerard Manley Hopkins to Robert Bridges*, London, 1935, p. 51.
20. G. F. Lahey, S. J., *Gerard Manley Hopkins*, Oxford, 1930, p. 10. The author draws attention to the influence of Keats in another early poem (pp. 11–13), but it is in *The Escorial* that the resemblance is most noticeable.
21. *Letters of Gerard Manley Hopkins to Richard Watson Dixon*, p. 6.
22. G. F. Lahey, *op. cit.*, p. 74.
23. Robert Bridges, *John Keats* (privately printed), 1895, pp. 38 and 92.

this plane of Keats's thought rather than his style. There are occasional passages which recall Keatsian phrasing, and oftentimes there are direct references, as for example, when he quotes from the *Ode to Psyche* on the title-page of his *Eros and Psyche* (1885), or in this description of an abbey in autumn:

> While in her leafy tower the langorous murmur
> floateth off heav'nward in a mellow dome of shade;—
> or when, *tho' summer hath o'erbrim'd their clammy cells.* . . .[24]

These lines are from *The Testament of Beauty*, a poem which although first published in 1929, nevertheless comes within the scope of a study of the Victorians, for Bridges is one of the last of them. The style of the poem reminds us of the more pedestrian epistemological passages in Wordsworth's *Prelude* rather than of Keats, but as a testament it represents an interesting expansion of some of Keats's ideas. Man finds God, says Bridges,

> . . . by the irresistible
> predominant attraction, which worketh secure
> in mankind's Love of Beauty and in the Beauty of Truth.
> (III, 1053–5)

Often in his letters Keats spoke of an awareness of beauty "without any irritable reaching after fact and reason" as the true basis of wisdom.[25] In *The Testament of Beauty* the same notion is emphasized and developed:

> Wisdom will repudiate thee, if thou think to enquire
> WHY things are as they are or whence they came:
> thy task
> is first to learn WHAT IS.
> (I, 128–30)

Whatever *The Testament of Beauty* may owe to Keats, its author as a critic was a severe judge of Keats's failings. His essay shows this clearly. Yet in the same essay he writes:

If one English poet might be recalled to-day from the dead to continue the work which he left unfinished on earth, it is probable that the crown of his country's desire would be set on the head of John Keats.[26]

These lines were one of the many tributes which appeared in 1895 on the centennial of Keats's birth. Most of the tributes, however, had actually made their appearance a year before on the occasion of the unveiling of a memorial to Keats in Hampstead Church.

24. *The Testament of Beauty*, New York, 1930, Book II, 353–5 (italics his).
25. *Letters of Keats*, p. 72.
26. Robert Bridges, *John Keats*, p. 5.

The memorial was a contribution from America, where Keats's fame had also developed extensively. James Russell Lowell, among others, was an early admirer, and it was at his suggestion that a committee was formed, in efficient American style, to collect funds for a monument to Keats. By 1894, it had secured over a hundred subscribers, and a bust of the poet was executed in Boston and shipped to England to be unveiled.

There was even talk for a while of having the memorial set up in Westminster Abbey,[27] but after some deliberation Hampstead Church was chosen. Edmund Gosse, who was in charge of the ceremony, made rather elaborate preparations for it, and from many points of view the results were most impressive. Announcements and invitations were printed by William Morris at the Kelmscott Press. On the following page appears a photograph of one of these announcements which was kindly lent to me by Mr. Carl Rollins. At the ceremony itself, as one observer noted, was the literary and artistic world of the Nineties. Aubrey Beardsley was there,[28] and so too were George Moore, Richard Garnett, Coventry Patmore, H. D. Traill, George du Maurier,[29] Watts-Dunton (representing Swinburne who was unable to come), Scawen Blunt and many others. As *The Times* account emphasizes, there was also the inevitable contingent of lords and ladies, no less than three bishops, and a general. Speeches were made by the representative of the American subscribers, and also by Gosse, Sidney Colvin, F. T. Palgrave, and Lord Houghton (the son of Keats's biographer).[30]

The ceremony had its amusing sides. It was not the first time that a certain incongruity marked the service within a Christian church in honour of a pagan poet. As Scawen Blunt noted in his diary,

. . . throughout the only allusion to religion was when one of the speakers enumerated what Keats was not, and included in the list that he was *not* a religious propagandist. When all was over the worthy vicar consoled himself with some prayers and an anthem.[31]

Blunt's diary goes on to complain that many of the speeches were dull, which is hardly surprising. Nevertheless in spite of its inescapable tediousness and formality, the ceremony represented a very real tribute. As Gosse and others pointed out, it was a belated one. Byron's bitter lines (translating Martial) on the fame of poets might be recalled:

27. See "The Keats Memorial," *Saturday Review*, LXXVIII (1895), 66.
28. Haldane Macfall, *Aubrey Beardsley*, p. 17.
29. See *The Times*, July 17, 1894, p. 8.
30. *The Times* report includes summaries of each of the speeches. Gosse's is reprinted in full in his *Critical Kit-Kats* (pp. 21–8) and also in *The Critic*, xxv (1894), 78–9.
31. Wilfred Scawen Blunt, *My Diaries*, I, 145.

AN AMERICAN MEMORIAL TO KEATS.

O N the afternoon of Monday, the sixteenth of July, at four o'clock, will be unveiled, in the Parish Church of Hampstead, the first memorial to the poet John Keats upon English ground. For some years the scheme of such a memorial has been promoted in America. Mr. Lowell was one of the earliest to encourage it, & it has been urged forward by Professor Charles Eliot Norton, Mr. Aldrich, Mr. R. W. Gilder, the late Dr. Parsons, and indeed most of those who now represent poetical literature in America.

N O W, through the generosity of these friends, a bust of the poet, executed in marble by Miss Anne Whitney, of Boston, Massachusetts, is presented to the English people. The donors comprise nearly a hundred persons, who will, it is hoped, be represented on this occasion by Mr. Bret Harte, while the memorial will be received on behalf of English men of letters by Mr. Edmund Gosse.

After the address of acceptance, there will be a performance upon the organ of the church of selections from Dr. Alexander C. Mackenzie's symphony "La Belle Dame sans Merci."

"The soul of Adonais, like a star,
Beacons from the abode where the Eternal are."

ANNOUNCEMENT OF THE KEATS MEMORIAL

PRINTED AT THE KELMSCOTT PRESS
1894

> While living
> Give him the fame thou wouldst be giving;
> So shall he hear, and feel, and know it—
> Post-obits rarely reach a poet.

Byron lived to taste his fame: Keats had little inkling of his. Yet if the "post-obits" of 1894 did not reach Keats, it was not for lack of good intentions on the part of the Victorian literary world, to whom he was now in danger of becoming only too much an idol. Some of his own lines on fame are in a different spirit from those of Byron:

> Bards of Passion and of Mirth,
> Ye have left your souls on earth! . . .
> And the souls ye left behind you
> Teach us, here, the way to find you. . . .

It is highly tempting to continue this account into the twentieth century, but except for one or two items, the story of Keats's rise to fame finds its logical stopping-point in 1894–95. His influence continues after 1900 and constitutes an important strand in twentieth-century poetry. It is especially noticeable in the work of Amy Lowell and other Imagists, and is also marked in some of the poems of Rupert Brooke. A more significant poet of the last war, Wilfred Owen, had a passion for Keats amounting to idolatry.[32] In a more general sense, the early work of Yeats has many affinities with Keats, but it would be foolish to assume from this, as some critics have done,[33] that the Keats-tradition exists in the twentieth century in anything like the same force which it had in the Victorian age. "We were the last romantics" writes Yeats in 1931:

> But all is changed, that high horse riderless,
> Though mounted in that saddle Homer rode
> Where the swan drifts upon a darkening flood.

The horse has not been riderless, but a different kind of horseman has been in the saddle from those poets who resemble Keats. The change was already taking place in 1894 at the time of the Keats Memorial ceremony. Thomas Hardy might pay warm tribute to the earlier poet,[34] but the wheezy harshness of his own verse represents a different world from that which Keats (and more especially Keats's successors) calls to mind. The main tradition of poetry since the turn of the century marks a great turning away from the influence of his work. Twentieth-century verse is closer to Browning than to any

32. See *The Poems of Wilfred Owen* (ed. Edmund Blunden), London, 1933, pp. 3–9.
33. Cf. "John Keats as the Master Spirit in Victorian Poetry," *Current Opinion,* LXX (1921), 526.
34. In his poems *At the Pyramid of Cestius Near the Graves of Shelley and Keats* (1877), and his contribution to the *Keats Memorial Volume* (1923).

other nineteenth-century writer, and Browning, much as he might admire Keats, is perhaps less close to his style of poetry than was any other major Victorian poet.

In spite of this diminishing of influence, Keats's fame has not been affected in the process. Twentieth-century studies such as those by Thorpe, Fausset, Finney, and Murry, have considerably strengthened his position by detailed examination of his mind in relation to his art. They have also discovered, what few of the Victorians realized, the real basis of his affinities to Shakespeare. They have further enhanced his fame by emphasizing the greatness of *Hyperion,* but for most of the poetry itself they have not added much to what the Victorians had already discovered. The level of enthusiasm which developed among many Victorians, both early and late, would be difficult to surpass in any age. As for the poets, in Arnold's phrase Keats was an indispensable part of the *Zeit-Geist.* If a Keats had not existed, the Victorians would have had to invent one.

APPENDIX TO CHAPTER VIII

A List of Victorian Paintings with Subjects Taken from Keats

THE following list is by no means meant to be complete, but some of the items may be of assistance to anyone interested in tracing out, in further detail, how frequently Victorian painters drew subjects from Keats's poems.

ARTHUR HUGHES, *The Eve of St. Agnes.* 1856.
HOLMAN HUNT, *The Eve of St. Agnes.* 1846–1848.
HOLMAN HUNT, *Isabella and the Pot of Basil.* 1868.
HOLMAN HUNT, Drawings from *Isabella.* 1847–1850.
C. H. LEAR, Painting from the *Ode on a Grecian Urn.* 1850.
J. E. MILLAIS (with Hunt), Drawings from *Isabella.* 1847–1850.
J. E. MILLAIS, *Lorenzo and Isabella.* 1848.
D. G. ROSSETTI, Sepia drawing of *La Belle Dame sans Merci.* 1848. See *Dante Gabriel Rossetti as Designer and Writer*, p. 274. (This drawing is presumably lost.)
D. G. ROSSETTI, Water-colour of similar design. 1855.
D. G. ROSSETTI, India ink sketch: *La Belle Dame sans Merci.* 1855(?). In this sketch, he pictures the lovers on horseback. According to his brother, the picture is much closer to Keats than the previous one.
J. M. STRUDWICK, *Isabella.* 1880(?).
J. M. STRUDWICK, *Peona—From Keats's "Endymion."* (See Walter Hamilton, *The Aesthetic Movement*, p. 26.)
G. F. WATTS, *Echo.* (From Keats's *Endymion.*)

BIBLIOGRAPHY

PART I: TEXTS, LETTERS, AND REMINISCENCES

ALLINGHAM, WILLIAM, *The Diary of William Allingham*, London, 1907.

ARNOLD, MATTHEW, *The Poems of Matthew Arnold 1840–1867* (ed. Sir Arthur T. Quiller-Couch), London, 1926.

The Works of Matthew Arnold, London, 1903–04, 15 vols.

Culture and Anarchy, Cambridge, 1935.

Discourses in America, London, 1885.

Essays in Criticism, First Series, London, 1935..

Essays in Criticism, Second Series, London, 1935.

Essays in Criticism (the so-called *Third Series*), Boston, 1910.

Matthew Arnold's Notebooks, London, 1902.

On the Study of Celtic Literature, New York, 1883.

The Letters of Matthew Arnold to Arthur Hugh Clough (ed. Howard Foster Lowry), London, 1932.

Unpublished Letters of Matthew Arnold (ed. Arnold Whitridge), New Haven, 1923.

BLUNT, WILFRED SCAWEN, *My Diaries*, New York, 1931, 2 vols.

BRIDGES, ROBERT, *The Testament of Beauty*, New York, 1930.

BROWNING, ROBERT, *The Poetical Works of Robert Browning*, London, 1903, 2 vols.

Letters of Robert Browning and Elizabeth Barrett Barrett, New York, 1899, 2 vols.

Letters of Robert Browning (coll. Thomas J. Wise), New Haven, 1933.

The Shorter Poems of Robert Browning (ed. W. C. DeVane), New York, 1934.

BURNE-JONES, EDWARD, *Memorials of Edward Burne-Jones* (ed. G. B-J.), New York, 1904, 2 vols.

CAINE, SIR T. HALL, *Recollections of Dante Gabriel Rossetti*, London, 1883.

My Story, New York, 1909.

Recollections of Rossetti, London, 1928.

CARLYLE, THOMAS, *Critical and Miscellaneous Essays*, London (Chapman and Hall), n. d., 5 vols.

CLARKE, CHARLES and MARY COWDEN, *Recollections of Writers*, London, 1878, pp. 120–58.

COLERIDGE, JOHN DUKE, *Life and Correspondence of John Duke Coleridge*, London, 1904, 2 vols.

DILKE, CHARLES WENTWORTH, *Papers of a Critic*, London, 1875, 2 vols.

DUNN, HENRY TREFFRY, *Recollections of Dante Gabriel Rossetti and His Circle*, London, 1904.

FITZGERALD, EDWARD, *Letters and Literary Remains of Edward Fitzgerald* (ed. W. A. Wright), London, 1889, 3 vols.

More Letters of Edward Fitzgerald, London, 1901.

GISSING, GEORGE, *Letters of George Gissing to Members of His Family*, London, 1927.

HAYDON, BENJAMIN ROBERT, *The Autobiography and Memoirs of Benjamin Robert Haydon*, London, 1926, 2 vols.
Correspondence and Table Talk, London, 1876, 2 vols.

HOOD, THOMAS, *The Complete Poetical Works of Thomas Hood*, Oxford, 1911.
The Prose Works of Thomas Hood, New York, 1878.

HOPKINS, GERARD MANLEY, *Letters of Gerard Manley Hopkins to Robert Bridges*, London, 1935.
Letters of Gerard Manley Hopkins to Richard Watson Dixon, London, 1935.

HORNE, RICHARD HENGIST, *Orion* (ed. Eric Partridge), London, 1928.

HUNT, LEIGH, *Autobiography*, London, 1850, 3 vols.

HUNT, W. HOLMAN, *Pre-Raphaelitism and the Pre-Raphaelite Brotherhood*, London, 1905, 2 vols.

KEATS, JOHN, *The Poetical Works of John Keats*, with a *Life of Keats* by J[ames] R[ussell] L[owell], Boston, 1854.
The Poems of John Keats (ed. E. de Sélincourt), London, 1905.
The Poetical Works of John Keats (ed. H. W. Garrod), Oxford, 1939.
The Letters of John Keats (ed. M. B. Forman), Oxford, 1935.

LANDOR, WALTER SAVAGE, *The Complete Works of Walter Savage Landor* (ed. T. Earle Welby), London, 1927–1936, 16 vols.

LANG, ANDREW, *Poetical Works*, London, 1923, 4 vols.

MARTINEAU, HARRIET, *Autobiography*, Boston, 1877, 2 vols.

MEREDITH, GEORGE, *Poems*, London, 1851.

MORRIS, WILLIAM, *The Collected Works of William Morris*, London, 1910–1915, 24 vols.
A Note by William Morris on his Aims in Founding the Kelmscott Press, Kelmscott Press, 1898.

PALGRAVE, G. F., *Francis Turner Palgrave, His Journals and Memories of his Life*, London, 1899.

PATER, WALTER, *Works*, London, 1920–1922, 10 vols.
Appreciations, London, 1920.
Sketches and Reviews, New York, 1919.

REID, SIR T. WEMYSS, *The Life, Letters, and Friendships of Richard Monckton Milnes*, New York, 1891, 2 vols.

ROBINSON, HENRY CRABB, *On Books and Their Writers* (ed. Edith J. Morley), London, 1938, 3 vols.

ROSSETTI, DANTE GABRIEL, *The Works of Dante Gabriel Rossetti* (ed. W. M. Rossetti), London, 1911.
Letters of Dante Gabriel Rossetti to William Allingham 1854–1870, London, 1897.
John Keats: Criticism and Comment (Rossetti's letters to H. B. Forman), London, 1919 (privately printed).
Letters from Dante Gabriel Rossetti to Algernon Charles Swinburne, London, 1921 (privately printed).

The House of Life (ed. with an introduction by Paull Franklin Baum),
Cambridge (U.S.A.), 1928.
The Letters of Dante Gabriel Rossetti to His Publisher F. S. Ellis,
London, 1928.
The Ballad of Jan Van Hunks, London, 1929.
An Analytical List of Manuscripts in the Duke University Library (ed.
Paull Franklin Baum), Duke University Press, 1931.
*The Blessed Damozel: The Unpublished Manuscript, Texts and
Collation* (ed. with an introduction by Paull Franklin Baum), Chapel
Hill, 1937.
Poems, Ballads, and Sonnets (ed. with an introduction by Paull
Franklin Baum), New York, 1937.
Letters to Fanny Cornforth, Baltimore, 1940.
ROSSETTI, WILLIAM MICHAEL, *Dante Gabriel Rossetti as Designer and
Writer,* London, 1889.
Dante Gabriel Rossetti: His Family Letters, with a Memoir, London,
1895, 2 vols.
Ruskin: Rossetti: Preraphaelitism: Papers 1854–1862, London, 1899.
Preraphaelite Diaries and Letters, London, 1900.
Rossetti Papers, New York, 1903.
Some Reminiscences, New York, 1906, 2 vols.
RUSKIN, JOHN, *The Works of John Ruskin* (ed. E. T. Cook and Alexander
Wedderburn), London, 1903–1912, 39 vols.
SCOTT, WILLIAM BELL, *Poems,* London, 1875.
Autobiographical Notes, New York, 1892, 2 vols.
SHARP, WILLIAM, *The Life and Letters of Joseph Severn,* London, 1892.
SMITH, ALEXANDER, *Poetical Works,* Edinburgh, 1909.
SWINBURNE, ALGERNON CHARLES, *The Complete Works of Algernon
Charles Swinburne* (Bonchurch edition, ed. Sir Edmund Gosse and T. J.
Wise), London, 1925–1927, 20 vols.
TENNYSON, ALFRED LORD, *Tennyson* (ed. W. J. Rolfe), New York, 1898.
The Early Poems of Alfred, Lord Tennyson (ed. John Churton Collins),
London, 1900.
The Works of Tennyson (Eversley edition), London, 1908–1920, 9 vols.
TENNYSON, HALLAM, *Alfred, Lord Tennyson: A Memoir by his Son,*
London, 1898, 2 vols.
WATTS-DUNTON, THEODORE, *Old Familiar Faces,* London, 1916.
WILDE, OSCAR, *Works,* Boston, 1909, vols. I, IX, XII.

PART II: CRITICISM, HISTORY, AND BIOGRAPHY

AUSTIN, ALFRED, *The Poetry of the Period,* London, 1870.
BABBITT, IRVING, *The New Laokoon,* New York, 1910.
Rousseau and Romanticism, Cambridge, 1935.
BAKER, A. E., *A Concordance to the Poems of Alfred, Lord Tennyson,*
London, 1914.
BALDWIN, DANE L., and Collaborators, *A Concordance to the Poems of
John Keats,* Washington, 1917.
BARING, MAURICE, *Lost Lectures,* London, 1932.

BATHO, EDITH C., and DOBRÉE, BONAMY, *The Victorians and After: 1830–1914*, London, 1935.

BEACH, JOSEPH WARREN, *The Concept of Nature in Nineteenth-Century English Poetry*, New York, 1936.

BEERBOHM, MAX, *Rossetti and His Circle*, London, 1922 (22 pictures).

BENN, ALFRED WILLIAM, *The History of English Rationalism in the Nineteenth Century*, London, 1906, 2 vols.

BENSON, ARTHUR C., *Rossetti*, London, 1926.

BINKLEY, ROBERT C., *Realism and Nationalism: 1852–1871*, New York, 1935.

BLOOMFIELD, PAUL, *William Morris*, London, 1934.

BLUNDEN, EDMUND, *Shelley and Keats as They Struck Their Contemporaries*, London, 1925.

Keats's Publisher: A Memoir of John Taylor, London, 1936.

BODKIN, MAUD, *Archetypal Patterns in Poetry*, London, 1934.

BRANDES, GEORG, *Main Currents in Nineteenth Century Literature*, London, 1916, vol. IV.

BRIDGES, ROBERT, *John Keats* (privately printed), 1895.

BRINTON, CRANE, *The Political Ideas of the English Romantics*, London, 1926.

BROOKE, STOPFORD A., *Tennyson*, London, 1894.

BROWN, CHARLES ARMITAGE, *Life of John Keats* (ed. Dorothy Hyde Bodurtha and William Bissell Pope), Oxford, 1937.

BROWNELL, W. C., *Victorian Prose Masters*, New York, 1901.

BROWNING, ROBERT, *Shelley*, Hull, n. d.

BUCHAN, JOHN, *Homilies and Recreations*, London, 1926.

BURDETT, OSBERT, *The Beardsley Period*, London, 1925.

BUSH, DOUGLAS, *Mythology and the Romantic Tradition*, Cambridge, 1937.

CAINE, T. HALL, *Cobwebs of Criticism*, London, 1883.

CHESTERTON, G. K., *The Victorian Age in Literature*, New York, 1913.

Varied Types, New York, 1921.

CHEW, SAMUEL S., *Byron in England*, London, 1924.

CHOISY, L. F., *Alfred Tennyson: son spiritualisme, sa personalité morale*, Genève, 1912.

CHRISTIE, O. F., *The Transition from Aristocracy: 1832–1867*, London, 1927.

CLUTTON-BROCK, A., *William Morris: His Work and Influence*, London, 1931.

COLVIN, SIDNEY, *Keats*, London, 1915 (E.M.L.S.)

Keats, London, 1917.

COMPTON-RICKETT, ARTHUR, *William Morris*, London, 1913.

COOK, E. T., *The Life of John Ruskin*, London, 1912, 2 vols.

CRUZE, AMY, *The Victorians and Their Books*, London, 1935.

DEVANE, WILLIAM CLYDE, *A Browning Handbook*, New York, 1935.

EGAN, ROSE FRANCES, "The Genesis of the Theory of 'Art for Art's Sake' in Germany and in England," *Smith College Studies in Modern Languages*, II, no. 4, 1921, pp. 5–61, and V, no. 3, 1924, pp. 1–33.

ELIOT, T. S., *The Use of Poetry and the Use of Criticism*, London, 1934.

ELTON, OLIVER, *A Survey of English Literature: 1830–1880*, London, 1932, 2 vols.

ESHELMAN, LLOYD WENDELL, *A Victorian Rebel: The Life of William Morris*, New York, 1940.

EVANS, B. IFOR, *English Poetry in the Later Nineteenth Century*, London, 1933.

FARMER, A. J., *Le mouvement esthétique et "décadent" en Angleterre (1873–1900)*, Paris, 1931.

FAUSSET, HUGH I'ANSON, *Keats*, London, 1922.

Tennyson, London, 1923.

FEHR, BERNARD, *Studien zu Oscar Wilde's Gedichten*, Berlin, 1918.

FINNEY, CLAUDE LEE, *The Evolution of Keats's Poetry*, Cambridge, 1936, 2 vols.

GARROD, H. W., *Keats*, Oxford, 1926.

GHOSE, S. N., *Dante Gabriel Rossetti and Contemporary Criticism (1849–1882)*, Dijon, 1929.

GOSSE, EDMUND, *Robert Browning: Personalia*, Cambridge, 1890.

Critical Kit-Kats, London, 1896.

The Life of Algernon Charles Swinburne, New York, 1917.

GRIERSON, H. J. C., *The Background of English Literature*, London, 1925.

Lyrical Poetry from Blake to Hardy, London, 1928.

GRIFFIN, W. H., and MINCHIN, H. C., *The Life of Robert Browning*, London, 1910.

GUÉRARD, ALBERT, *Art for Art's Sake*, New York, 1936.

HALÉVY, ELIE, *A History of the English People*, London, 1938, vol. III.

HAMILTON, WALTER, *The Aesthetic Movement*, London, 1882.

HERFORD, C. H., *The Age of Wordsworth*, London, 1897.

HILDYARD, M. CLIVE, *Lockhart's Literary Criticism*, Oxford, 1931.

HORN, KURT, *Zur Entstehungsgeschichte von Dante Gabriel Rossettis Dichtungen*, Bernau, 1909.

HOVELAQUE, HENRI-LÉON, *La jeunesse de Robert Browning*, Paris, 1932.

HUEFFER, FORD MADOX, *Rossetti. A Critical Essay on His Art*, London, 1902.

HUNT, LEIGH, *Lord Byron and Some of his Contemporaries*, London, 1828, 2 vols.

Selections from the British Poets, Philadelphia, 1856.

HUNT, VIOLET, *The Wife of Rossetti: Her Life and Death*, London, 1936.

HUTTON, R. H., *Brief Literary Criticisms*, London, 1906.

JACKSON, HOLBROOK, *William Morris*, London, 1926.

The Eighteen Nineties, London, 1939.

JERROLD, WALTER, *Thomas Hood: His Life and Times*, New York, 1909.

KEATS HOUSE COMMITTEE, *The John Keats Memorial Volume*, London, 1921.

KNIGHT, JOSEPH, *Life of Dante Gabriel Rossetti*, London, 1887.

KUSTER, ELISABET C., *Mittelalter und Antike bei William Morris*, Berlin, 1928.

LADD, HENRY, *The Victorian Morality of Art*, New York, 1932.

LAFOURCADE, GEORGES, *Swinburne's Hyperion and other Poems, With an Essay on Swinburne and Keats*, London, 1927.
La jeunesse de Swinburne (1837–1867), Paris, 1928, 2 tomes.
Swinburne: A Literary Biography, London, 1932.
LAHEY, G. F., S. J., *Gerard Manley Hopkins*, Oxford, 1930.
LAND, DAVID, *Trial by Virgins*, London, 1933.
LA SIZERRANNE, ROBERT DE, *Ruskin et la religion de la beauté*, Paris, 1897.
LEVELOH, PAUL, *Tennyson und Spenser: Eine Untersuchung von Spensers Einfluss auf Tennyson mit Berücksichtigung von Keats*, Marburg, 1909.
LOUNSBURY, THOS. R., *The Life and Times of Tennyson*, New Haven, 1915.
LOWELL, AMY, *John Keats*, New York, 1925, 2 vols.
LUCAS, E. V., *The Life of Charles Lamb*, London, 1905, 2 vols.
The Colvins and Their Friends, London, 1928.
LUCAS, F. L., *Eight Victorian Poets*, Cambridge, 1930.
LYND, ROBERT, "Keats: The Matthew Arnold View," in *Old and New Masters*, London, 1919, pp. 64–9.
MACFALL, HALDANE, *Aubrey Beardsley*, New York, 1927.
MACKAIL, J. W., *The Life of William Morris*, London, 1899, 2 vols.
William Morris and His Circle, Oxford, 1907.
MARILLIER, H. C., *Dante Gabriel Rossetti*, London, 1899.
MASON, FRANCIS CLAIBORNE, *A Study in Shelley Criticism*, privately printed at Mercersburg, Pennsylvania, 1938.
MASSINGHAM, H. J., and HUGH (editors), *The Great Victorians*, London, 1937, 2 vols.
MÉGROZ, R. L., *Dante Gabriel Rossetti*, London, 1928.
MILNES, RICHARD MONCKTON, *Life and Letters of John Keats*, New York, 1848.
MORE, PAUL ELMER, *Shelburne Essays, Seventh Series*, New York, 1910.
MORRIS, MAY, *William Morris: Artist, Writer, Socialist*, Oxford, 1936, 2 vols.
MURRY, JOHN MIDDLETON, *Keats and Shakespeare*, Oxford, 1925.
Studies in Keats, Oxford, 1930.
MUSTARD, W. P., *Classical Echoes in Tennyson*, New York, 1904.
NICOLL, W. R., and WISE, T. J., *Literary Anecdotes of the Nineteenth Century*, London, 1895, 2 vols.
NICOLSON, HAROLD, *Tennyson*, London, 1922.
Swinburne, New York, 1926.
NORDAU, MAX, *Degeneration*, New York, 1895.
OWEN, FRANCES MARY, *John Keats: A Study*, London, 1880.
PALGRAVE, FRANCIS T., *Landscape in Poetry*, London, 1897.
POTTLE, FREDERICK A., *Shelley and Browning: A Myth and Some Facts*, Chicago, 1923.
PRAZ, MARIO, *The Romantic Agony*, London, 1933.
PYRE, J. F. A., *The Formation of Tennyson's Style* (University of Wisconsin Studies), Madison, 1921.
RANNIE, DAVID WATSON, *Keats's Epithets*, in *Essays and Studies by Members of the English Association*, III, 1912, pp. 92–113.

RIEGEL, JULIUS, *Die Quellen von William Morris' Dichtung The Earthly Paradise*, Leipzig, 1890.

ROBERTSON, JOHN M., *Modern Humanists*, London, 1901.

ROE, FREDERICK WILLIAM, *Thomas Carlyle as a Critic of Literature*, New York, 1910.

ROSENBLATT, LOUISE, *L'idée de l'art pour l'art dans la littérature anglaise pendant la période victorienne*, Paris, 1931.

ROSSETTI, WILLIAM MICHAEL, *Life of John Keats* (with a Bibliography by John P. Anderson), London, 1887.

ROUTH, H. V., *Money, Morals and Manners as Revealed in Modern Literature*, London, 1935.

Towards the Twentieth Century, Cambridge, 1937.

RUSSELL, G. W. E., *Matthew Arnold*, London, 1904.

SAINTSBURY, GEORGE, *Matthew Arnold*, London, 1902.

A History of English Prosody, London, 1910, vol. III.

SCOTT, DIXON, *Men of Letters*, London, 1917.

SHERMAN, STUART P., *Matthew Arnold: How to Know Him*, New York, 1932.

SPENDER, STEPHEN, "Keats and Shelley," in *From Anne to Victoria* (ed. Bonamy Dobrée), London, 1937, pp. 574–88.

TAYLOR, HENRY, Preface to *Philip van Artevelde*, London, 1834.

THORPE, CLARENCE DEWITT, *The Mind of John Keats*, New York, 1926.

TINKER, CHAUNCEY B., and ROLLINS, CARL C., *Addresses Commemorating the One Hundredth Anniversary of the Birth of William Morris*, Overbrook Press, 1935.

TINKER, C. B., and LOWRY, H. F., *The Poetry of Matthew Arnold: A Commentary*, Oxford, 1940.

TRILLING, LIONEL, *Matthew Arnold*, New York, 1939.

TROXELL, JANET CAMP, *Three Rossettis*, Cambridge (U.S.A.), 1937.

VAN DYKE, HENRY, *The Poetry of Tennyson*, New York, 1915.

VILLARD, LÉONIE, *The Influence of Keats on Tennyson and Rossetti*, Paris, 1914.

WALKER, HUGH, *The Literature of the Victorian Era*, Cambridge, 1931.

WALLER, R. D., *The Rossetti Family: 1824–1854*, Manchester, 1932.

WARD, MRS. HUMPHRY, *A Writer's Recollections*, London, 1919.

WATKIN, RALPH GRANGER, *Robert Browning and the English Pre-Raphaelites*, Breslau, 1905.

WATSON, WILLIAM, *Excursions in Criticism*, London, 1893, pp. 23–45.

WAUGH, EVELYN, *Rossetti: His Life and Works*, London, 1928.

WEBER, MAX, *Gesammelte aufsätse zur Religionssoziologie*, Tübingen, 1922, vol. I.

WELBY, T. EARLE, *The Victorian Romantics: 1850–1870*, London, 1929.

WILLIAMS, STANLEY T., *Studies in Victorian Literature*, New York, 1923.

WILSON, J. DOVER, *Leslie Stephen and Matthew Arnold as Critics of Wordsworth*, Cambridge, 1939.

WINWAR, FRANCES, *Poor Splendid Wings*, Boston, 1933.

Oscar Wilde and the Yellow Nineties, New York, 1940.

YOUNG, G. M., *Early Victorian England: 1830–1865*, London, 1934, 2 vols.

PART III: PERIODICALS

ANON., "John Keats as the Master Spirit in Victorian Poetry," *Current Opinion,* LXX (1921), 526–531.

"Matthew Arnold," *TLS,* Dec. 21, 1922, 1092.

APP, A. J., "How Six Famous Poets Were Treated," *Catholic World,* CXIV (1937), 582–589.

The Athenaeum, "An Elegy on the Death of the Poet Keats," [by 'Barry Cornwall,'] no. 228 (1832), p. 162.

"Atalanta in Calydon, by A. C. Swinburne," no. 1953 (1865), 450–1.

BABBITT, IRVING, "Matthew Arnold," *The Nation,* CV (1917), 117–21.

BAYNE, PETER, "Mr. Arnold and Mr. Swinburne," *The Contemporary Review,* VI (1867), 338–356.

Blackwood's Magazine, "Cockney School of Poetry, No. IV," III (1818), 519–524.

"John Keats," VII (1820), 665.

"Shelley's Prometheus Unbound," VII (1820), esp. p. 686.

"Poems by Coventry Patmore," LVI (1844), 331–42.

BROWN, ANNA R., "The Celtic Element in Tennyson's 'Lady of Shalott,'" *Poet Lore,* 1892, 408–15.

BROWN, E. K., "Matthew Arnold and the Elizabethans," *University of Toronto Quarterly,* I (1932), 333–52.

"Swinburne: A Centenary Estimate," *University of Toronto Quarterly,* VI (1937), 215–35.

"Matthew Arnold and the Eighteenth Century," *University of Toronto Quarterly,* IX (1940), 202–13.

CHEW, SAMUEL C., "Keats After a Hundred Years," *The New Republic,* XXVI (1921), 49–50.

CORNELIUS, ROBERTA D., "Two Early Reviews of Keats's First Volume," *PMLA,* XL (1925), 193–210.

COURTHOPE, WILLIAM JOHN, "Keats' Place in English Poetry," *National Review,* X (1887), 11–24.

The Critic, "The Keats Memorial," XXV (1894), 78–9.

DECKER, CLARENCE R., "The Aesthetic Revolt Against Naturalism in Victorian Criticism," *PMLA,* LIII (1938), 844–56.

DE QUINCEY, THOMAS, "John Keats," *Tait's Edinburgh Magazine,* XIII (1846), 249–54.

DEVANE, WILLIAM CLYDE, "The Harlot and the Thoughtful Young Man," *Studies in Philology,* XXIX (1932), 463–84.

The Edinburgh Review [Rev. of *Endymion* and *Lamia* vols.], XXXIV (1820), 203–14.

[Rev. of Milnes's Life of Keats.] XC (1849), 424–33.

ELLIOT, G. R., "The Real Tragedy of Keats," *PMLA,* XXXVI (1921), 315–31.

ETIENNE, LOUIS, "La poésie paienne en Angleterre," *Revue des Deux Mondes,* LXIX (1867), 291–317.

EVANS, B. IFOR, "Tennyson and the Origins of the Golden Treasury," *TLS* (Dec. 8, 1932), 941.

GRENDON, FELIX, "The Influence of Keats Upon the Early Poetry of Tennyson," *Sewanee Review*, XV (1907), 285–96.

HARRIS, ALAN, "Matthew Arnold: The Unknown Years," *Nineteenth Century and After*, CXIII (1933), 498–509.

HARRISON, FREDERIC, "Culture, A Dialogue," *Fortnightly Review*, VIII (1867), 608.

KNICKERBOCKER, R. L., "Rossetti's 'The Blessed Damozel,'" *Studies in Philology*, XXIX (1932), 485–504.

The London Magazine, "Lamia and Other Poems," II (1820), 315–21.

"The Death of Mr. John Keats," III (1821), 426–7, and 526.

MABBOTT, T. O., "Keats in America," *Notes and Queries*, CLXIII (1932), 97.

MARSH, GEORGE L., and WHITE, NEWMAN I., "Keats and the Periodicals of his Time," *Modern Philology*, XXXII (1934), 37–53.

MASSON, DAVID, "The Life and Poetry of Keats," *Macmillan's Magazine*, III (1860), 1–16.

"The Story of Gifford and Keats," *The Nineteenth Century*, XXXI (1892), 586–605.

MASSON, EUGENE, "The Influence of Keats," *The Bookman* (London), LIX (1921), 185–7.

MILNER, GEORGE, "On Some Marginalia made by Dante G. Rossetti in a Copy of Keats' Poems," *Manchester Quarterly*, II (1883), 1–11.

MYERS, F. W. H., "Rossetti and the Religion of Beauty," *Cornhill Magazine*, XLVII (1883), 213–24.

The New Monthly Magazine, "The Faults of Recent Poets," XXXVII (1833), 69–74.

Notes and Queries, IX (1854), 421.

OLIVERO, FREDERIC, "Hood and Keats," *MLN*, XXVIII (1913), 233–5.

PARRY, JOHN J., "A Note on the Prosody of William Morris," *MLN*, XLIV (1932), 306–9.

[PATMORE, COVENTRY,] "Keats," *St. James's Budget* (July 2, 1887), 21.

The Quarterly Review, "*Endymion* by John Keats," XIX (1818), 204–8.

"Lord Byron and Some of his Contemporaries," XXXVII (1828), esp. 416–19.

"Poems by Alfred Tennyson," XLIX (1833), 81–96.

"Poems by Richard Monckton Milnes," LXIV (1839), 59–64.

[Rev. of Poems by Swinburne, Morris, and Rossetti.] CXXXII (1872), 60.

Rev. of Ward's *English Poets*.] CLIII (1882), esp. 459–60.

"*Keats*," by Sidney Colvin, CLXVI (1888), 308–38.

"The Poetry of Tennyson," CLXXVI (1893), 2–39.

"Fathers of Literary Impressionism in England," CLXXXV (1897), esp. 186–93.

ROBERTS, JOHN HAWLEY, "The Significance of Lamia," *PMLA*, L (1935), 550–61.

ROUTH, JAMES, "Parallels in Coleridge, Keats, and Rossetti," *Modern Language Notes*, XXV (1910), 33–7.

The Saturday Review, "The Keats Memorial," LXXVIII (1895), 66.

SEVERN, JOSEPH, "On the Vicissitudes of Keats' Fame," *Atlantic Monthly*, XI (1863), 402.

Sharpe's London Magazine [Rev. of Milnes's Life of Keats.], VIII (1849), 55–60.

SHINE, HILL, "The Influence of Keats Upon Rossetti," *Englische Studien*, 61 (1926), 183–219.

SWINBURNE, ALGERNON C., "Mr. Arnold's New Poems," *The Fortnightly Review*, VIII (1867), 414–28.

THORPE, CLARENCE D., "Wordsworth and Keats—A Study in Personal and Critical Impression," *PMLA*, XLII (1927), 1010–26.

"Keats's Interest in Politics and World Affairs," *PMLA*, XLVI (1931), 1228–45.

The Times, "The Keats Memorial," July 2 and July 17, 1894.

TINKER, CHAUNCEY B., "Arnold's Poetic Plans," *Yale Review*, XXII (1933), 782.

TURNER, ALBERT MORTON, "Rossetti's Readings and His Critical Opinions," *PMLA*, XLII (1927), 465–91.

Victoria Magazine, "The Daintiest of Poets—Keats," XV (1870), 55–67.

WALLER, R. D., "The Blessed Damozel," *Modern Language Review*, XXVI (1931), 129–41.

The Westminster Review, "Life and Works of John Keats," L (1894), 349–71.

WILDE, OSCAR, "The Tomb of Keats," *Irish Monthly*, V (1887), 476–8.

WILLIAMS, STANLEY T., "Walter Savage Landor as a Critic of Literature," *PMLA*, XXXVIII (1923), 906–28.

INDEX